CHARMION VON WIEGAND

Edited by Maja Wismer
With contributions by Martin Brauen,
Lori Cole, Haema Sivanesan,
Nancy J. Troy, and Felix Vogel

EXPANDING

PRESTEL
Munich · London · New York

Kunstmuseum Basel

MODERNISM

FOREWORD

Charmion von Wiegand (1896–1983) was an American journalist, art critic, and painter. Although largely unknown today, she won international acclaim beginning in the 1950s for paintings and collages in which she combined Far Eastern iconography with geometric abstraction. Yet it was as an art critic and member of New York's literary circles of the 1920s that she initially made a name for herself. It was in this capacity that she had her first encounter with Piet Mondrian, who, having first gone into exile in London, emigrated to New York in 1940. Von Wiegand's engagement with Mondrian's transcendental, geometrically abstract art prepared the ground for her own work. The fascination she holds for us today rests as much on her colorful compositions inspired by her spirituality as on her legacy as an open-minded, cosmopolitan intellectual. As Haema Sivanesan describes in this publication, Charmion von Wiegand developed a visual language for a "transcultural, modern Buddhism."

In *Charmion von Wiegand. Expanding Modernism*, the Kunstmuseum Basel presents her oeuvre of diverse works spanning a fifty-year period from the 1920s to the 1970s. This book was produced in preparation for an exhibition of the same name—the first institutional exhibition of Charmion von Wiegand's work outside the United States. Unlike previous approaches to this artist, which have tended to concentrate on specific phases of her career, our project is broad in scope and embraces the whole of her creative life, including a selection of her early artwork.

Charmion von Wiegand began painting after a psychotherapy session in 1927. Those early paintings grew out of her interactions with influential American artists of the interwar period, such as the painter Joseph Stella and the poet Hart Crane. Of crucial importance to any overview of Charmion von Wiegand's multifaceted legacy are her texts, most of which she wrote as a left-leaning journalist and art critic in the 1930s. Her writings give us an impression of her interests and of the larger historical context of Great Depression America in which her career began. What impresses us today about Von Wiegand, alongside her fascinating and hitherto rarely exhibited paintings and collages, is her consistent openness to the new and the unknown.

What is not widely known is that during her lifetime and in the nearly four decades since her death there have indeed been critics, dealers, and collectors who believed—and still believe—in her art and who have sought to bring it the attention it deserves. Named here in chronological order, these include the American gallerists Rose Fried, Eleanore B. Saidenberg, Zoe Dusanne, Howard Wise, Andre Zarre, Marilyn Pearl, and Michael Rosenfeld. It is thanks to them and their collectors that works by Charmion von Wiegand are now to be found in the collections of several major American museums, even if the majority of them have for too long languished in the vaults. At the international level, too, there were gallerists who threw their weight behind Charmion von Wiegand, at least for a while, among them Fiamma Vigo in Rome and Venice, Gisèle Real of the gallery Cittadella d'Arte Internazionale e d'Avanguardia in Ascona, Susanne Bollag in Zurich, and the legendary London-based gallerist Annely Juda. In the late 1970s, the International Women's Arts Festival in New York honored Von Wiegand for her "outstanding cultural contribution" along with other illustrious women of the American art scene, such as Georgia O'Keeffe, Louise Nevelson, and Betty Parsons. In the early 1980s and 1990s, her work was the subject of monographic exhibitions in Florida and Connecticut. The 1990s also saw Jennifer Newton Hersh write a wide-ranging and in-depth dissertation on the life and work of Charmion von Wiegand, while in more recent years the New York-based art historian Aliza Edelman has authored a number of important essays on the artist. Von Wiegand's works were included in thematic group shows at the Newark Museum of Art in 2010 and at the Solomon R. Guggenheim Museum in New York in 2019.

In 2010, the then chief curator of New York's Rubin Museum of Art, Martin Brauen, included several works by Charmion von Wiegand in the show *Grain of Emptiness: Buddhism-Inspired Contemporary Art*. It was again Martin Brauen who urged me, when I took over as director of the Kunstmuseum Basel, to consider staging an exhibition on Von Wiegand here. He even introduced me to Khyongla Rato, the founder of the Tibet Center in New York and Charmion von Wiegand's Buddhist teacher, whom she appointed the heir to her estate. Yet, given how little known Charmion von Wiegand is to a wider audience, it was clear to me that any exhibition of her work would have to command the full backing and commitment of everyone at the museum. I therefore decided to place the project in the hands of Maja Wismer, then an assistant curator, who prepared the show for the Kunstmuseum Basel in collaboration with Martin Brauen. Thanks to the generous support pledged by the Terra Foundation for American Art, Maja Wismer was able to conduct a research colloquium at the Kunstmuseum Basel, in the course of which the authors assembled here presented the results of their research that were later revised and reworked for inclusion in this book. Students from the Department of Art History at the University of Basel also took part in the project and two of them became co-authors of the detailed biographical chronology published here. It serves as a further contribution to this first comprehensive monograph of Charmion von Wiegand's work and is likely to prove valuable to any future engagement with Von Wiegand the artist and the intellectual.

Charmion von Wiegand's work is not currently represented in the collection of the Kunstmuseum Basel. This is a point that was raised on multiple occasions during the project's preparatory phase. There are, nevertheless, good reasons for pursuing this project in Basel. For one, the museum's ongoing interest in the development of new perspectives in the study and promulgation of our extensive holdings. This is especially the case with the impressive collection of non-figurative art from the early twentieth century, which includes works by Piet Mondrian, as well as Theo van Doesburg, Fritz Glarner, Sophie Taeuber-Arp, Hans Arp, and Kurt Schwitters, all of whom influenced Charmion von Wiegand her whole life long. Secondly, our commitment to American art, which we have cultivated assiduously since a now legendary and expansive acquisition in the late 1950s, is one that we would like to foster and enrich by raising awareness of lesser-known artists and historical trends. This was also the background to our recent retrospective of the early works of Sam Gilliam (b. 1933) and our purchase of a representative group of works by Sari Dienes (1898–1992).

Finally, it is worth mentioning that—at least theoretically—Charmion von Wiegand's works might indeed have entered the collection of the Kunstmuseum Basel at one point in the past. The small canvas called *New York* (1957; fig. 16) that she gave her friend and fellow artist, Hans Arp, and the Basel-born collector, Marguerite Hagenbach, as a wedding gift in 1957 now belongs, along with another work by Von Wiegand, to the collection of the Fondazione Marguerite Arp in Locarno. Could those two paintings have been among the many works by their artist friends that Arp and Hagenbach surrounded themselves with during their final years in Ticino? The photos of Hagenbach's birthday celebration in 1968 certainly suggest as much. Perhaps, it could be speculated, this was one of the reasons why the works by Charmion von Wiegand were not included in Arp-Hagenbach's very generous donation to the Kunstmuseum Basel, the exact composition of which my predecessor Franz Meyer was invited to fashion according to his own wish list.

It is certainly true that here at the Kunstmuseum Basel, the works of Charmion von Wiegand would be close to those of many of the artists with whom she felt an affinity. Furthermore, as the texts and collections of documents and materials that inform this volume make clear, any engagement with Charmion von Wiegand as an artist and woman cannot help but broaden our view of the highly innovative handling of geometric abstract art, with its European origins, as seen from the other side of the Atlantic. What could be more appropriate than a change of perspective, coming at a time when art history is at last shifting away from its decades-long Eurocentric narrative?

I would especially like to thank all our lenders, this book's authors, its designer, Julia Born, Zurich, and its publisher, Prestel Verlag. Sincere thanks are also due to Martin Brauen, halley k harrisburg, Khyongla Rato, Michael Rosenfeld, and Nicholas Vreeland. My greatest debt of thanks, however, is to Maja Wismer, who developed this project with passion and intelligence.

Josef Helfenstein, Director

Addendum: Due to the global pandemic in 2020 and 2021, the exhibition *Charmion von Wiegand. Expanding Modernism* could not open as planned. It is scheduled to take place in 2023.

ACKNOWLEDGEMENTS

Khyongla Rato, Nicholas Vreeland, and Linda McClain, halley k harrisburg and Michael Rosenfeld, Estate of Charmion von Wiegand and Michael Rosenfeld Gallery LLC, New York

LENDERS

Albright-Knox Art Gallery, Buffalo, NY, Janne Sirén
Arithmeum/Forschungsinstitut für Diskrete Mathematik, Rheinische Friedrich-Wilhelms-Universität Bonn, Bonn, Ina Prinz
Sonam Dolma and Martin Brauen, Bern, Switzerland
Brooklyn Museum, New York, NY, Anne Pasternak
Cincinnati Art Museum, Cincinnati, OH, Cameron Kitchin
The Cleveland Museum of Art, Cleveland, OH, William M. Griswold
Estate of Charmion von Wiegand, Collection of Khyongla Rato
Estate of Charmion von Wiegand and Michael Rosenfeld Gallery LLC, New York, NY
Fondazione Marguerite Arp, Locarno, Switzerland, Simona Martinoli
Carol Brown Goldberg and Henry H. Goldberg
The Grey Art Gallery, New York, NY, Lynn Gumpert
Charles and Kathleen Harper, Chicago, IL
Hillenbrand Family Collection
Museum der Kulturen, Basel, Anna Schmid and Stephanie Lovász
The Museum of Modern Art, New York, NY, Glenn D. Lowry
The Newark Museum of Art, Newark, NJ, Linda C. Harrison
Collection of Nancy and Fred Poses, New York, NY
Seattle Art Museum, Seattle, WA, Kimerly Rorschach

Solomon R. Guggenheim Museum, New York, NY, Richard Armstrong and Tracey Bashkoff
Völkerkundemuseum, Universität Zürich, Zurich, Switzerland, Mareile Flitsch
Walker Art Center, Minneapolis, MN, Mary Ceruti
Whitney Museum of American Art, New York, NY, Adam D. Weinberg, David Breslin, and Kim Conaty

As well as those lenders who wish to remain anonymous.

THIS PUBLICATION HAS BEEN MADE POSSIBLE THROUGH THE SUPPORT OF:

KPMG AG

Vreni & Lukas Richterich

Foundation for the Kunstmuseum Basel

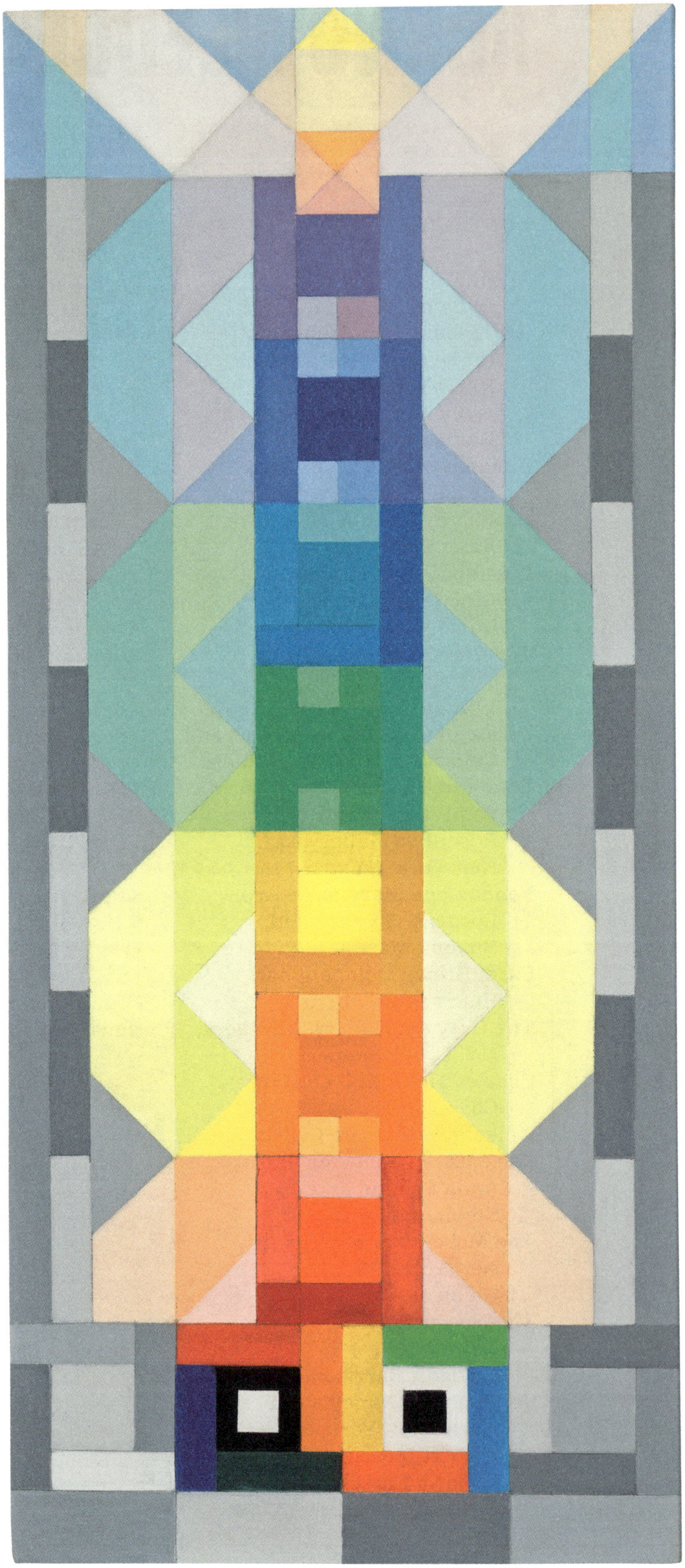

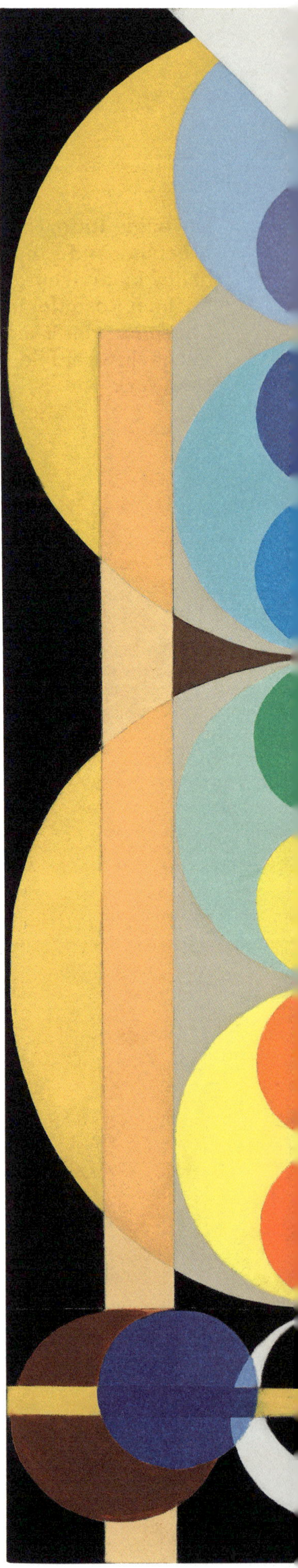

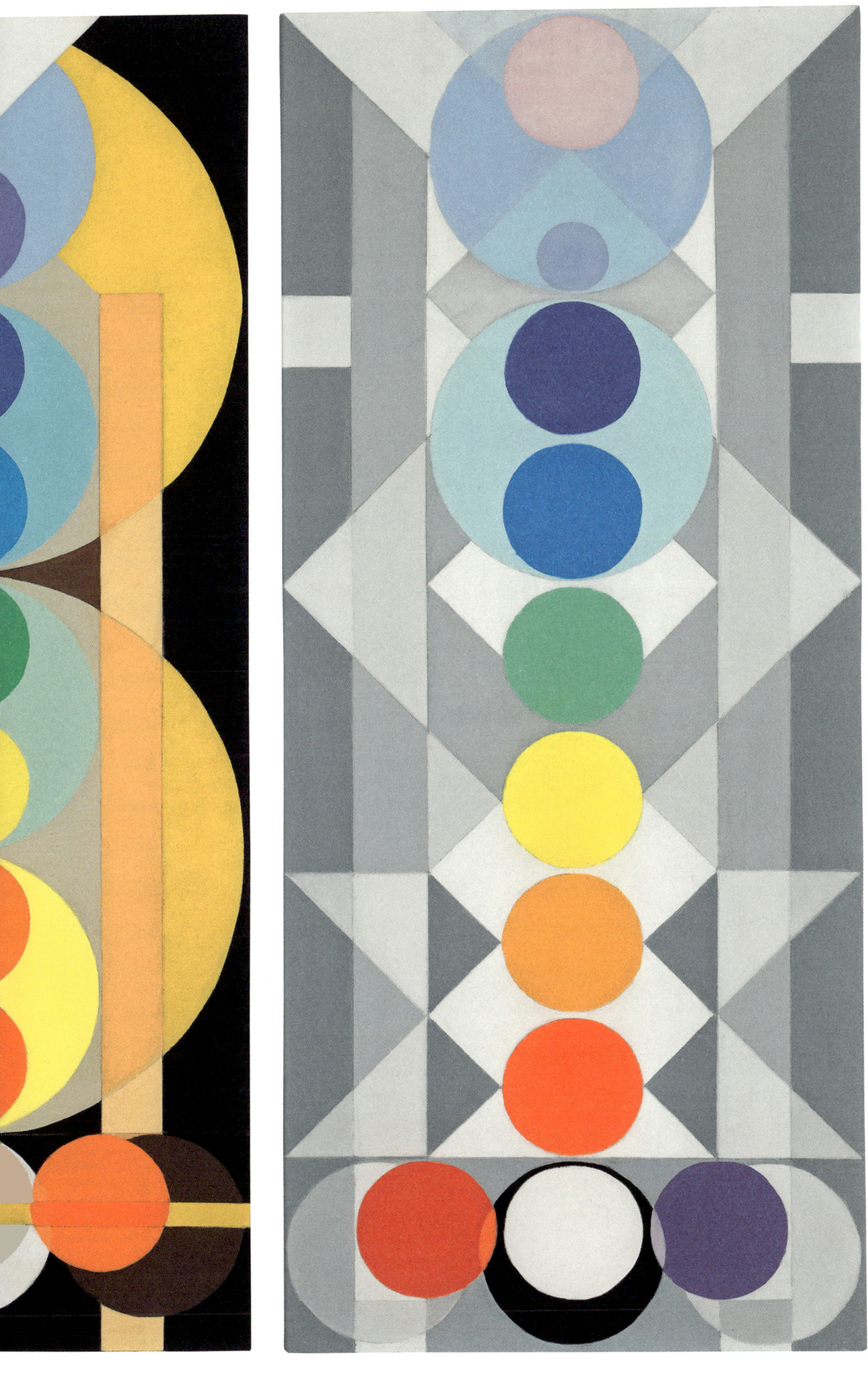

CONTENTS

Previous spread:
Charmion von Wiegand, *Triptych,
Number 700*, 1961, oil and pencil
on canvas, three parts,
overall 107.3 × 138 cm, Whitney
Museum of American Art,
Gift of Alvin M. Greenstein

MAJA WISMER

THE PARADOX OF TRANS- FORMATION

My first encounter with an artwork by Charmion von Wiegand took place in poorly lit conditions that, for a museum, would be considered anything but ideal. She was, at that point, an artist I had only just recently heard of. All the more surprising was the instantly engaging impact of that work consisting of roughly one-meter-tall vertical canvases arranged to form a triptych and full of brightly colored triangles, circles, and straight lines. In no way did these canvases conform to what my hasty search for the artist's name yielded by way of information: "Painter, whose work was inspired by Piet Mondrian's Neo-Plasticist painting style." The challenge of a visual language that, looking back at twentieth-century art, defies any obvious categorization was to be a constant companion in my engagement with Charmion von Wiegand and her artistic and intellectual legacy, as was the appendage "Mondrian." *Expanding Modernism* is the result of my attempts to grasp an oeuvre spanning a good three decades that consistently eludes any one definition or designation.[1]

Charmion von Wiegand's practice and work resist any straightforward categorizations. This is complicated by Von Wiegand herself assiduously cultivating the comparison with Mondrian's aesthetic her entire life and readily acknowledging the formative influence that this icon of the twentieth-century, trans-Atlantic art world had on her understanding of painting. This poses a methodological challenge, especially at a time when museums would prefer not to present the work of a woman artist in the shadow of a (more famous) male colleague. Yet it is this same challenging of convention that makes Von Wiegand such a relevant artist today—that and the powerful immediacy of her colorful, diagrammatic compositions (the aforementioned triptych, for example), which is a direct result of her own distinctive idiom. It is that idiom, that visual language that fascinates us most, and all the more so in view of the art world's current interest in works that have grown out of a (supposedly) spiritual experience or connection with a spiritual world.[2]

Charmion von Wiegand's true contribution to the history of twentieth-century art, it could be argued, taking the *classical* Modernist criterion of artistic innovation as a benchmark of quality, was her work to "produce an image of 'modern Buddhism'—that is, an image of Buddhism as a transcultural phenomena,"[3] which she developed in the atmosphere specific to New York in the 1960s and 1970s. Von Wiegand was initially active as a writer, however, and having arrived in Moscow in 1929, shortly after the forced collectivization of Soviet agriculture envisaged in the first Five-Year Plan began, she became the only female correspondent in the Soviet capital to work for the Hearst-owned American news agency Universal Service. What interested Von Wiegand about the USSR—unlike Alfred H. Barr, Jr., the founding director of New York's Museum of Modern Art, who visited Moscow shortly before her—was not so much the progressive art by the likes of Aleksandr Rodchenko and Varvara Stepanova as the immediate impact of the Russian Revolution on the everyday lives of the people there, as well as the art of socialist propaganda.[4] On returning to the United States in 1930, she took part as a journalist in the heated debates about the social status of artists and the social relevance of art, all against the backdrop of the Great Depression, during which time the periodicals in question, such as *Art Front* and the *New Masses*, weighed the relative advantages of figurative art against those of abstract art. As Lori Cole demonstrates, Von Wiegand wrote on a wide range of topics; however, the compatibility of revolutionary art and revolutionary politics was a special concern of hers in those days.[5] While she is known to have engaged in dialogue with artists such as Joseph Stella as early as the

---

1 The aim of this research has been to reach beyond both the standard attribution "Neo-Plasticism" and the "geometric-abstract," "Constructivist," or "Pop-Op" labels used on the countless gallery invitations and write-ups of the artist's exhibitions preserved in her archive.

2 Especially worthy of mention here are the exhibitions *Hilma af Klint: Paintings for the Future*, Solomon R. Guggenheim Museum, New York, 2018–2019; *World Receivers: Georgiana Houghton—Hilma af Klint—Emma Kunz*, Lenbachhaus, Munich, 2018–2019; *Emma Kunz—Visionary Drawings: An Exhibition Conceived with Christodoulos Panayiotou*, Serpentine Gallery, London, 2019; *Agnes Pelton: Desert Transcendentalist*, Whitney Museum of American Art, 2020; the book *Enchanted Modernities: Theosophy, the Arts and the American West*, edited by Christopher M. Scheer, Sarah Victoria Turner, and James G. Mansell (Somerset: Fulgur, 2019); as well as the omnipresence of Matt Mullican's large-format diagrams at the ARCO Madrid art fair, 2019.

3 For more on this, see the essay by Haema Sivanesan, "Charmion von Wiegand's Vision of Modern Buddhism," in the present publication, pp. 91–116, here p. 115.

4   This can be inferred from the notes preserved in her archive as well as a piece she wrote for the *New York Times* after her return: "In the Soviet Circus, Fun Goes Serious: The Many New Shows Mix Propaganda with Amusement, and the Clown Uses Satire for Social Ends," *New York Times*, November 26, 1933. See also Jennifer Newton Hersh, "Abstraction, Spiritualism, and Social Justice: The Art and Writing of Charmion von Wiegand," (PhD dissertation, City University of New York, 1998), 142, also quoted by Martin Brauen in his essay, "'You are a writer and I don't want to know about your painting': Charmion von Wiegand's Origins as an Artist," in the present publication, pp. 41–65.

5   See the essay by Lori Cole, "Charmion von Wiegand and the Creative Work of Criticism," in the present publication, pp. 31–40.

6   See the essay by Martin Brauen, pp. 62, 63–65.

7   Frederick Kiesler and Charmion von Wiegand were in constant contact beginning in the early 1930s; see Hersh, 220–224.

1920s, and she began drawing and painting around the same time, the first works that make up what is now considered her artistic oeuvre all date from the early 1940s.

Her first paintings show sweeping, organic forms rendered in a palette which, although often reductive, inasmuch as it consists of black, gray, white, and the primary colors, red, yellow, and blue, is used so expansively that it becomes a very powerful presence in her works. Among these is *Ominous Form* (1946; cat. 3) and *The Nuptial Form* (1946–1947; cat. 6). The graphic compositions of these works and even more so their titles leave us in no doubt that, contrary to the oft-repeated assertion of her indebtedness to Mondrian, Von Wiegand developed her first body of work in dialogue with Hans Richter, then active as a film maker, and the scenographer Frederick Kiesler. Preserved in the artist's archives are not only her diaries but also her correspondence with Mondrian, which began in April 1941 and ended only with the latter's death in February 1944. These sources afford us an insight into Von Wiegand's inner conflicts as well as giving us an inkling of why her own first steps as an artist were quite clearly inspired by sources very different than Mondrian. To judge by the excerpts from her diaries selected by Martin Brauen, Von Wiegand began painting works of her own in defiance of Mondrian's wishes.[6] She was encouraged in this endeavor, rather, by her aforementioned artist friends: Richter and Kiesler. It seems likely that the latter's staging of Peggy Guggenheim's collection at her gallery Art of This Century, which almost functioned more like a museum, was instrumental in shaping Von Wiegand's development as an artist in her own right.[7]

Writing in the mid-1960s, the art critic Lawrence Alloway remarked on how important "biomorphism" had been to the artistic and intellectual life of New York in the 1940s. He attributed this in part to the ubiquity of Surrealism—the majority of whose European

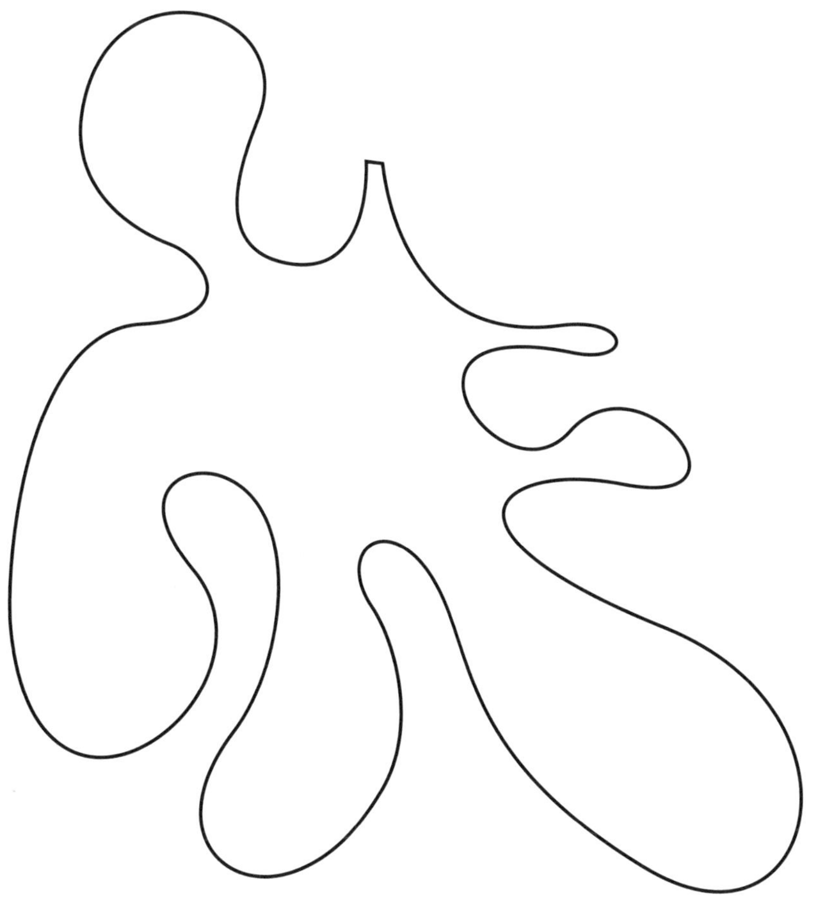

8   Lawrence Alloway, "The Biomorphic Forties," *Artforum* 4, no. 1 (September 1965), reprinted in Lawrence Alloway, *Topics in American Art Since 1945* (New York: W. W. Norton 1975), 17–24.

9   See Alfred H. Barr, Jr., "Two Main Traditions of Abstract Art," in *Cubism and Abstract Art* (New York: Museum of Modern Art, 1936; reprint 1966), 19.

10   See the essay by Nancy J. Troy, "'Mondrian was my Guru': Charmion von Wiegand and Piet Mondrian in the 1940s and 1950s," in the present publication, pp. 67–90.

11   Cf. Harry Cooper and Ron Spronk, *Mondrian: The Transatlantic Paintings* (Cambridge, MA: Harvard University Art Museums; New Haven, CT: Yale University Press, 2001), 12–14; Nancy J. Troy, *The Afterlife of Piet Mondrian* (Chicago: University of Chicago Press, 2013), esp. 28–29.

12   A term used in Mondrian scholarship since the mid-1980s, cf. Cooper and Spronk, 24.

13   See the essay by Nancy J. Troy, pp. 67–90.

14   See the essay by Felix Vogel, "Autonomy—Spirituality—Universalism: The Meaning of Abstraction," in the present publication, pp. 117–140, here p. 119.

15   See the essay by Nancy J. Troy, pp. 67–90.

protagonists had emigrated to the United States—and in part to the general interest at the time in the human psyche and the subconscious, as conveyed in the works of Sigmund Freud and Carl Jung.[8] Above all, Alloway argued, a language of forms tied to the unconscious, coming at a time when all new art was expected to break with the clear, geometric language of Constructivism, seemed to offer an alternative to figuration. Knowing that Von Wiegand created geometrically organized paintings parallel to her biomorphic compositions, Alfred H. Barr's 1936 description of the dynamics at work in abstract art as "The shape of the square confronts the silhouette of the amoeba" might even be read as a prescient characterization of those forces that Von Wiegand was even then developing in her art.[9] In contrast to artists like Jackson Pollock and Barnett Newman, who until just recently dominated the history of postwar American art, Charmion von Wiegand spent several years studying the legacy of what, it was generally agreed at the time, was the primarily European tradition of geometric, abstract art.[10]

Her share in Mondrian's revaluation of what, by the early 1940s, had become his well-established, iconic visual language and with it his shift toward a style of painting that was in no way referential and was defined by straight lines, a purist palette, and the resulting areas of color and the optical dynamism generated by these, has been amply documented elsewhere.[11] Mondrian's move first to London and then New York to escape the war in Europe played an important role in his late works and his "Transatlantic Paintings."[12] Like a number of other artists of the period, Von Wiegand witnessed the influence that the dynamic, pulsating megacity New York had on Mondrian's work and did what she could to promote its presence and reception in the city.[13] That the group of works by Von Wiegand that can be most readily associated with Mondrian, at least visually, grew out of her engagement with Mondrian himself and his works and hence her sensitization to the abstractive potential of urban space is scarcely surprising. *City Lights* (1947; cat. 10) and *Night Rhythm* (1948; cat. 11), which even without the explanatory titles are astonishingly representational, are all good examples of this. Felix Vogel describes this method as a kind of *"refiguration"* of the Neo-Plasticist approach.[14]

Apart from a few exceptions like *Radiating Plane* (1949; cat. 13) and *Composition* (1949; cat. 15), which for a short while put Von Wiegand in the company of artists like Burgoyne Diller, Fritz Glarner, and Carl Holty—in other words, the circle of those who have gone down in the annals of art history as disciples of Mondrian[15]—most of the works in her series of New York paintings can also be linked to a different American tradition, some of whose exponents were personal acquaintances of hers. Among them were Georgia O'Keeffe and Joseph Stella, who in the 1910s and 1920s used their perception of modern urban architecture as a starting point for more or less abstract compositions.[16] We are therefore bound, from a contemporary point of view, to wonder why Von Wiegand was not included in *American Artists Paint the City*, the 1956 group exhibit showcasing that very same tradition that Katharine Kuh curated at the American pavilion of the Venice Biennale. The answer probably has to do with Kuh's agenda, which was focused firmly on America: "Our cities amaze us, outlined against both coasts or seen from the distance across the vast plains of Texas, Illinois, and Iowa. The light in America, almost always brighter than in Europe."[17] Artists like Von Wiegand who had a socialist past and who were not only open to, but actively interested in Europe's artistic tradition were therefore seen as insufficiently representative. But as works like

16   Charmion von Wiegand, "Letter to the Editor: Joseph Stella," *New York Times*, Febuary 23, 1941, X9. See also Mary Kate O'Hare, "Constructive Spirit: Abstract Art in South and North America, 1920s–50s," in *Constructive Spirit: Abstract Art in South and North America, 1920s–50s* (Newark: Newark Museum; San Francisco: Pomegranate, 2010), 16; published in conjunction with an exhibition of the same title. The fact that Charmion von Wiegand featured prominently in this project (not least as one of her paintings was chosen as the cover motif) makes it all the more surprising that her *City* series had no role at all to play in it.

17   Katharine Kuh's press release about the exhibition, quoted in Mary Caroline Simpson, "American Artists Paint the City: Katharine Kuh, the 1956 Venice Biennale, and New York's Place in the Cold War Art World," *American Studies* 48, no. 4 (Winter 2007): 36.

18   Charmion von Wiegand, "The Oriental Tradition and Abstract Art," in *The World of Abstract Art*, ed. American Abstract Artists (New York: George Wittenborn, 1957), 55–67, here 55.

19   See Helen Molesworth, "Imaginary Landscape," in *Leap Before You Look: Black Mountain College, 1933–1957* (Boston: Institute of Contemporary Art, Boston; New Haven, CT: Yale University Press, 2015), 57; published in conjunction with an exhibition of the same title.

The Golden Flower (1951–1952; cat. 27), *The Great Field of Action or the 64 Hexagrams* (1953; cat. 19), and *The Wheel of the Seasons* (1957; cat. 22) clearly show, Von Wiegand had no interest in debates with nationalistic overtones in the mid-1950s. By then she believed the future to lie in the influence of East Asian art: "Today it is the arts of the Far East that are pervading the artistic atmosphere and whose influence we may expect to see growing."[18]

This broadening of her frame of reference was already apparent in Von Wiegand's works by the late 1940s. One good example of this is her collage *Transfer to Cathay* (1948; cat. 12), which is scarcely larger than a postcard and brings together her many different interests of that period in a complex, literally multilayered whole. Kurt Schwitters's collages, created out of the most basic materials, may have been an inspiration for her engagement with the medium, especially as we know that she had studied his work in great depth in her role as a curator. Just as her article on the "Biomorphic 40s," with its sweeping organic forms, and her fascination with Mondrian tie her voice as a progressive journalist to the specific context of creating work in the New York of the time, so much the same might be said of her interest in the collage method. The art historian Kobena Mercer has described the selection of elements from radically different sources and their piecing together to produce something new, as practiced by twentieth-century artists, as a "cosmopolitan" process.[19] *Transfer to Cathay* can certainly be read as a textbook demonstration of this principle: The work is dominated by vertically and horizontally arranged, variously colored strips of paper, some printed with fragments of text, others patterned and others still monochrome but with a range of haptic qualities—among them several tickets for New York mass transit—and seen vertically inevitably evokes Manhattan's north-south orientation. The date inscribed on

20   For more on this, see Mona Schieren, *Agnes Martin. Transkulturelle Übersetzung. Zur Rekonstruktion asianistischer Ästhetiken in der amerikanischen Kunst nach 1945* (Munich: Verlag Silke Schreiber, 2016), 141–155.

21   As Stanley K. Abe has shown, Clement Greenberg had been endeavoring to suppress any mention of Asian influences in discussions of Abstract Expressionism since the 1950s; Stanley K. Abe, "To Avoid the Inscrutable: Abstract Expressionism and the 'Oriental Mode,'" in *Discrepant Abstraction*, ed. Kobena Mercer (London: Institute of International Visual Arts; Cambridge, MA: MIT Press, 2006), 52–73. The Solomon R. Guggenheim Museum finally broke with that tradition with its 2009 show, *The Third Mind: American Artists Contemplate Asia, 1860–1989.* Astonishingly, the works by Charmion von Wiegand in the museum's own collection were not included in the exhibition catalog, although she herself was deemed to warrant a portrait in the chronology: Alexandra Munroe, ed., *The Third Mind: American Artists Contemplate Asia, 1860–1989* (New York: Guggenheim Museum, 2009), 395.

22   See Schieren, 146.

the work, as well as the monogram that the artist inserted into the grid fragment, locates the artist herself at the time of the collage's creation as a part of the metropolis's dynamism.

Knowing what we do of Von Wiegand's own broadening of her frame of reference in the late 1940s, the title of the piece—where "Cathay" is an antiquated name for China—can be read as a concrete pointer to the reorientation of her personal, and soon her artistic, compass. The collage thus evokes a certain interrelationship between New York City and Far Eastern philosophies and practices, the hyping of which in cosmopolitan circles had only just begun and would continue for many years to come.[20] Only in recent years have art historians focusing on postwar American art moved beyond the exclusive preoccupation, established in the 1950s, with its references to the Western tradition and begun to take an interest in those artists who engaged explicitly with Far Eastern philosophies of being and existence.[21] Among the examples of artists whose works contain "Asian" influences named by Charmion von Wiegand in the essay from 1957 quoted earlier are Mark Tobey, Ad Reinhardt, and Mark Rothko. Whereas these days we would not necessarily associate Rothko with the ideas and art of East Asia, one striking omission from the list is Agnes Martin.

Initially Von Wiegand's interest in Far Eastern philosophies, like that of the other artists mentioned here, was not a religious one. What fascinated her was the "poetic and ethical material" supplied by these hitherto unknown sources.[22] Her reading of Taoist texts, above all the *I Ching, Book of Changes*, sparked a surge of creativity. With works like the aforementioned *The Great Field of Action or the 64 Hexagrams, The Wheel of the Seasons*, and several other paintings, including *The Ancestral Altar from I Ching* (1954; cat. 21) and *The Sign of Keeping Still* (1953; cat. 18), she found artistically persuasive ways of injecting new energy into her interest in geometric abstraction.

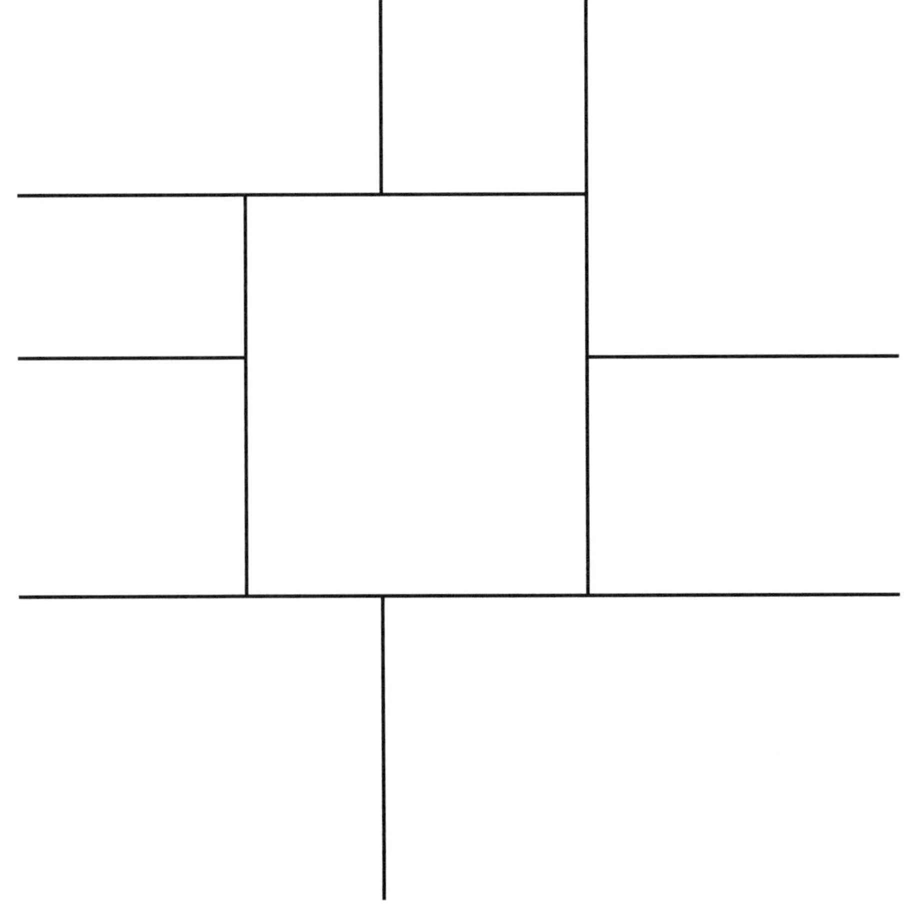

16

Continue on p. 29

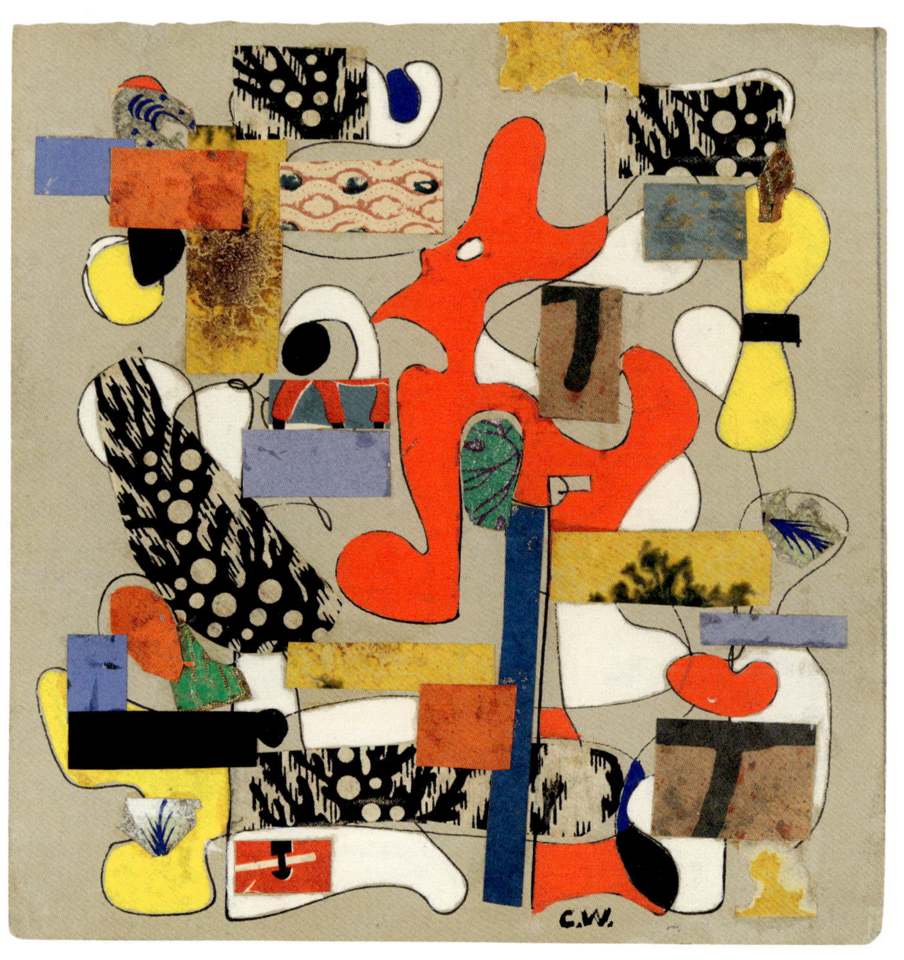

Untitled, ca. 1942
mixed media, collage on paper, 21.6 × 20.5 cm
Whitney Museum of American Art, Gift of Alice and Leo Yamin

Cat. 1   18

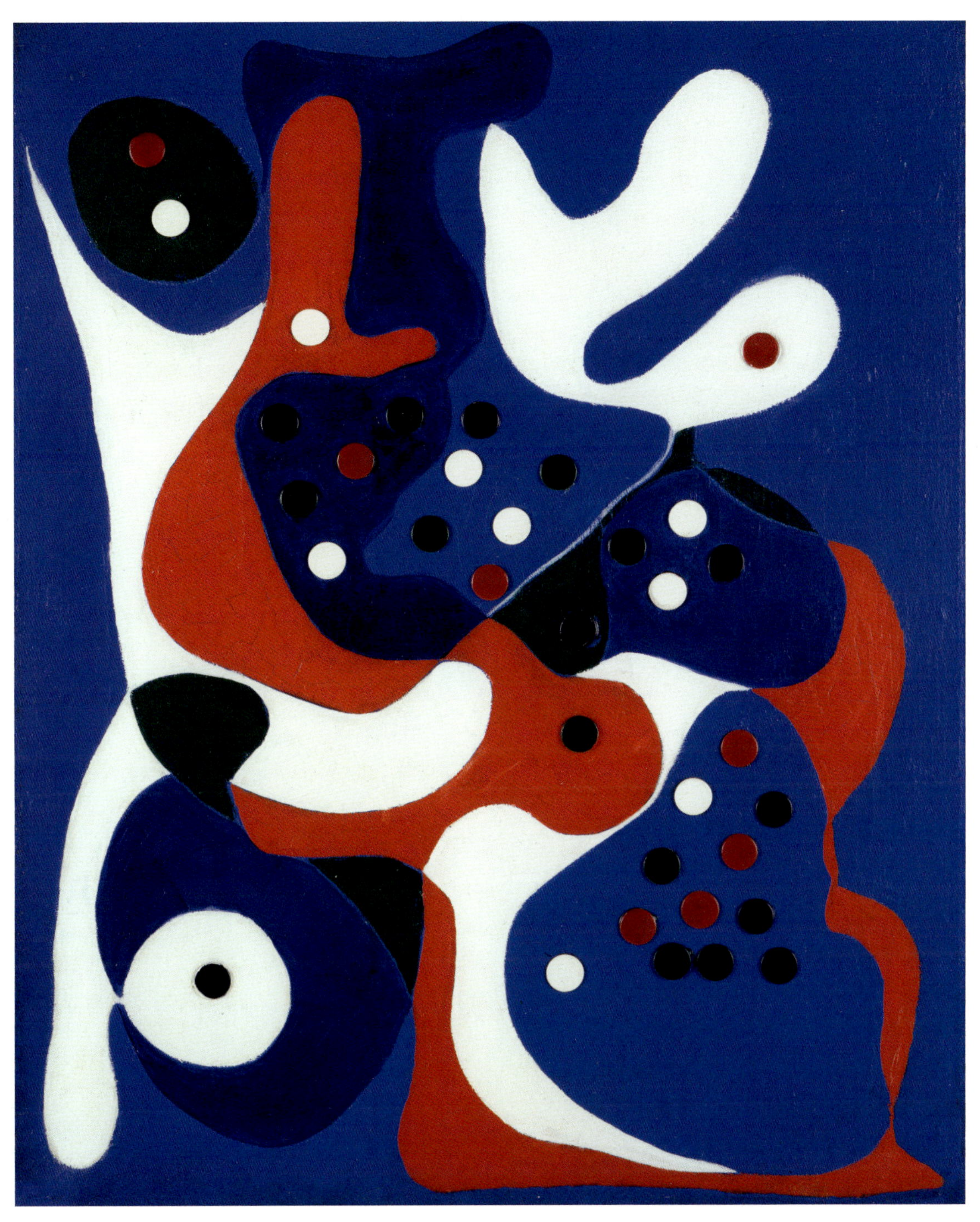

Untitled, ca. 1945
oil with round plastic tiles on canvas, 50.8 × 40.6 cm
Private Collection, New York

Cat. 2   19

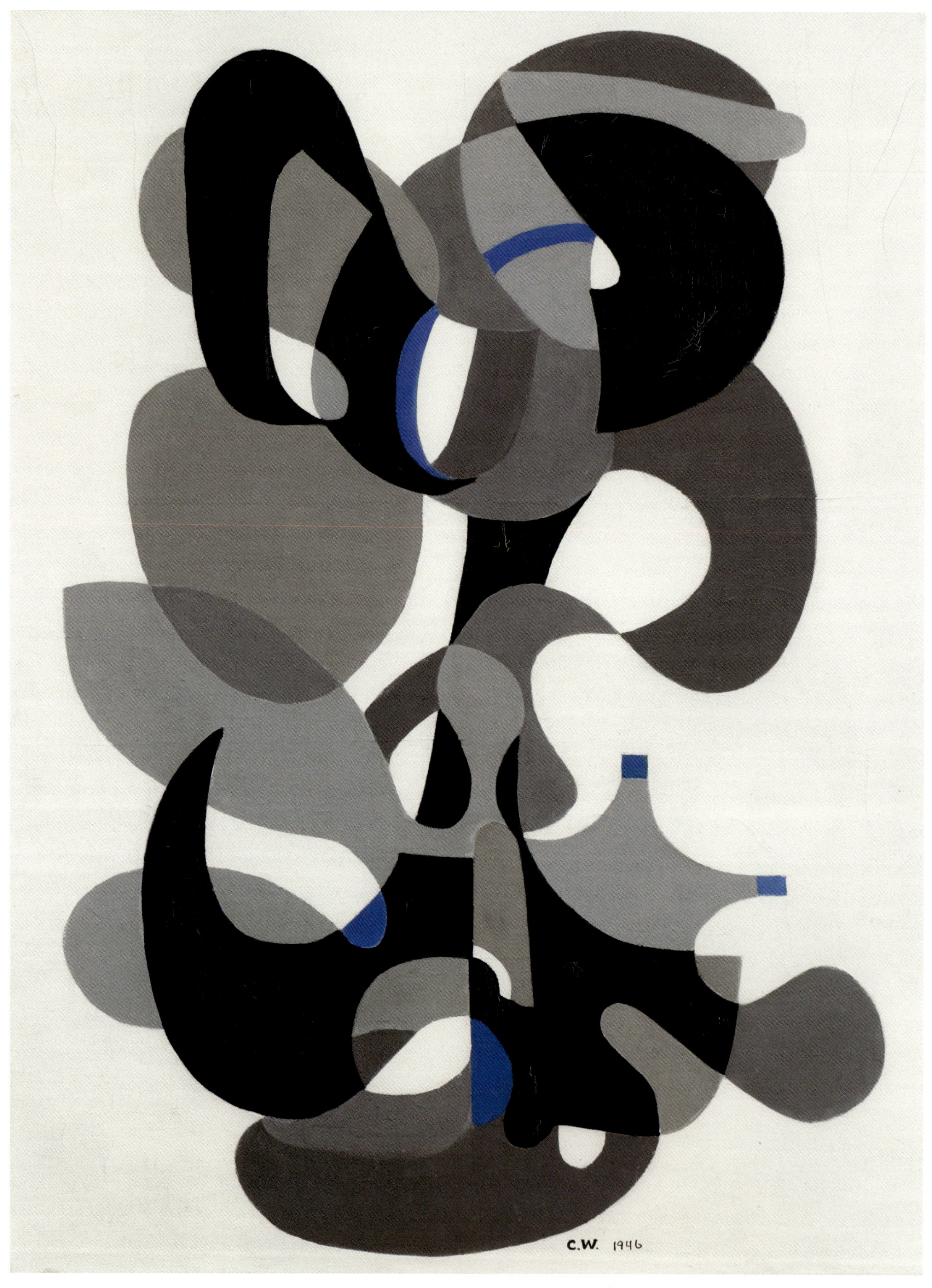

Ominous Form, 1946
oil on canvas, 88.9 × 63.2 cm
Seattle Art Museum, Gift of Zoe Dusanne

Cat. 3   20

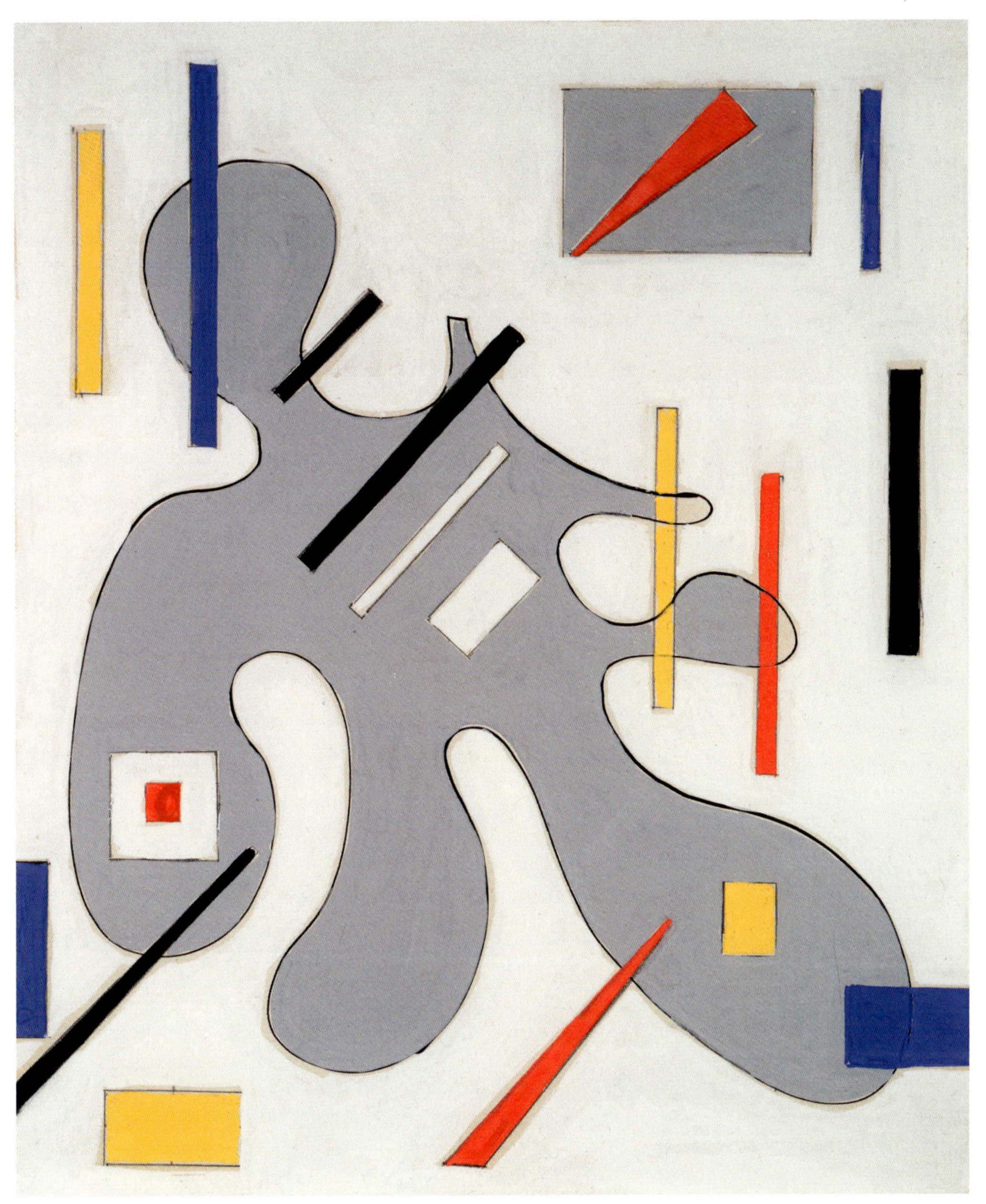

Untitled, 1945
gouache on paper, 42.9 × 35.2 cm
Private Collection, New York

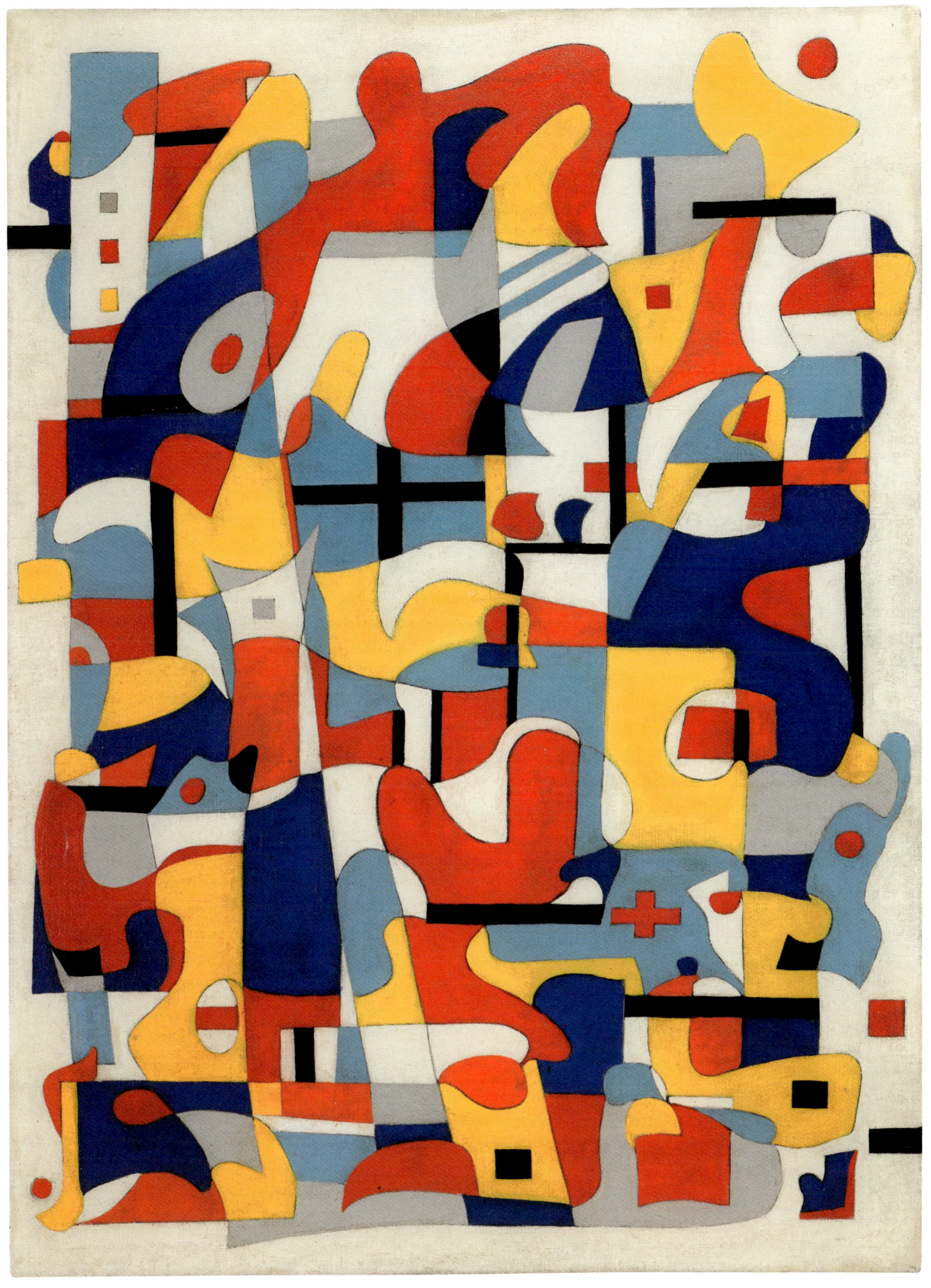

Forms #6, Disparate Forms, 1946
oil on canvas, 89.5 × 63.8 cm
Seattle Art Museum, Gift of Gladys and Sam Rubinstein

Cat. 5

23

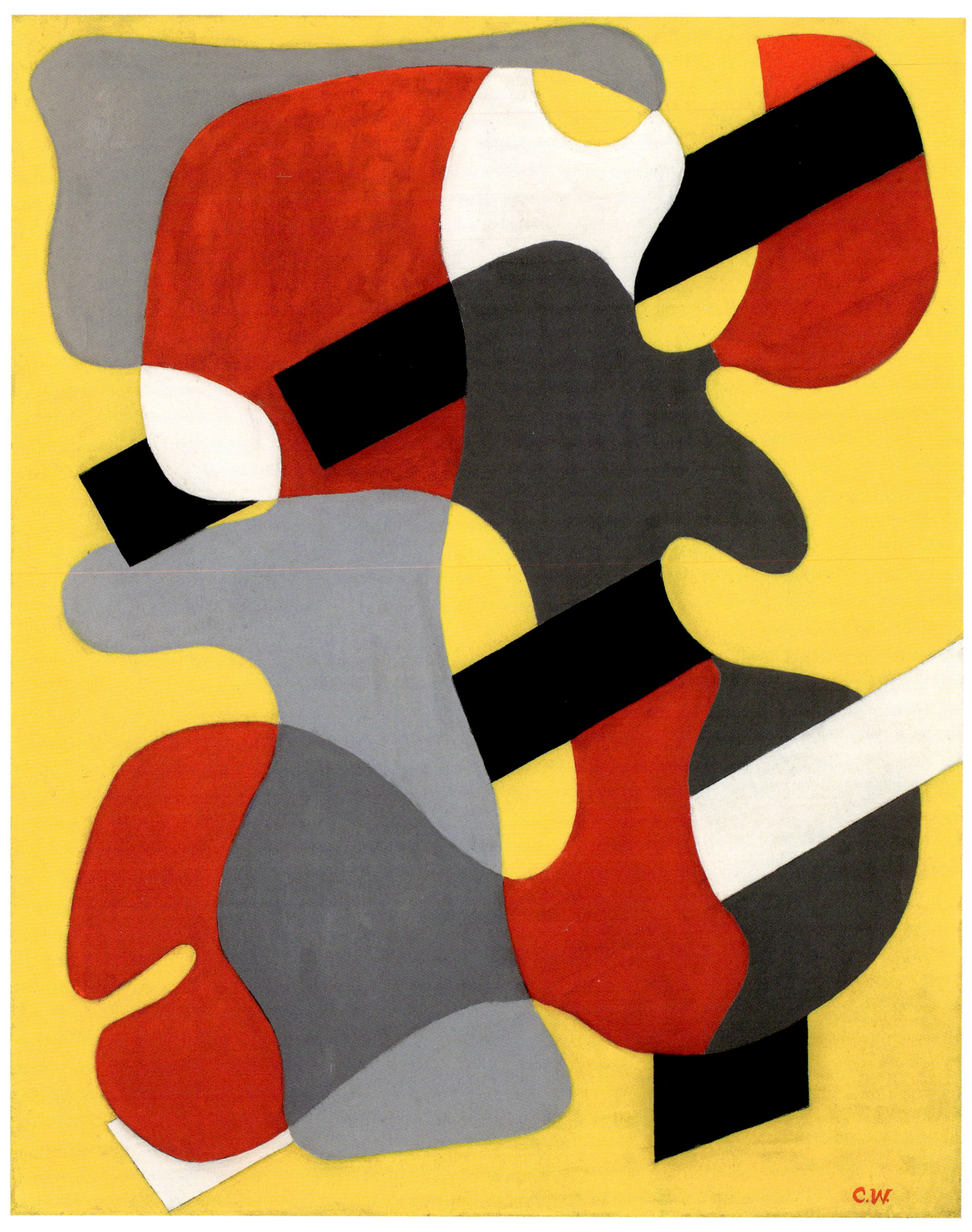

The Nuptial Form, 1946–1947
oil on canvas, 71.1 × 55.9 cm
Estate of Charmion von Wiegand, Courtesy of
Michael Rosenfeld Gallery LLC, New York

Cat. 6   24

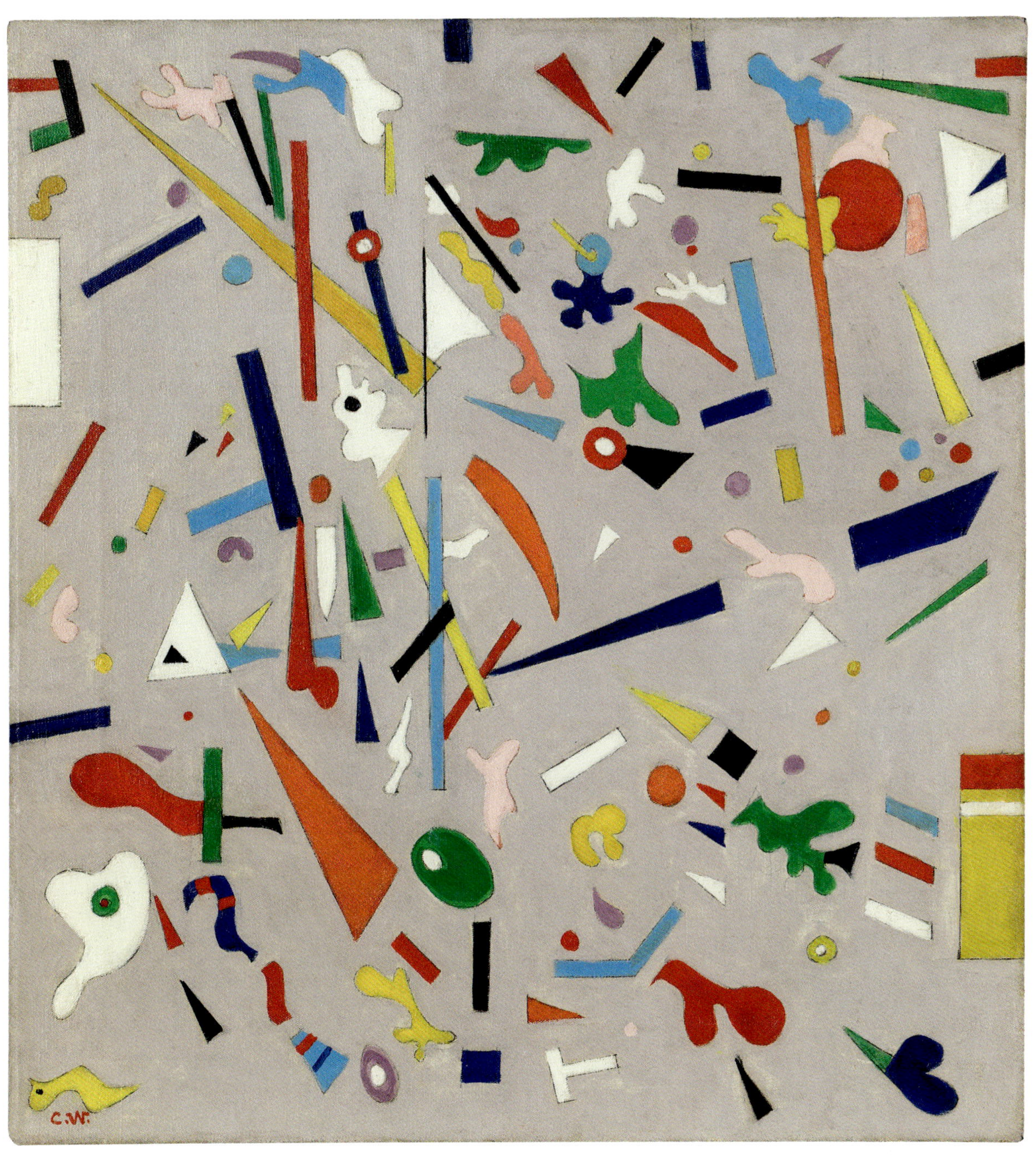

Untitled, 1946
oil on canvas, 50.8 × 45.7 cm
Estate of Charmion von Wiegand, Courtesy of
Michael Rosenfeld Gallery LLC, New York

Cat. 7

25

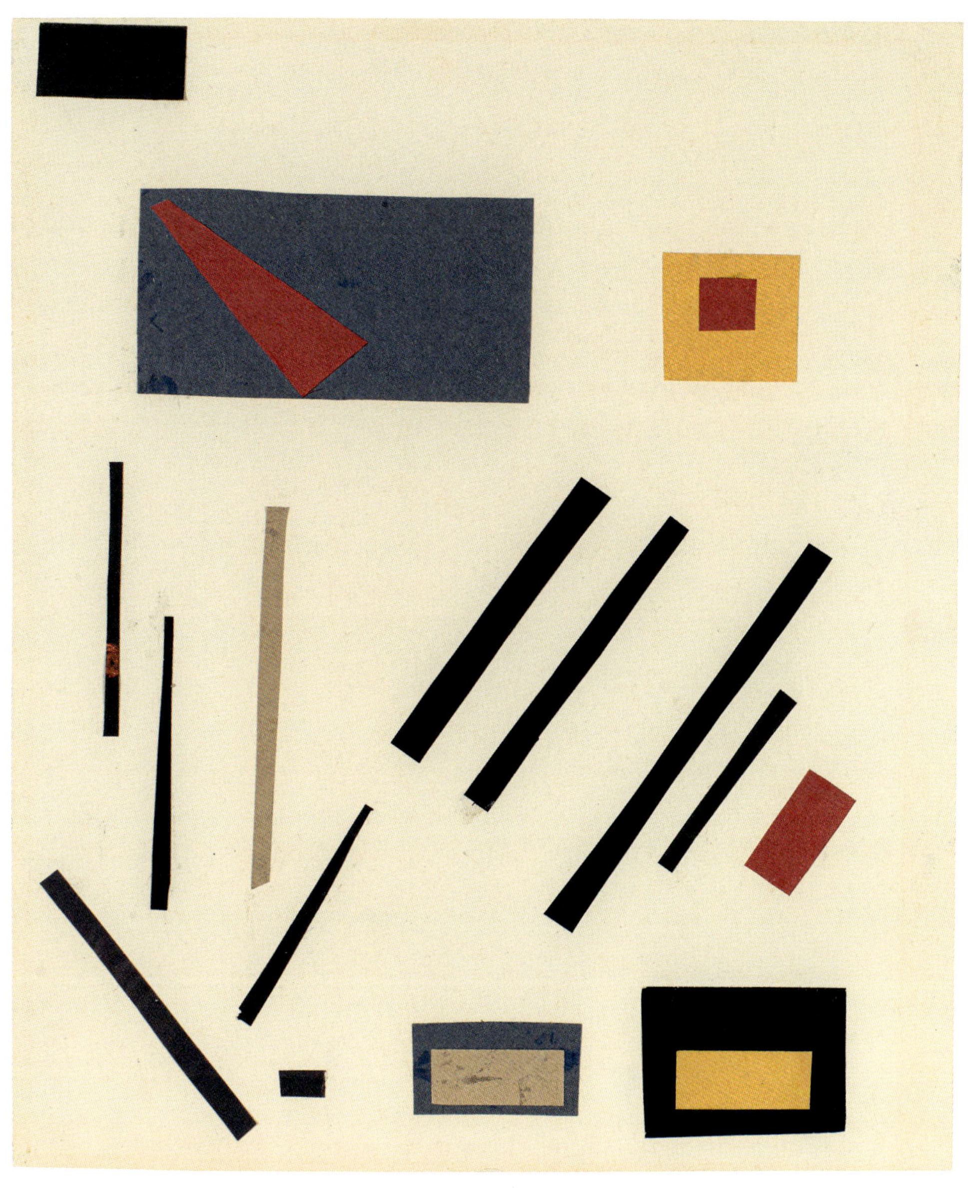

Untitled, ca. 1950
collage on paper, 34.6 × 27.9 cm
Estate of Charmion von Wiegand, Courtesy of
Michael Rosenfeld Gallery LLC, New York

23   See the essay by Felix Vogel, p. 114, and Charmion von Wiegand, "The Oriental Tradition and Abstract Art," 55–67: "For certain painters nothing exists but the canvas, the artist and the operation of painting—the establishment of direct, immediate, bodily, or psychic sensation with the minimum of conscious determination," 60.

24   E-mail to the author, September 29, 2019.

25   See the essay by Haema Sivanesan, pp. 91–116.

26   James Elkins, *On the Strange Place of Religion in Contemporary Art* (New York: Routledge, 2004), 79–80.

27   Donald Kuspit, "Concerning the Spiritual in Contemporary Art," in *The Spiritual in Art: Abstract Painting, 1890–1985* (Los Angeles: Los Angeles County Museum of Art; New York: Abbeville Press, 1986), 319; published in conjunction with an exhibition of the same title.

28   Owen McNally, "A Mondrian Influence, but Wiegand an Original," *Hartford Courant*, November 21, 1993, quoted by Nancy J. Troy in her essay in the present publication, p. 89.

29   Lee Krasner suffered a similar fate. On a visit to Krasner's studio in 1959, Clement Greenberg saw that she had begun changing her work to avert the risk of becoming stuck in the "Krasner style." This displeased Greenberg so much that he cancelled the exhibition he was planning for her. See Suzanne Hudson, "Present Conditional," in *Lee Krasner: Living Colour*, (London: Thames & Hudson, 2019), 42; published in conjunction with an exhibition of the same title at the Barbican Art Gallery, London, and the Schirn Kunsthalle, Frankfurt am Main, among other planned venues.

For Von Wiegand, as for several other New York-based artists of her generation (including John Cage, Sari Dienes, and Yoko Ono), the principle of sixty-four hexagrams explained in the *I Ching* and their interpretation by means of chance provided a set of rules for the development of a creative approach that did not rest exclusively on authorial subjectivity or choice. Thus, she once again positioned herself outside the dominant discourse that would go down in history to great acclaim as Abstract Expressionism.[23]

Charmion von Wiegand's study of Tibetan Buddhism enabled her to broaden the scope of this creative combination of codified parameters around establishing a superstructure to accommodate artistic content. By a circuitous route, what first aroused her interest in the subject were the "Orientalized" writings of Helena Petrovna Blavatsky, founder of the Theosophical Society. Von Wiegand's most copious source of material when preparing her own visual interpretation of a modern, transcultural Buddhism were Madame Blavatsky's appropriative reinterpretations, color codes, and schemata published post-humously by her successors, Annie Besant and Charles Webster Leadbeater, as well as various ethnological publications. Typical of this phase of her work, which Haema Sivanesan has referred to as one of "Book Buddhism,"[24] are paintings like *Sanctuary of the Four Directions* (1959–1960; fig. p. 97) and *The Ascent to Mt. Meru* (1962; cat. 31), which stand out on account of their stark contrasts and clearly delineated geometric forms, and whose titles alone are an acknowledgment of her sources. As a pupil of one of the first yogis in the West, Von Wiegand devoted much of the late 1950s to the attainment of a tantric state of consciousness, fully outside the body. The work *Triptych, Number 700* (1961; fig. pp. 6/7) described at the start of this essay already belongs to that phase of her life in which she was grappling more intensely with the practice of Tibetan Buddhism in the Gelug tradition. Her *Gouache #233: To the Goddess of Spring Vasantadevi* (1964; cat. 35), *Offering of the Universe* (1964; cat. 38), and *To the Adi Buddha* (ca. 1968–1970; cat. 39) all attest to this. Unlike her fellow artists mentioned above, Von Wiegand did not use the visual representations common to Tibetan Buddhism as "aesthetic material," but instead worked with her own experience as a practicing Buddhist. The result is not religious art in the sense of a ritual object, but rather art that *tells* of religious experience.[25]

Charmion von Wiegand's artistic position and work elude any easy categorization using the selection criteria common to the twentieth century—criteria such as identifiable style or artistic innovation. In her late works, however, she comes close to breaking altogether with what, since 1800, has been one of the paradigms of Western autonomous art, namely its detachment from a religious context. This is also the paradigm underlying those various traditions, which the curator Maurice Tuchman brought together in 1986 in *The Spiritual in Abstract Art*, a show that drew much criticism at the time but that from today's perspective counts as a groundbreaking exhibition.[26] The catalog contains an essay by Donald Kuspit that gives us an inkling of why Charmion von Wiegand's work was not included in that exhibition. Spiritually powerful contemporary art, Kuspit writes, "is not the vehicle of communication of religious dogma but of a certain kind of irreducible, nondiscursive experience."[27]

A reviewer writing about an exhibition of Von Wiegand's works in Hartford, Connecticut, in the early 1990s asked the following question: "So why just 10 years after her death isn't she a better known figure?"[28] Any answer to that question would almost certainly include mention of the stylistic diversity of her works[29] and their position both within

30 Cf. Kuspit, "Concerning the Spiritual in Contemporary Art."

31 The case of Hilma af Klint is similar: "[R. H.] Quaytman: But it's always women artists who get the biographical treatment. [Helen] Molesworth: I totally accept that. Why strip the women of their biographies rather than insist upon Jackson Pollock's biography before speaking about his paintings?" in "Art for Another Future: Learning from Hilma af Klint," a conversation with the artist R. H. Quaytman moderated by Helen Molesworth, in *Hilma af Klint: Paintings for the Future*, 33–47, here 44. On Charmion von Wiegand's use of her own biography, see the essay by Nancy J. Troy in the present publication, pp. 67–90. Her deliberate "cultivation" of her biography is attested to by a stack of curriculum vitae contained in the records of the Marilyn Pearl Gallery; see Marilyn Pearl Gallery records, 1925–2000, bulk 1976–1993. Archives of American Art, Smithsonian Institution.

32 She is certainly known to have had contact with Mail Art pioneer Ray Johnson, with whom she had a joint exhibition at the Sid Deutsch Gallery in New York in 1977; see the illustration in Haema Sivanesan's essay on p. 115 and the biographical chronology on p. 153 of the present publication.

33 Adrian Piper, "On Wearing Three Hats," 1996, 117, http://www.adrianpiper.com/docs/Website NGBK3Hats.pdf.

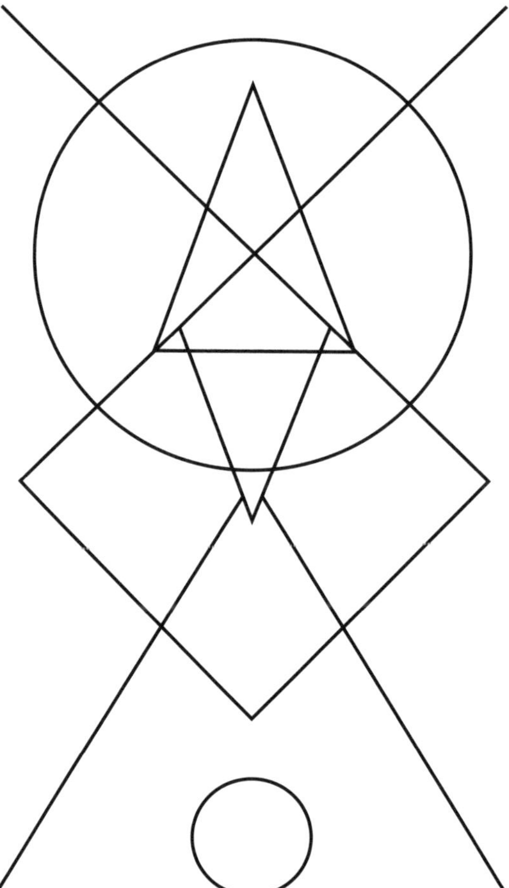

the Western tradition of autonomous, abstract art and in relation to a field that lies outside the purview of Western art historiography.[30] Then there is her work as a curator, journalist, and organizer, and her careful cultivation of her own biography and attempts to correlate it to her artistic output,[31] all of which are factors that only now show off Von Wiegand's role within the American art scene from the 1940s to the 1970s.

Future projects regarding Charmion von Wiegand should aim to connect her work not just to geometric, abstract art, but also to artists such as George Brecht, Robert Filliou, and Ray Johnson, artists to whom Von Wiegand could well have had contact, given their shared interest in Buddhist practice.[32] Comparisons with the contemporary artist Adrian Piper, who, since the late 1960s, has been producing art concerned with gender, xenophobia, and social activism in parallel to her work as a professor of analytical philosophy and her yoga practice might also prove fruitful. Asked "Do you keep your different 'selves' separate, or do you integrate them?" Piper answered:

> There are no discrete selves to separate or integrate. My variety of professional activities are all different, equally essential expressions of one self. When I am alone in the solitude of my study or my studio, I am completely out of the closet: I move back and forth easily among art, philosophy and yoga (my third hat). It's the only time I feel completely free to be who I am.[33]

Presumably Charmion von Wiegand would have subscribed to that statement. But our aim here shall be first to introduce today's audiences to the multifaceted legacy, which spanned nearly the entirety of the twentieth century, of this artist and intellectual open to the world's influences.

LORI COLE

CHARMION VON WIEGAND AND THE CREATIVE WORK OF CRITICISM

1   Charmion von Wiegand, "Playwright into Critic," *New Theatre* 3, no. 4 (April 1936): 35.

2   Charmion von Wiegand, "The Box of Pandora," *The Double Dealer* 4, no. 22 (October 1922): 197–199; Letter, Hart Crane to Charmion von Wiegand, October 9, 1922, quoted in Jennifer Newton Hersh, "Abstraction, Spiritualism, and Social Justice: The Art and Writing of Charmion von Wiegand" (PhD dissertation, City University of New York, 1998), 64.

3   In the early 1920s, Von Wiegand published her work in *Poet Lore*, *The Buccaneer*, *The Double Dealer*, *Lyric West*, and *Casements*. See Hersh, 523–527, for a list of her published work.

4   Charlotte Streifer Rubinstein, "Charmion von Wiegand," in *American Women Artists* (Boston: G.K. Hall, 1982), 297, quoted in Hersh, 75.

5   Von Wiegand, "Playwright into Critic," 35–36.

Cover of the New York publication *Art Front*, February 1936, with an illustration by the Mexican artist David Alfaro Siqueiros (1896–1974)

"Criticism actually plays the first creative role in art," Charmion von Wiegand declared in 1936.[1] In her own career, Von Wiegand's experience as a critic was inextricable from her artistic development. Writing for leftist New York-based periodicals such as the *New Masses* (1926–1948) and *Art Front* (1934–1937), she advocated for the compatibility of revolutionary art and politics, covering Cubism, Mexican muralism, Expressionism, and Surrealism, and their reception in the United States. Through her writing, Von Wiegand developed a critical vocabulary to reconcile her commitment to social change with her burgeoning interest in abstraction.

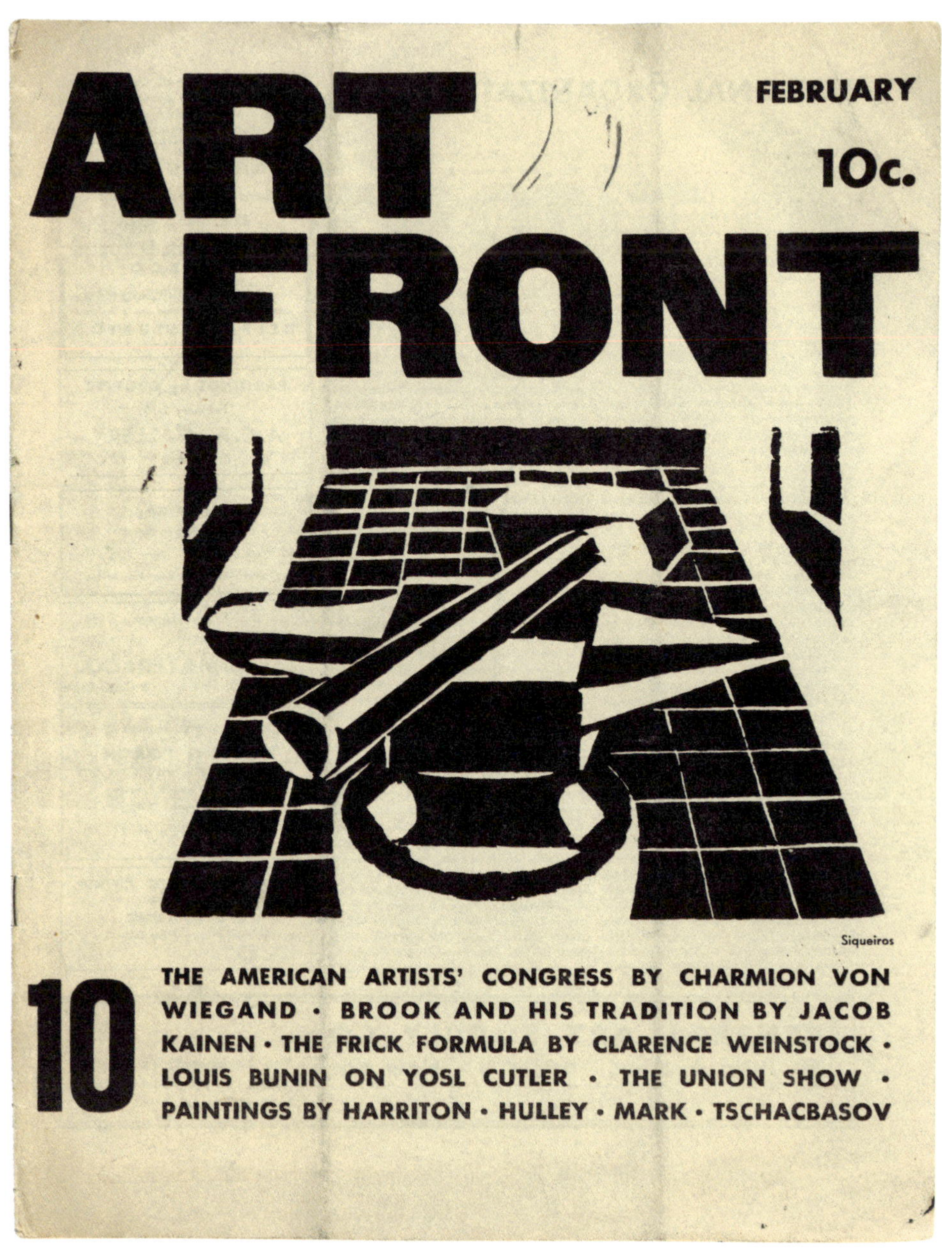

Von Wiegand published her first piece of criticism in 1922 in the New Orleans-based magazine *The Double Dealer* (1921–1926), which prompted the poet Hart Crane to chide, "Say farewell to peace from hence forth, fair lady. Once you have seen yourself between the covers of the magazine you will never be content again without burning oil for it—by which, I mean, 'encores.'"[2] As Crane predicted, Von Wiegand continued to publish art, film, and theater criticism, as well as poetry and plays.[3] At roughly the same time, she began painting; when asked by her psychoanalyst in 1927 what she would do if she could do anything she desired, she proclaimed, "why I'd paint, of course."[4]

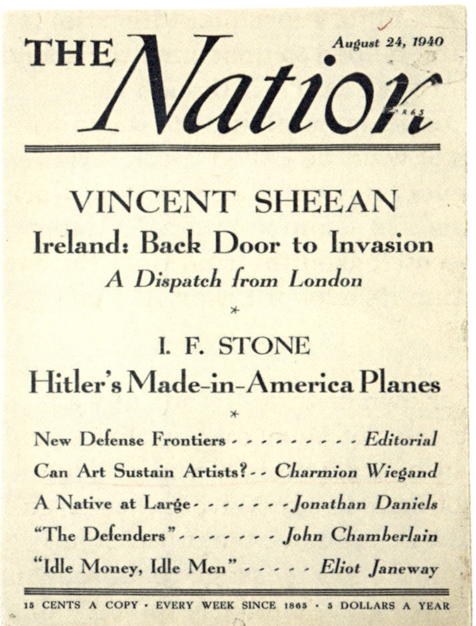

Cover of the weekly magazine *The Nation*, August 24, 1940

6   The European Hearst Service likely hired Von Wiegand because her father, Karl von Wiegand, was a successful journalist who worked for them (Hersh, 148).

7   Von Wiegand became familiar with the *New Masses* as a member of the Workers' Drama League and the New Playwrights' Theatre before her trip to Russia where she met Freeman (Hersh, 192).

8   Arshile Gorky according to his wife, Agnes Gorky Phillips, to Patricia Passlof, December 29, 1956, quoted in Robert Vitz, "Struggle and Response: American Artists and the Great Depression," *New York History* 57, no. 1 (January 1976): 86.

9   Charmion von Wiegand, "Can Art Sustain Artists?," *The Nation* (New York: August 24, 1940): 150.

10   Vitz, 89.

11   Von Wiegand, "Can Art Sustain Artists?," 152.

12   Vitz, 80–98.

Later, in an essay for the leftist *New Theatre* magazine, she would affirm that criticism was productive for artistic practice.[5]

Von Wiegand was the only female correspondent for the Hearst-owned Universal Service in Moscow, where she first went in 1929 and then returned in 1930; she also contributed to the *Moscow Daily News*, an English-language Russian Communist publication, among other outlets.[6] In Russia, Von Wiegand met Joseph Freeman, an editor of the *New Masses*, and she came back with him to New York in 1932 and began contributing to the magazine.[7]

American artists at the time were in acute economic distress; one described "the futility of such paralyzing poverty."[8] As Von Wiegand herself wrote for the leftist political weekly *The Nation* in 1940, "most artists cannot make a living" and "their status remains precarious."[9] These economic and political conditions—and artists' responses to them—informed Von Wiegand's criticism. The Society of Independent Artists staged an art market at the Grand Central Palace in New York in 1931; in 1932, the Artists' Aid Committee organized an open-air show in Washington Square, and similar outdoor shows were organized across the United States.[10] She describes how artists "joined labor and radical protest groups, changed the contents of their pictures to reflect the life around them, and like other affected trades and professions demanded economic relief from the government."[11] From 1933 to 1934, the federal government ran the Public Works of Art Project (PWAP), which treated artists as workers, a model which carried over to the Federal Art Project (1935–1943), overseen by the Works Progress Administration (WPA) as part of President Franklin D. Roosevelt's New Deal policies.[12] Artists formed the Artists' Union and the American Artists' Congress; publications such as the *New Masses* and *Art Front* were extensions of such collective self-organizing.

As a regular contributor to the "Fine Arts" column and one of only two women on staff at the *New Masses*—a successor to the

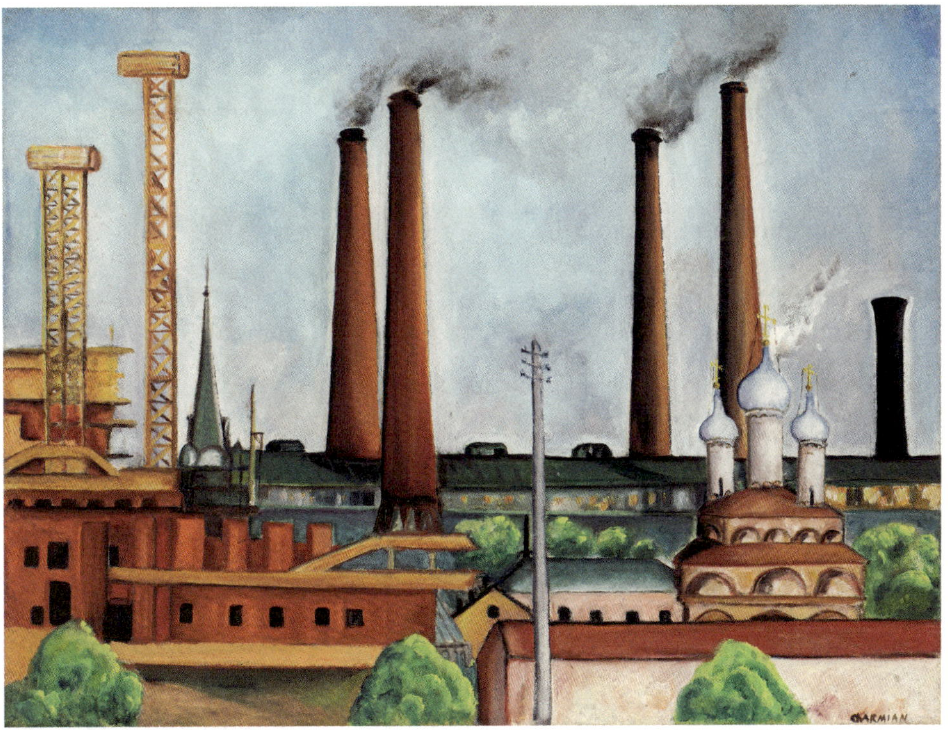

Charmion von Wiegand, *New Russia*, 1929, oil on canvas, 54.6 × 71.1 cm, signed, Estate of Charmion von Wiegand, Courtesy of Michael Rosenfeld Gallery LLC, New York

13　　Virginia Hagelstein
Marquardt, "Art on the Political
Front in America: From
The Liberator to *Art Front*,"
Art Journal 52, no. 1, Political
Journals and Art, 1910–40
(Spring 1993): 72.

14　　Michael Gold, "Notes of the
Month," *New Masses* (New York)
6, no. 4 (September 1930): 5,
quoted in Virginia Hagelstein
Marquardt, "Art on the Left
in the United States, 1918–1937,"
in *Art and Journals on the
Political Front, 1910–1940*, ed.
Virginia Hagelstein Marquardt
(Gainesville: University Press
of Florida, 1997), 228.

15　　David Peck, "'The Tradition
of American Revolutionary
Literature': The Monthly *New
Masses*, 1926–1933," *Science
and Society* 42, no. 4 (Winter
1978/1979): 393, 398.

16　　Charmion von Wiegand,
"David Alfaro Siqueiros," *New
Masses* (New York) 11, no. 5
(May 1, 1934): 18.

17　　Ibid.

18　　Charmion von Wiegand,
"The Fine Arts," *New Masses*
(New York) 24, no. 3 (July 13,
1937): 29.

19　　Charmion von Wiegand,
"The Fine Arts," *New Masses*
(New York) 23, no. 4 (April 20,
1937): 38.

20　　Charmion von Wiegand,
"Letter to the Editor: The
Strongly Native American Art
of Marsden Hartley," *New York
Times* (April 14, 1940): 133;
Charmion von Wiegand,
"Letter to the Editor: Joseph
Stella," *New York Times*
(February 23, 1941): X9.

21　　Gerald M. Monroe, "Art
Front," *Archives of American
Art Journal* 13, no. 3 (1973): 13.

socialist weekly *The Masses* (1911–1917) and its subsequent iteration,
The Liberator (1918–1924)—Von Wiegand helped to articulate the social
and political role of art, a subject of fierce debate.[13] Although the
New Masses was initially artistically experimental, in 1928 its editor
Michael Gold refashioned it in service of what he called "proletarian
art," noting in 1930 that "Every poem, every novel and drama [and work
of art], must have a social theme, or it is mere confectionery."[14] Later
that year, the magazine joined the Moscow-based International Bureau
of Revolutionary Artists (IBRA), orienting its artwork even further
toward a proletarian model.[15]

In her reviews, Von Wiegand offered her own criteria for socially engaged art. For example, she lauded the work of Mexican muralist David
Alfaro Siqueiros as "one form of revolutionary action."[16] She praised
his use of exterior walls and of automobile paint and airbrushes, argu-
ing that "we must cease to be enslaved by expensive technical equip-
ment; we must learn to convey the revolutionary message to masses in
any medium that comes to hand."[17] Von Wiegand similarly linked Pablo
Picasso's political engagements with his formal innovations, writing,
"Like the sensitive seismograph, which records a catastrophe in nature,
Picasso, the artist, registers the social earthquake of fascism and re-
coils from its violence."[18] Von Wiegand's criticism focused primarily on
painting and what she called the turn "away from representational
painting" toward abstraction.[19] "Abstract art has become a vital issue
in the USA," she notes in 1937. Elsewhere, Von Wiegand drew attention
to work by artists such as Joseph Stella and Marsden Hartley.[20]

As the *New Masses* shifted in orientation toward Russia, *Art Front*
emerged as an outlet for politically-engaged American artists in the
1930s and became "the liveliest art periodical of the time."[21] Von Wiegand
was the magazine's only female editor and one of its few women
contributors.[22] *Art Front* began as a joint venture of the Artists'
Committee of Action, formed in 1934 to protest Nelson Rockefeller's
destruction of Diego Rivera's mural *Man at the Crossroads*,

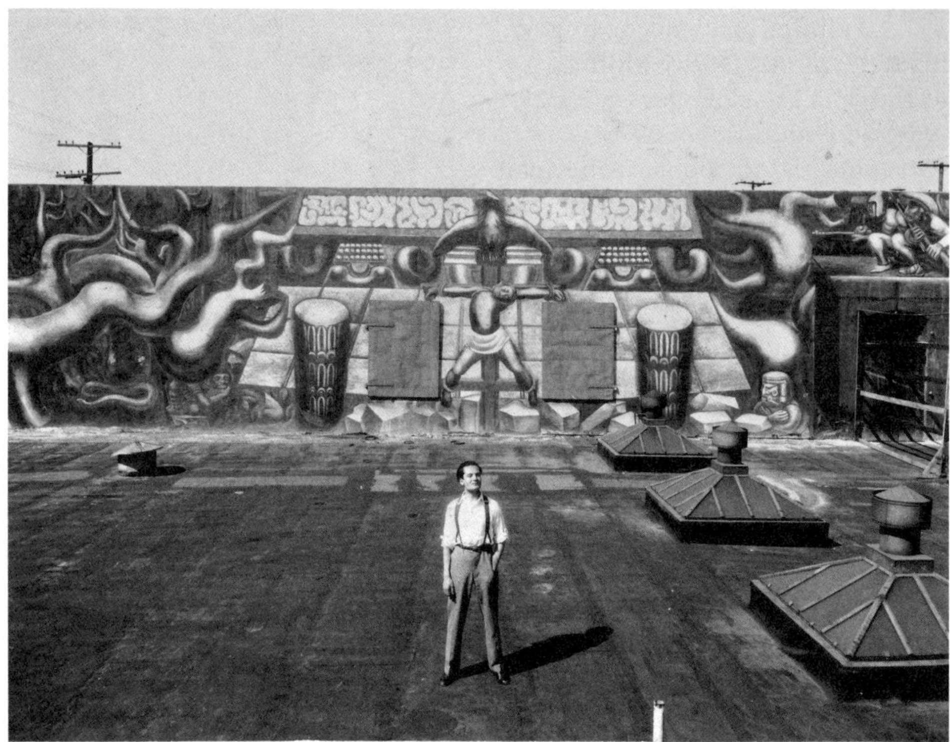

The Bolivian artist Roberto Berdecio (1910–1996) in front of David Alfaro Siqueiros
mural *América Tropical*, Los Angeles, 1932

22   Von Wiegand was listed on the masthead starting in November 1936 (Hersh, iv); Berenice Abbott and Elizabeth McCausland (writing as "Elizabeth Noble") also wrote for *Art Front*.

23   *Art Front* (November 1934): 2; by April 1935, it became the "Official Publication of the Artists' Union," though the masthead had both symbols until January 1937 (Monroe, 13); Marquardt, "Art on the Left in the United States," 235.

24   Monroe, 13, 16–17.

25   Ibid., 13, quoting Grievance Committee of the Artists' Union, "Jobs and Adequate Relief," *Art Front* (November 1934): 3.

26   Charmion von Wiegand, "American Artists' Congress," *Art Front* (February 1936): 8.

27   Marquardt, "Art on the Political Front in America," 79; Monroe, 15.

28   Marquardt, "Art on the Left in the United States," 235.

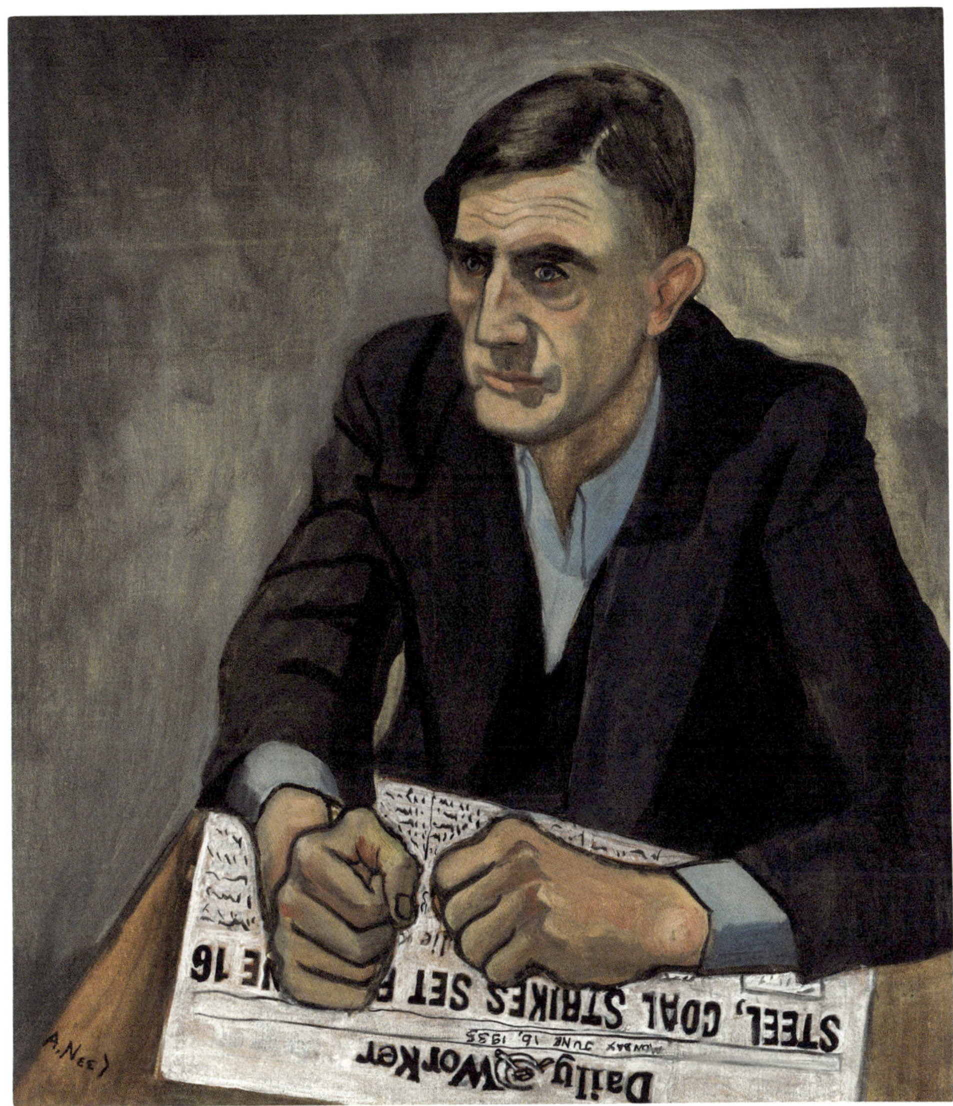

Alice Neel, *Pat Whalen*, 1935, oil, ink, and newspaper on canvas, 68.9 × 58.7 cm, Whitney Museum of American Art, Gift of Dr. Hartley Neel

along with the Artists' Union, also established in 1934, to advocate for unemployed artists.[23] At first resembling a union publication, *Art Front* initially consisted of eight-page issues in an 11- by 16-inch format, but by December 1935 it was reformatted as a 9- by 12-inch art journal. Roughly sixteen to thirty-two pages in length, it published writing by Louis Aragon, Frederick Kiesler, and Berenice Abbott, and reproduced artwork by Alexander Calder, Alice Neel, and Isamu Noguchi.[24]

As its name suggests, *Art Front* foregrounded the arts and alluded to the popular front, an alliance formed in the 1930s between leftist and centrist parties. It announced itself as a publication that "speaks for the artist, battles for his economic security, and guides him in his artistic efforts."[25] Von Wiegand's first piece for *Art Front* anticipated the inaugural meeting of the American Artists' Congress in 1936, an organization founded "to safeguard art and culture against the threats of war and fascism." As Von Wiegand notes, "This is the first time in American history that artists have organized on so wide a scale for the purpose of protecting their crafts, and culture in general, in a social situation fraught with danger."[26]

Those writing for *Art Front* were particularly concerned with representing America in a way that reflected their politics. Many opposed Regionalism, the American-focused scene painting embodied by the work of Thomas Hart Benton, Grant Wood, and John Steuart Curry.[27] They viewed such work as "romantic and escapist in its virtual disregard for the problems facing workers during the depression."[28]

35

29   Ibid., 236; see Stuart Davis, "The New American Scene in Art," *Art Front* (February 1935): 6; Jacob Burck, "Benton Sees Red," *Art Front* (February 1935): 5, 8; Thomas H. Benton, "On the American Scene," *Art Front* (February 1935): 4, 8; John Steuart Curry, "A Letter from Curry," *Art Front* (February 1935): 1.

30   Stuart Davis, "A Medium of 2 Dimensions," *Art Front* (May 1935): 6; Marquardt, "Art on the Left in the United States," 237.

31   Charmion von Wiegand, "The Fine Arts," *New Masses* (New York) 23, no. 12 (June 15, 1937): 29.

32   Angela Miller, "'With Eyes Wide Open': The American Reception of Surrealism," in *Caught by Politics: Hitler Exiles and American Visual Culture*, ed. Sabine Eckmann and Lutz Koepnick (New York: Palgrave Macmillan, 2007), 64; Monroe, 15.

33   Fernand Léger, "The New Realism," trans. Harold Rosenberg, *Art Front* (December 1935): 10.

34   Balcomb Greene, "Abstract Art at the Modern Museum," *Art Front* (April 1936): 8.

35   Clarence Weinstock [Clarence Humboldt, pseud.], "Freedom in Painting," *Art Front* (January 1936): 10.

36   Charmion von Wiegand, "Expressionism and Social Change," *Art Front* (November 1936): 12.

Writing in *Art Front*, artists like Stuart Davis and Jacob Burck condemned Regionalism, while Benton and Curry defended it.[29] Davis, an editor of *Art Front*, argued in favor of abstraction: "The abstract artist might be best equipped to provide artistic expression to social problems because he 'has already learned to abandon the ivory tower in his objective approach to materials.'"[30] Davis's 1935 cover for *Art Front* features these materials: paint brushes, tubes of paint, a palette knife, a saw, and a pencil. As for Von Wiegand, she took the measured position that "The rise of regionalism in painting, while in many respects reactionary, has had the good effect of directing attention toward artists in other parts of the United States."[31]

However, if some condemned "the xenophobia of Regionalism," others criticized abstraction as a "servile imitation of Europe."[32] The magazine's debates on the merits of abstraction coalesced around Fernand Léger's 1935 talk at the Museum of Modern Art (MoMA) titled "The New Realism," which he delivered in French, excerpts of which were then translated into English for *Art Front* by Harold Rosenberg, who later became an influential art critic. Léger defined abstraction as a "new realism," asserting that color and geometric form have "a reality in itself, independent and plastic."[33] In response, Balcomb Greene, an abstract artist, hailed Léger as "the complete revolutionist."[34] By contrast, the artist Clarence Weinstock wrote that painting cannot free art from subject matter until "subject matter itself is free."[35] Such exchanges—over whether or not explicitly social subject matter was needed to constitute truly "revolutionary" art—served as the backdrop against which Von Wiegand developed her own critical and painterly sensibilities. "Neither abstract art nor academic pictorialism are satisfactory means to embody the social struggle of our time as it assumes ever more dramatic and violent form in the United States," she wrote in 1936. Expressionism, she argued, was a form of abstraction infused with spiritual urgency, which could communicate political exigencies, noting that "its activism is a vehicle suited to American vitality."[36]

Although Von Wiegand favored Expressionism over Cubism, she continued to champion the work of Picasso. In her analysis of *Guernica*

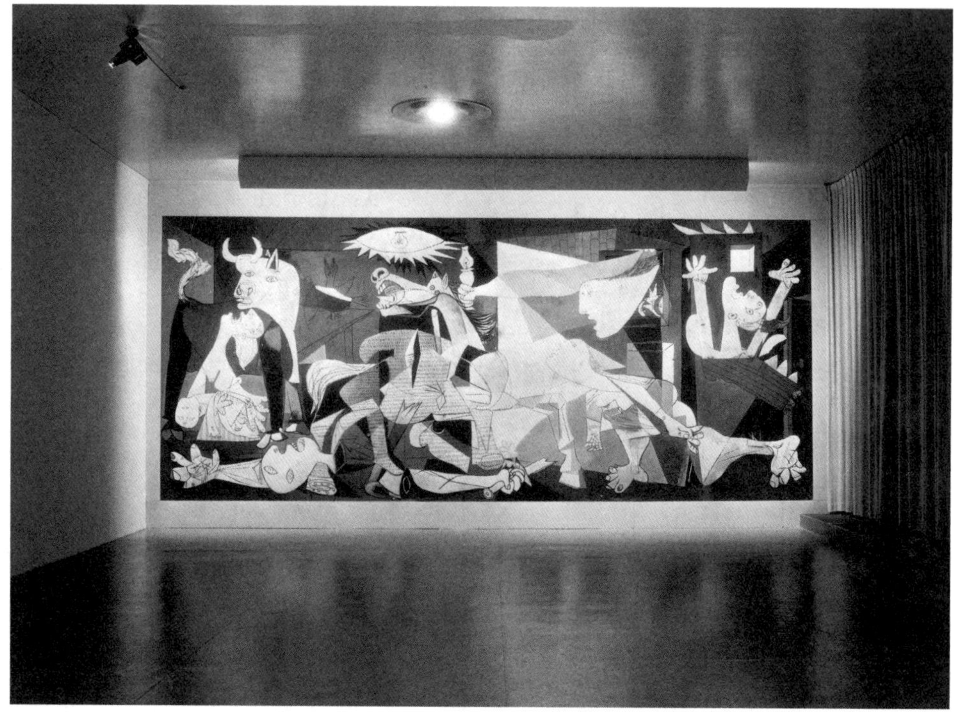

View of Pablo Picasso's *Guernica* (1937) exhibited in *Picasso Forty Years of His Art*, Museum of Modern Art, New York (November 15, 1939–January 7, 1940)

THE SURREALISTS
By Charmion Van Wiegand

MASK OF FEAR

PAUL KLEE

Courtesy Museum of Modern Art

THE present exhibition now on at the Museum of Modern art called Fantastic Art, Dada, and Surrealism arouses belated echoes of the post-war controversies which rocked the European art world more than a decade ago. The shell-shocked imagination of the continental artists exposed for over four years to the unendurable reality of destruction and war, the disintegration and social chaos which grew out of the bloody slaughter, revolted and found relief in a fantastic world where the usual logical and rational concepts ceased to be valid. If the explosive anarchism of Dadaism (born in 1916) intent upon wiping out existing notions of beauty and obliterating all individuality was mad, madder still was the world it reflected where millions of human beings were perishing and the whole cultural heritage of man was overthrown in the ruthless struggle for power.

The museum has arranged its exhibition in historical sequences and if you have the sardonic humor of Dada, you may see it with the eyes of the visitor, who termed it "just four floors of good clean fun." But if you are more seriously inclined, you may see in the astonishing potpourri of paintings, collages, sculpture and unesthetic objects in general, the heroic effort of man to adjust himself in a tragic dilemma, the need to find release from the unbearable confusion and contradictions inherent in a dying social order.

Fantastic art has always existed in all peoples and all societies. Its two great branches—grotesque and erotic art— are inevitable manifestations where human energy is not reduced to the minimum of self preservation. Good as the present exhibition is, it is a sterilized version of fantasy, in which the extreme aberrations of the grotesque and particularly the erotic have been politely eliminated. But the addition of a section devoted to fantastic art in Europe since the end of the middle ages with examples of Bosch, Duerer, Hogarth, Blake, Goya and the belated romantics, despite many astonishing resemblances to surrealist images, only serves particularly in the early old masters to bring into sharp contrast the tremendous difference between the robust imagination of a growing society disengaging itself from medieval superstition and "the sickness of the world" which is surrealism self-styled.

It is impossible in small space even to review this enormous collection of "art" objects of all times and of varied esthetic worth from fur-covered cups, zipper-eyed suede maidens, bearded grapes, mathematical objects, rotating glass machines, bird-cages filled with sugar, collages of all sorts, architectural photographs, prints, paintings and sculpture. A serious omission is the lack of photomontage—in particular, the work of John Heartfield—the one phase of modern fantastic art which has received universal approbation and has been incorporated in our everyday existence.

Is it possible to rescue sense out of confusion and discover the meaning behind the surrealist efflorescence of fantasy in a hard-headed and rational age? The Cubists, we know, reduced the human body into separate parts, analyzing and dissecting it with surgical precision until they had destroyed its organic unity. The Surrealists seem to wish to perform the same task for the human mind. Their work coming after Cubism represents and reflects an even more acute crisis in the disintegration of the individual in capitalist society.

Three events in the beginning of this century hastened the death of the old order of society. They were the destruction of the concepts of the physical world with Einstein's discovery of the theory of relativity; the destruction of the moral concepts of our social life by Freud's theory of psychoanalysis; the destruction of existing political structures with the

First page of Charmion von Wiegand's review of the exhibition *Fantastic Art, Dada, Surrealism* in the publication *Art Front*, January 1937

37   Charmion von Wiegand, "Picasso's Last Period," *Direction* 3, no. 6 (Summer 1940): 38.

38   Ibid., 40; Margit Rowell, "Interview with Charmion von Wiegand, June 20, 1971," in *Piet Mondrian, 1872–1944: Centennial Exhibition* (New York: Solomon R. Guggenheim Foundation, 1971), 78.

39   Von Wiegand, "Picasso's Last Period," 39.

40   In the catalog to *Fantastic Art, Dada, Surrealism*, Barr reinforces the tension between the two exhibitions, even though many of the same artists were included in both shows. Alfred H. Barr, Jr., ed., *Fantastic Art, Dada, Surrealism* (New York: Museum of Modern Art, 1936), 9; Isabelle Dervaux, "A Tale of Two Earrings: Surrealism and Abstraction, 1930–1947," in *Surrealism USA*, ed. Isabelle Dervaux (Ostfildern-Ruit: Hatje Cantz, 2005), 50.

41   Von Wiegand, "Picasso's Last Period," 40.

42   Charmion von Wiegand, "The Surrealists," *Art Front* (January 1937): 12.

43   Ibid., 14.

44   Louis Aragon, "Painting and Realism," trans. James Johnson Sweeney, *Art Front* (January 1937): 10; Salvador Dalí, "I Defy Aragon," *Art Front* (March 1937): 7.

45   Clarence Weinstock [Clarence Humboldt, pseud.], "The Man in the Balloon," *Art Front* (March 1937): 10; Samuel Putnam, "Marxism and Surrealism," *Art Front* (March 1937): 10–11; Miller, 65.

for the magazine *Direction* in 1939, she writes, "We see Picasso build the gaunt forms of dynamic cubism into gigantic machines of energy."[37] By contrast, she saw Mondrian's work as more mathematical than expressive: "While Mondrian was pushing Cubist principle to its logical conclusion in an art as pure as mathematics [...] Picasso was searching for a new way to create pictorial reality."[38] Von Wiegand reflects on *Guernica*'s implications for abstraction, claiming, "It is one of many contemporary absurdities that this art built on the most concrete pictorial reality should bear the name 'abstract.'" She compares the work to a photograph, making a case for such abstraction's relationship to the real, as well as its political and emotional heft.[39]

Such a reckoning with the legacy of Cubism and other European movements mirrored the kinds of exhibitions that were on view in New York at the time. MoMA held *Cubism and Abstract Art* (March–April 1936) and then *Fantastic Art, Dada, Surrealism* (December 1936–January 1937).[40] In her *Direction* essay, Von Wiegand describes how Surrealists "turned their backs on external reality [...] to delve into the world of the unconscious and of the dream."[41] Yet in her review of *Fantastic Art, Dada, Surrealism* for *Art Front*, Von Wiegand argues that the movement's turn inward still reflected a "crisis in the disintegration of the individual in capitalist society." She suggests that Surrealist experiments with automatism, for example, were a response to their lived experiences, noting that the "shell-shocked imagination of the continental artists exposed for over four years to the unendurable reality of destruction and war [...] found relief in a fantastic world where the usual logical and rational concepts ceased to be valid."[42] She enumerates Giorgio de Chirico and Picasso's contributions as well as those of Wassily Kandinsky, George Grosz, Paul Klee, Marcel Duchamp, Francis Picabia, and Man Ray, and analyzes work by Max Ernst and Salvador Dalí. Yet, while she praises Surrealism for "pictorializing the destructive and creative processes of the subconscious mind," she argues that ultimately, "the art of the future, which will strive for a new humanism on a social basis will inevitably turn its face toward the world of reality again."[43]

Defining and conveying what constituted "reality" was integral to these debates. Surrealism was pitted against realism again in articles written by Aragon and Dalí for *Art Front*. Aragon argued for a realism not "dominated by nature" but rather reflective of a "conscious expression of social realities." He states, "In a word, it will either be a socialistic realism or painting will cease to exist," to which Dalí responded, "the true laboratory wherein one pursues the systemic exploration of uncharted regions of the human mind is 'Surrealism.'"[44] Clarence Weinstock then condemned Dalí's "miserable eclectic art," and the writer Samuel Putnam agreed that "only truly Marxist art is a socialist realism."[45] Many distrusted Surrealism in the United States because of its ties to commercialism, as evidenced by Dalí's entanglements with advertising, and instead championed "social surrealism" produced by American artists like Walter Quirt (whom Von Wiegand had reviewed favorably in the *New Masses*).[46] Abstract artists faced similar hurdles. As Jacob Kainen writes in *Art Front*, "For various reasons, abstract painters in this country have had to put up with a fierce cross-fire of general opposition."[47] Much as in Europe where the artists' group Cercle et Carré was founded to defend, as Michel Seuphor wrote, "a mental attitude diametrically opposed to the troubled climate of Surrealism," similarly the American Abstract Artists group (AAA) was founded in 1936 in New York.[48]

46   Charmion von Wiegand, "The Fine Arts," *New Masses* (New York) 18, no. 13 (March 24, 1936): 25; Charmion von Wiegand, "Quirt," *Art Front* (April 1936): 13; Miller, 68–69; see *I Dream about an Evening Dress*, Dalí's contribution to *Vogue*'s "3 Man Show," *Vogue* (March 15, 1937): 80, quoted in Sandra Zalman, "The Vernacular as Vanguard: Alfred Barr, Salvador Dalí, and the U.S. Reception of Surrealism in the 1930s," *The Journal of Surrealism and the Americas* 1 (2007): 49.

47   Jacob Kainen, "American Abstract Artists," *Art Front* (April/May 1937): 25.

48   Dervaux, 48; It was the dispute between abstraction and Surrealism that influenced the rise of Abstract Expressionism in the United States (Dervaux, 51–55).

49   Charmion von Wiegand, review of *Five on Revolutionary Art*, *Art Front* (September–October 1936): 10.

50   Rowell, "Interview with Charmion von Wiegand," 78.

51   Ibid.

Edward McKnight, study of cover for the publication *Five on Revolutionary Art*, 1935, graphite and gouache on paper, 18.9 × 13 cm, Cooper Hewitt, Smithsonian Design Museum

The debate over the value of abstraction was further addressed in the 1935 pamphlet *Five on Revolutionary Art*, published by the leftist British organization Artists International Association (AIA), which Von Wiegand reviewed for *Art Front*. She notes that Herbert Read "offers Miró and Mondrian as the only 'true revolutionary artists.'" Yet she criticizes Read's view of the abstract artist as "the custodian of the formal values dedicated to the future socialist society." Instead, Von Wiegand contends, "if the forms of abstract art are to have relevancy for the future society, they must inevitably undergo profound changes during a period of social revolution."[49] However, after Herbert Read declared Mondrian to be one of the only true revolutionary artists, Von Wiegand decided that she had to meet him.[50] Their meeting, on April 12, 1941, led to a mutually enriching conversation about art and ideas that changed the course of Von Wiegand's work: "from that first meeting, my eyes were transformed," she said.[51] Conversely, as a painter and critic, she offered Mondrian an entry point into the New York arts

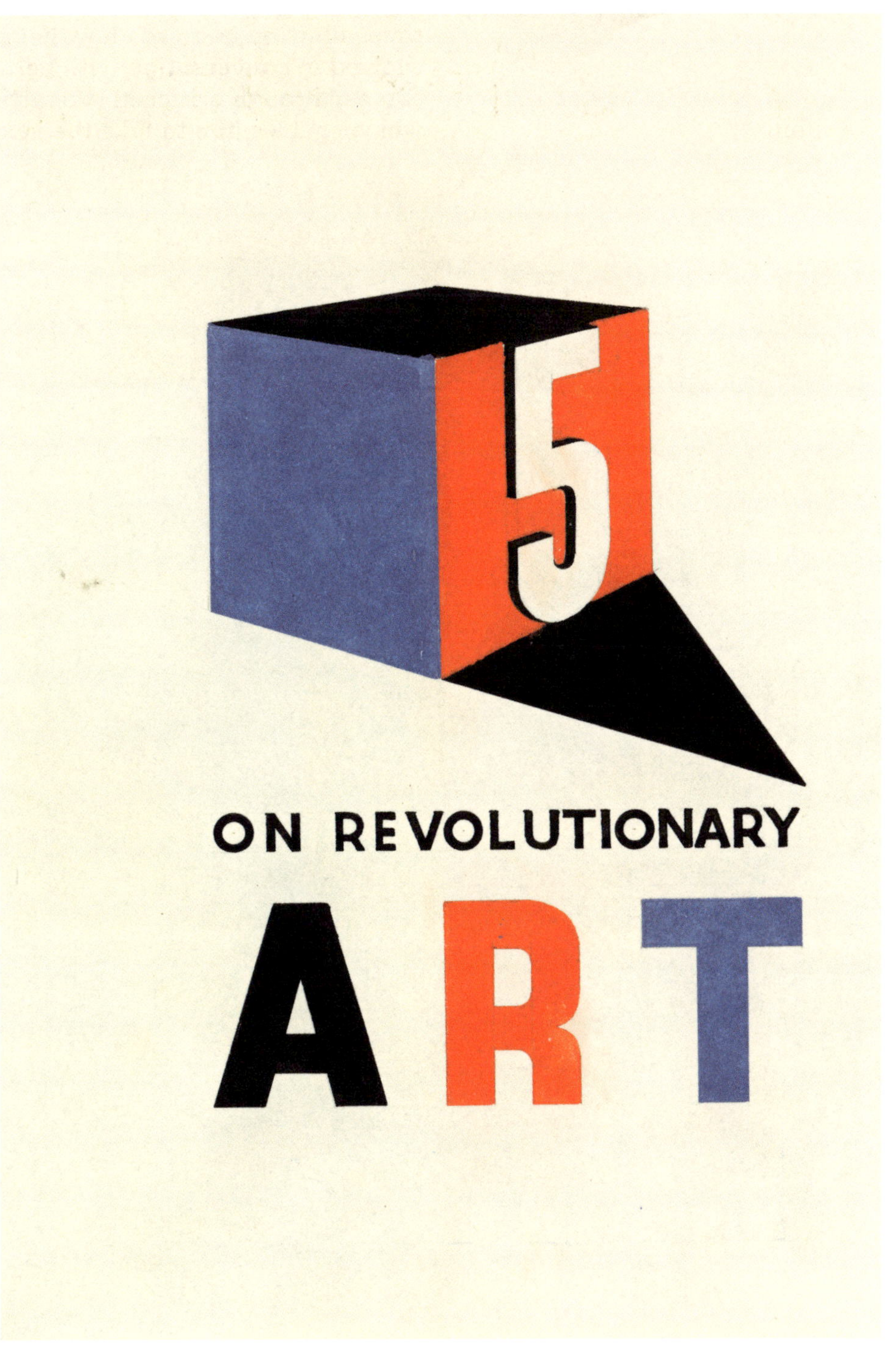

community and worked with him to translate his writing into English for an American audience.[52] Their discussions, which led to Von Wiegand's deep engagement with his ideas, also provided the basis for her article, "The Meaning of Mondrian," published in the *Journal of Aesthetics and Art Criticism* in 1943. In it, Von Wiegand calls Mondrian's work "a new beginning" for American art.[53]

While Von Wiegand's encounter with Mondrian reinvigorated her commitment to painting, she also continued to write for a variety of publications, including *Art News*, *Arts Magazine*, and the *Arts Yearbook*, where she reflected on work by Mark Tobey, Marsden Hartley, Picasso, as well as Mondrian. She found that her criticism sharpened and contributed to her artistic development. As she noted in 1936, "the best critics have always been creators."[54]

Her criticism was a catalyst for her own work as well. Through her writing, she engaged in the central political and aesthetic debates of her time, allowing us to see how her position on abstraction, in particular, evolved in conversation with her contemporaries. As Von Wiegand observes, through criticism "the artist achieves a necessary clarification, which enables him to take the next step forward in his creative work."[55]

52   Hersh, 259–260.

53   Charmion von Wiegand, "The Meaning of Mondrian," *Journal of Aesthetics and Art Criticism* 2, no. 8 (Fall 1943): 62.

54   Von Wiegand, "Playwright into Critic," 35.

55   Ibid.

MARTIN BRAUEN

"YOU ARE A WRITER AND I DON'T WANT TO KNOW ABOUT YOUR PAINTING"[1]

CHARMION VON WIEGAND'S ORIGINS AS AN ARTIST

1   Charmion von Wiegand, Diary, October 29, 1942. The diary and letters of Charmion von Wiegand cited below are housed in the artist's estate: Estate of Charmion von Wiegand, Collection of Khyongla Rato.

2   Oral history interview with Charmion von Wiegand by Paul Cummings, October 9 and November 3, 1968. Archives of American Art, Smithsonian Institution, 10, quoted in Jennifer Newton Hersh, "Abstraction, Spiritualism, and Social Justice: The Art and Writing of Charmion von Wiegand" (PhD dissertation, City University of New York, 1998), 75.

3   Charmion von Wiegand, letter to her father, Karl von Wiegand, September 2, 1927, quoted in Hersh, 78.

4   Charmion von Wiegand, letter to Karl von Wiegand, September 6, 1927, quoted in Hersh, 79; as a young woman, Charmion von Wiegand was in contact with various artists—among them Joseph Stella, Jules Pascin, and the poet Hart Crane—who contributed greatly to her knowledge of both art and literature. Also influential were the artists David Burliuk, Jure Labaš, and Adolf Wolff.

5   Charmion von Wiegand, letter to Karl von Wiegand, August 8, 1929, quoted in Hersh, 132.

6   Here in Russia only the human being is of value-- the abstract has no meaning--the struggle above for some end is unreal. Only the brotherhood of man--man in his relation to his fellow beings. This is the living reality of Russia. See Hersh, 142.

7   Hersh, 178; the concept of "socialist realism" was coined only later, in 1932.

8   Hersh, 180–181; see Lori Cole's essay, "Charmion von Wiegand and the Creative Work of Criticism," in the present publication, pp. 31–40.

The beginnings of Charmion von Wiegand's artistic creativity seem to date back to 1927, while she was undergoing psychoanalysis. Asked by her analyst, Dr. L. Pierce Clark, what she would do if she could choose freely, she immediately replied, "Why I'd paint, of course." And when Dr. Clark pressed her on the question of why she was not doing that already, she answered, "It's too late in life to be a painter."[2]

All the same, the thirty-year-old Von Wiegand went out and bought some paints and began painting at her suburban home in Darien, Connecticut. And although she never had a brush or pencil in my hand till about eight weeks ago, she told her father in a letter, she could scarcely wait to get up in the morning to paint.[3] In fact, I never had so much enjoyment out of anything.[4]

Two years later, during a six-month-long visit to Moscow at the end of the 1920s, Von Wiegand wrote that her most important activity there consisted in painting and drawing: I have only the [one] desire--painting.[5] Her preferred subjects were landscapes, factory buildings, churches, interiors, and window views, although she regretted not being able to depict the brotherhood of man, which is what *revolutionary artists* were doing in their art.[6]

Von Wiegand returned to Moscow in September 1930 after a short intermezzo in New York. This time she was in the Soviet capital as a journalist, and her artistic output seems to have decreased notably when compared to her first six-month-long Russian sojourn. An avid reader of Marx, Lenin, Trotsky, and Engels, she was firmly persuaded of the need for fundamental social and political change based on communist principles and of rebellion against the bourgeoisie. She held proletarian art—also referred to

9   Von Wiegand, Diary, June 10, 1941 (or June 12, 1941): I felt he [Piet Mondrian] was tired and I planned to go home at 10.30. Our conversation flagged a bit. I forgot to say that before I had told him about <u>Art Front</u> and how I had once attacked him in that review <u>Five on Revolutionary Art</u>. And his eyes flashed for the moment--he can be very angry--and then he laughed and playfully struck at me. So I told him it was only about that old chestnut form and how we leftists always thought abstract art was devoid of content.

10   Von Wiegand, Introduction to the Diary, dated March 26, 1960.

11   Ibid.: But in 1940, there was still a hiatus--a period of stagnation, of uncertainty and groping. In my own work, I felt at an impasse. The last landscapes I had made in the country had become ever more simplified, and preferably painted in winter, they were white with trees and buildings as structural accents. More and more I was troubled by the fact, that I could not any longer as formerly paint great distances, that the horizon line refused to lie back, and that top and bottom came together in a kind of plane. This unconscious destruction of the perspective was perturbing--against my will--and I felt that I was retrograding instead of advancing. It was thus that I had taken to writing to find a new vantage point. And with curiosity I looked at modern painting in a new way.

12   Hersh, 221.

13   Von Wiegand, letter to Piet Mondrian, June 5, 1941: For when I first saw them, I felt them as beautiful design merely and saw their relation to life as in architecture and in design.

as revolutionary art—in high esteem and was thrilled with the socialist philosophy of art.[7] Von Wiegand took the view that artists should be socially aware and that art should reflect the artist's own political views;[8] and as a self-avowed leftist, she was absolutely convinced that abstract art was devoid of content.[9]

The Crisis and Rediscovery of Art

Charmion von Wiegand's attitude to art changed fundamentally in the late 1930s when, as an artist, she experienced a hiatus--a period of stagnation, of uncertainty and groping.[10] She felt herself to be at an impasse and was troubled by her inability to paint landscapes with spatial depth and perspective as she had done previously without coming into conflict with naturalism and the striving for ever greater abstraction. This unconscious destruction of the perspective was perturbing--against my will-- and I felt that I was retrograding instead of advancing. Hence her decision to dedicate herself more to writing. Her decision to begin again permitted her to look at modern painting from a new vantage point, with greater curiosity and in a new way.[11]

At the time Von Wiegand suggested to a publisher that she write an article based on an interview with Piet Mondrian. She had seen only a few of his works in the original, specifically those that had been shown at Albert Eugene Gallatin's Gallery of Living Art[12] and at the *Cubism and Abstract Art* exhibition at New York's Museum of Modern Art in 1936; however, they had not impressed her much, and she had categorized them rather as beautiful design.[13]

It was through a friend of hers, the artist Carl Holty, that

14   See also Nancy J. Troy's essay "'Mondrian was my Guru': Charmion von Wiegand and Piet Mondrian in the 1940s and 1950s," in the present publication, pp. 67–90. Charmion von Wiegand's diary, her "Notes on Mondrian," her letters to Piet Mondrian, and his letters to her are published in a separate book: Martin Brauen, ed., *A Sameness Between Us: The Friendship of Charmion von Wiegand and Piet Mondrian in Letters and Memoirs* (Stuttgart: Arnoldsche Art), 2020.

15   Von Wiegand, letter, June 5, 1941: It seems to me that the problem of creating unity through an equilibrium established through the equivalence of unequal oppositions has always been the basic problem of life and of art. But today it assumes a new and more vital importance, because it expresses the need of all human beings in a moment of destruction and disintegration, when the very fabric of society is being rent apart. But the very intensity of this destruction must bring forth an equal intensity of creation. And I believe that in every field of endeavor, people are working and struggling over the problem, of a new unity through a new integration of the creative energies in the world.

Letter by Piet Mondrian to Charmion von Wiegand, December 8, 1941, Collection of Khyongla Rato

Von Wiegand first met Mondrian in person. That momentous encounter in April 1941 marked the beginning of a checkered relationship that would endure right up to Mondrian's death.

Though Von Wiegand's interview with Mondrian was never actually published, it would lead to a close collaboration in the months to come. She edited and revised those texts by the artist written in English, while also translating a number of his other texts from the French. This turned out to be a difficult undertaking, given that she lacked the necessary vocabulary to understand his ideas and express them. The more she studied Mondrian's art and immersed herself in his conceptual world, however, the more she began to understand and appreciate his work, as can be inferred from her increasingly euphoric utterances. On her many visits to him, moreover, she also began commenting on his works and even hazarding her own verdicts of them.[14]

Von Wiegand's understanding of art had changed and was no longer identical with that of her past revolutionary phase. Her meetings and discussions with Mondrian definitely left their mark on her and persuaded her that one of art's most basic functions had always been, as she would formulate it, creating unity through an equilibrium established through the equivalence of unequal oppositions.[15] The war then raging had consequently lent a new urgency and importance to art, Von Wiegand argued, because it expresses the need of all human beings in a moment of destruction and disintegration, when the very fabric of society is being rent apart.

Mondrian's work, she explained in a letter to him from August 1941, had made her aware of something she had long been

Continue on p. 57

45

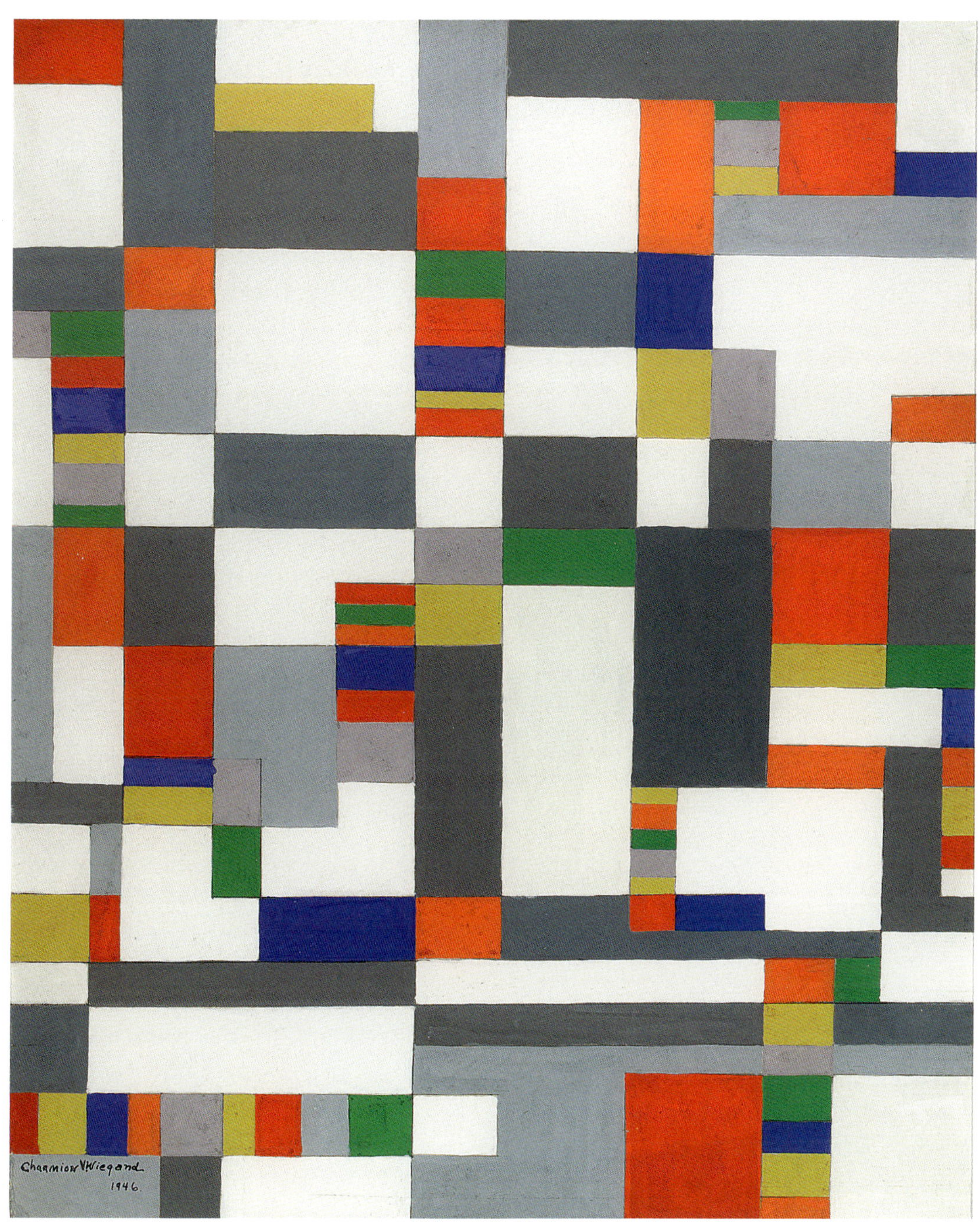

City Lights, 1946
pencil and gouache on board, 50.2 × 40.6 cm
Collection of Charles and Kathleen Harper, Chicago

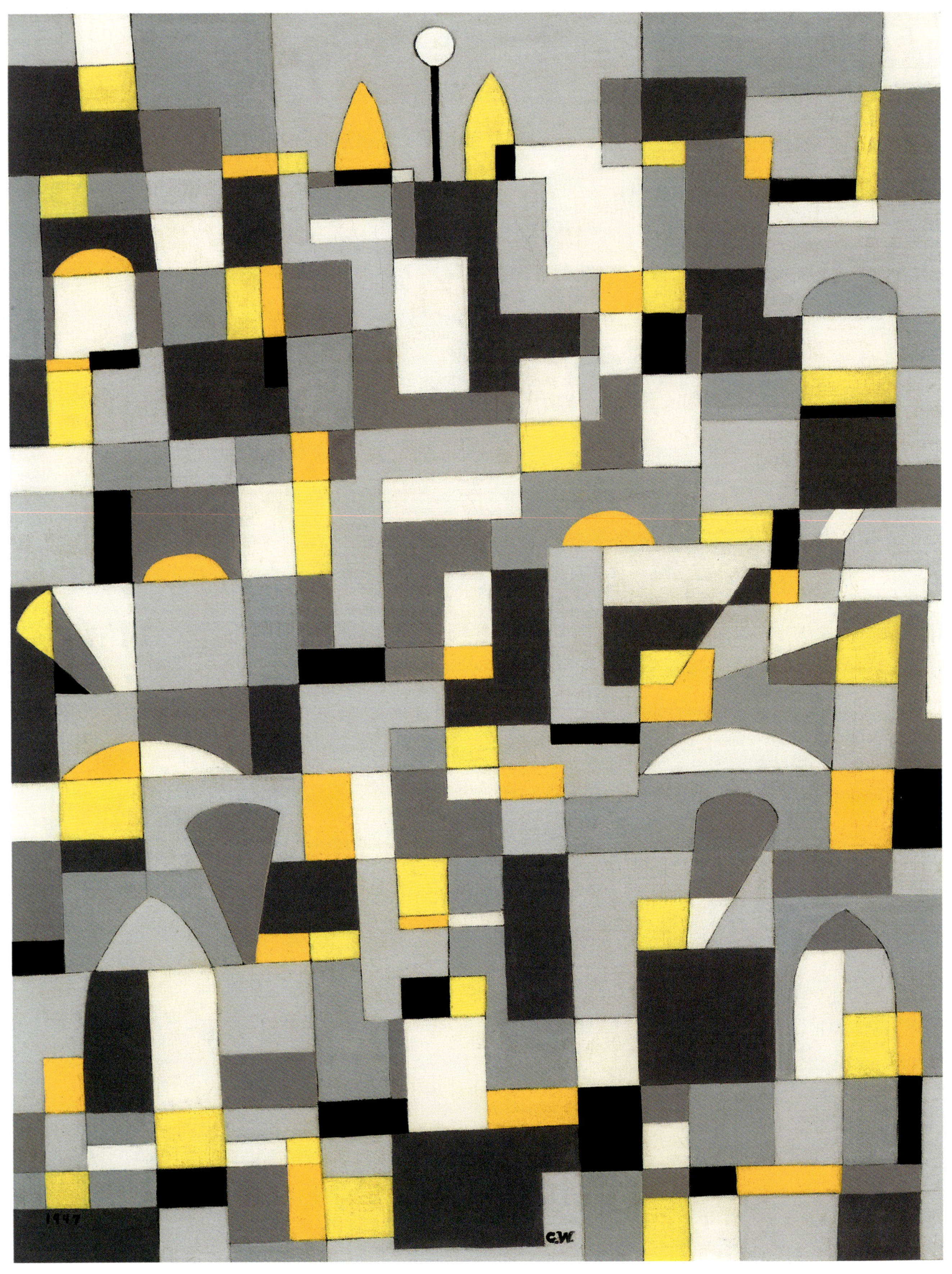

City Lights, 1947
oil on canvas, 81.9 × 61.8 cm
Whitney Museum of American Art, New York,
Gift of Ruth Stephan Franklin

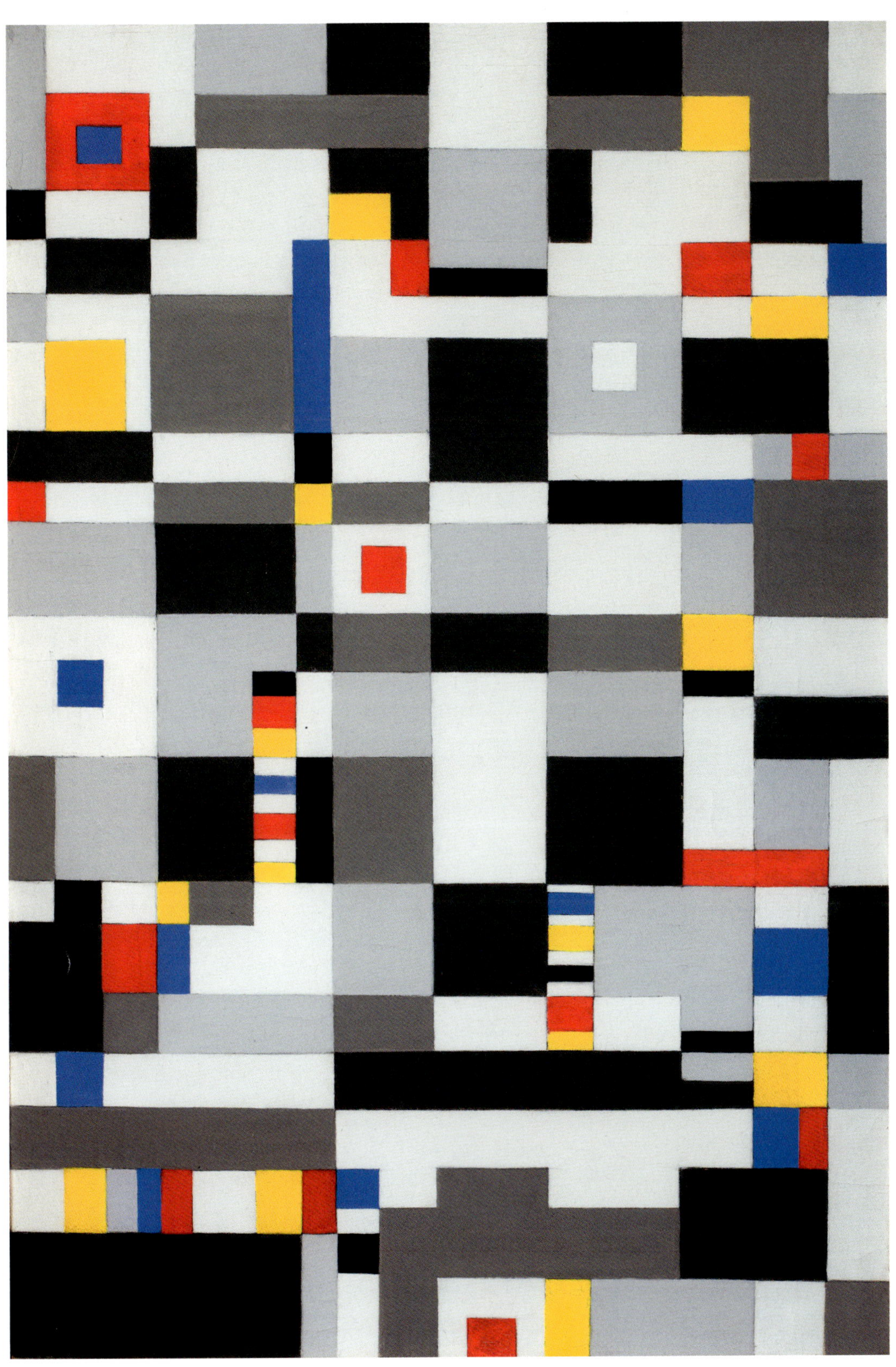

Night Rhythm, 1948
oil on canvas, 76 × 50 cm
Collection of the Fondazione Marguerite Arp, Locarno

Cat. 11

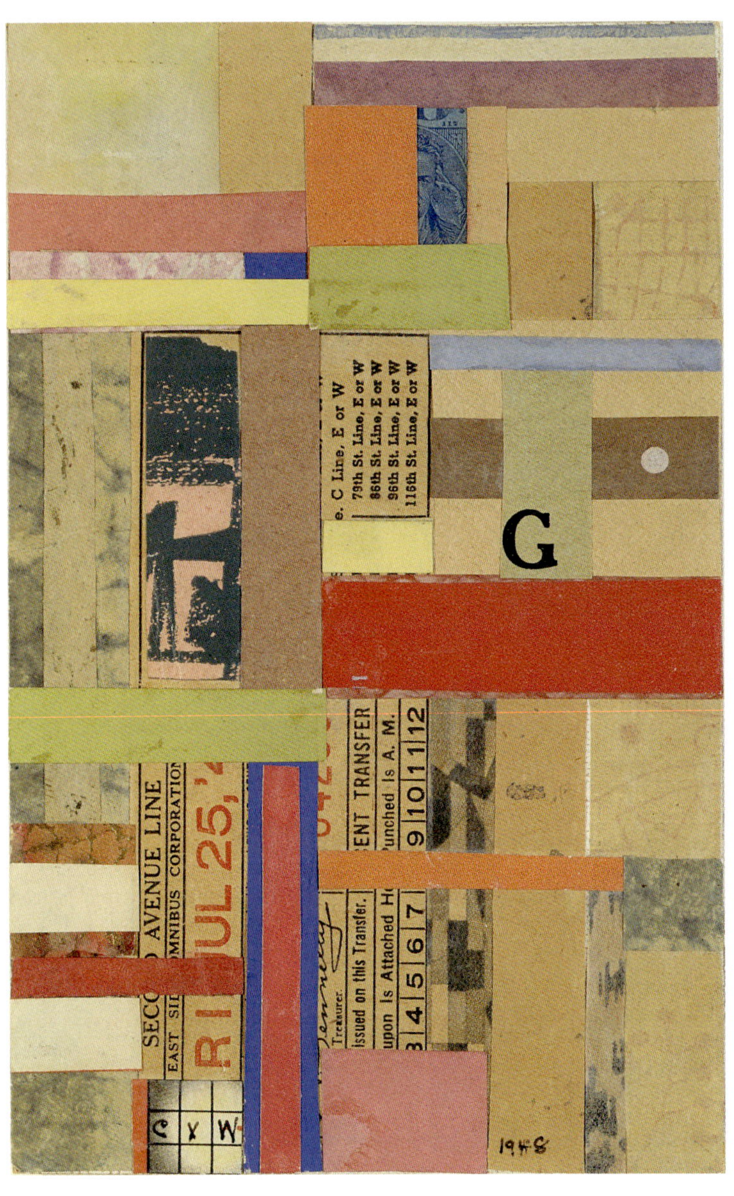

Transfer to Cathay, 1948
collage, paper on paper, 19 × 11.6 cm
Smithsonian American Art Museum,
Gift of Patricia and Philipp Frost

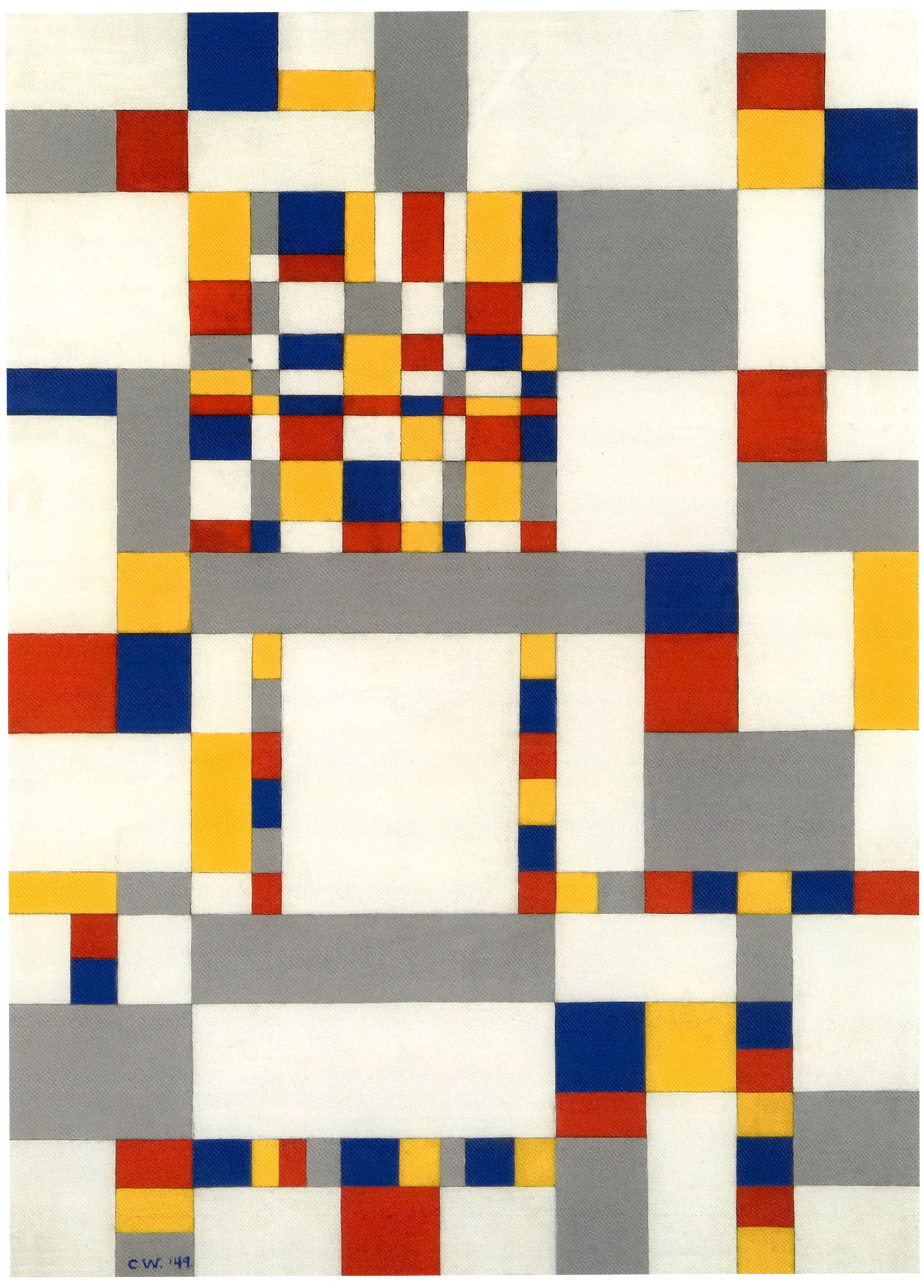

Radiating Plane, 1949
oil on canvas, 88.9 × 64.1 cm
Grey Art Gallery, New York University Art Collection,
Gift of Howard Wise

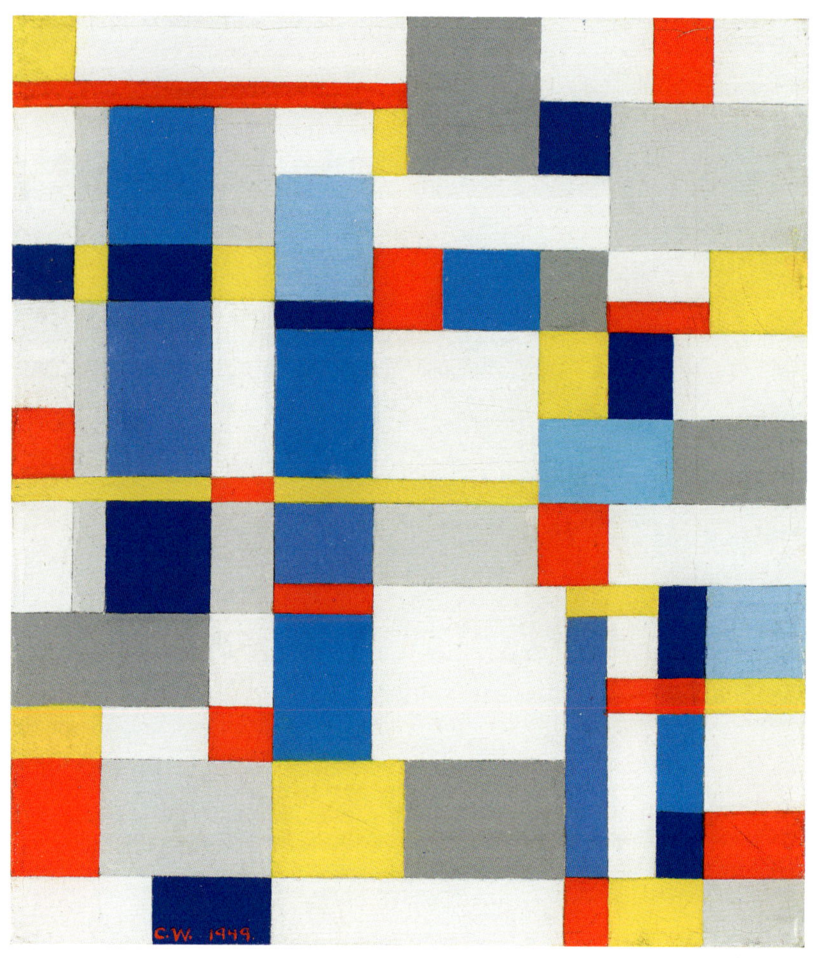

The Citadel, 1949–1950
oil on canvas, 36.8 × 31.8 cm
Private Collection, New York

Cat. 14

52

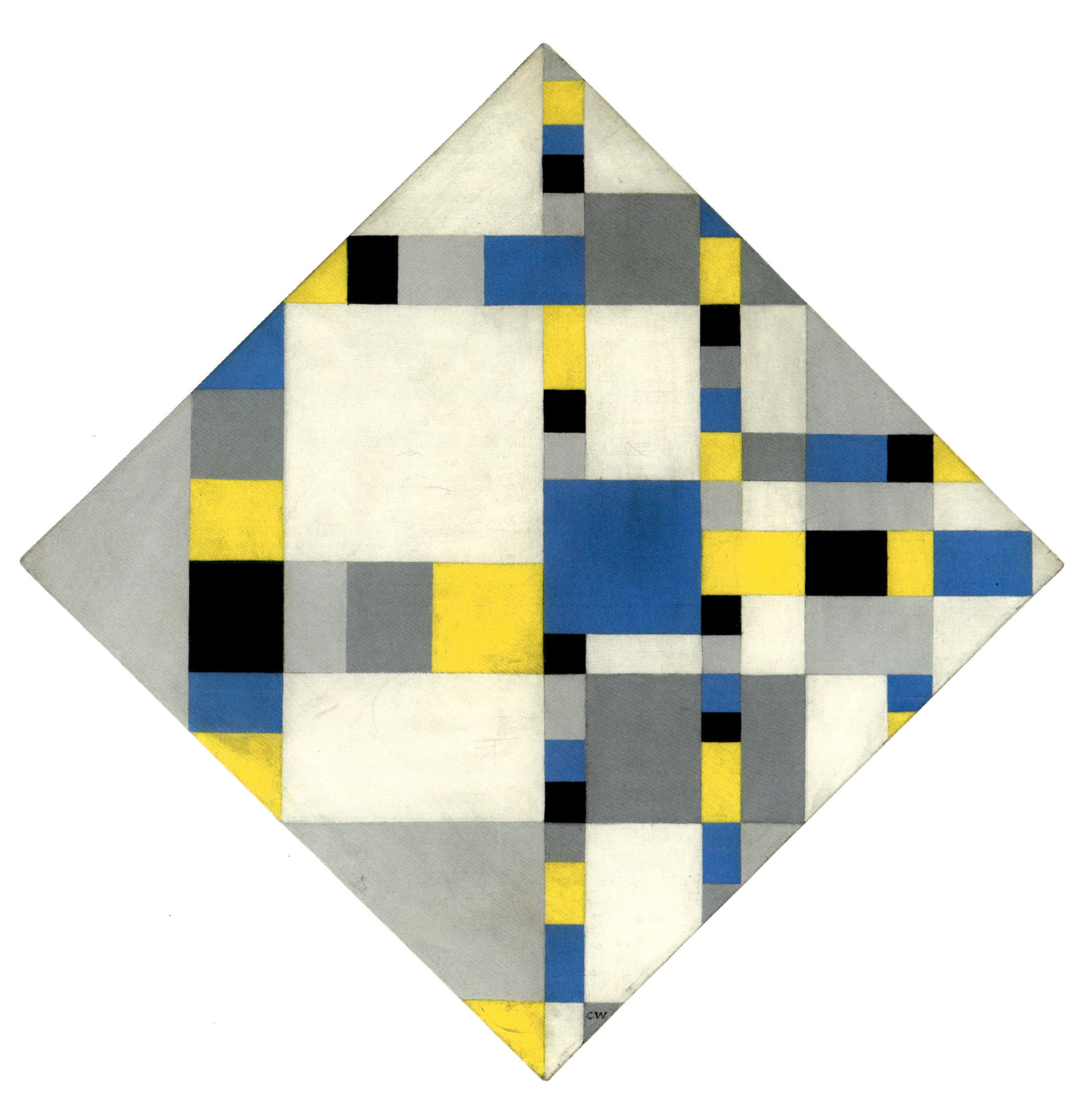

Composition, 1949
oil on canvas, 64.8 × 64.8 cm
The Metropolitan Museum of Art, New York,
Gift of William Benenson, 1991

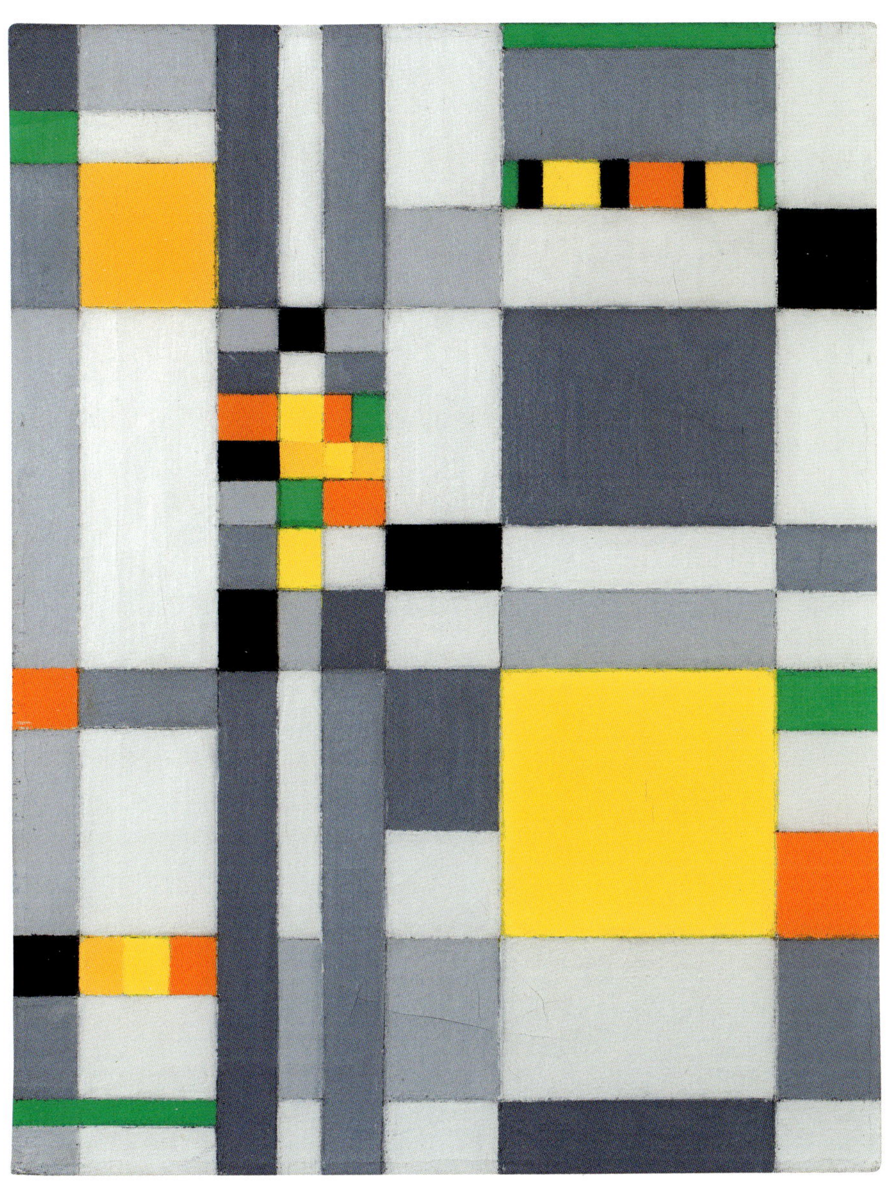

New York, 1957
oil on canvas, 40.5 × 30.5 cm
Collection of the Fondazione Marguerite Arp, Locarno

Cat. 16

16   Von Wiegand, letter to Piet Mondrian, August 17, 1941.

17   Ibid. See also Piet Mondrian, "Neo-Plasticism: The General Principle of Plastic Equivalence," 1920, in *The New Art—The New Life: The Collected Writings of Piet Mondrian*, ed. Harry Holtzman and Martin S. James (Boston: G. K. Hall, 1986), 132–147; and Piet Mondrian, "Plastic Art and Pure Plastic Art," 1936, in *The New Art— The New Life*, ed. Harry Holtzman and Martin S. James, 288–300.

PURE ABSTRACT ART.

Unconsciouly every true artist has always been moved by the beauty of line, color, and relationships for their own sake—and not by what they may represent. He has always tried to express all energy and all vital richness by these means alone. Nevertheless, consciously, he has followed the form of things. Consciously, he has tried to express their things and sensations through modelling and technique. But unconsciously, he has established planes: he has augmented the tension of the line and purified the color. Thus, gradually, through centuries, the culture of painting has led to the total abolition of the limiting form and the particular representation. In our time, art has been liberated from everything that prevents it from being truly plastic. This liberation is of the greatest importance for art, whose purpose is to conquer individual expression and to establish, as far as possible, the universal manifestation of life.

Every expression of art has its own laws, which are in accord with the principal law of art and of life: that of equilibrium. On these laws depends the degree of equilibrium that is realized and therefore, also at what point disequilibrium is destroyed. This is clear to us if we compare the different expressions of past and contemporary art. Both is tried to express equilibrium, always in a different way - yet identical in the search for and creation of universal expression. The aspirations toward equilibrium and toward disequilibrium constantly oppose

Manuscript page of Piet Mondrian's text "Pure Abstract Art" annotated by Charmion von Wiegand, Collection of Khyongla Rato

feeling: `And what I felt was such a violent and sudden change when I first saw your work directly, was after all only a long process of unconscious development which suddenly became conscious in finding the work that answered the need.`[16]

Art, as Mondrian himself had postulated, had to be "absorbed into concrete life. In a world where the concentration of interest is no longer on the object itself [. . .] the 'art' object too must of necessity disappear—that is the work of art as picture, statue, musical composition, book. They represent static objects, intact and limited, vessels for creative energy, but in a world where dynamic energies can function freely, their forms must be dissolved and the creative feeling expressed more directly and more concretely."[17]

Charmion von Wiegand as a Visionary Thinker

Charmion von Wiegand and Piet Mondrian discussed not only the translation of his texts and the paintings he was working on, but also earlier works of his, exhibitions that were currently showing in New York, works of literature, and their mutual friends. Every now and then, Von Wiegand also afforded him a glimpse of her own flashes of inspiration. In May 1941, for example, she described to him how she awoke with a crazy but wonderful idea: a second Armory Show organized by the artists themselves. The first one, held in New York in 1913 on the eve of the First World War, had introduced the American public to an array of Modernist stances from Cézanne to Picasso. Yet no one had given any thought to showing how modern art had developed during the thirty years since then. And surely now, with Europe once again at war, artists should be focused on the future, on the

THE RELATIONSHIP MACHINE.

Portable Size.

Based on the oppositions of LINE (Verticals and Horizontals)
and COLOR (Color and Non-Color)

For the Establishment of a new Dynamic System of Proportion based on
MONDRIAN's theory of NEO*PLASICISM.

For the use of all Painters, Designers and Architects.

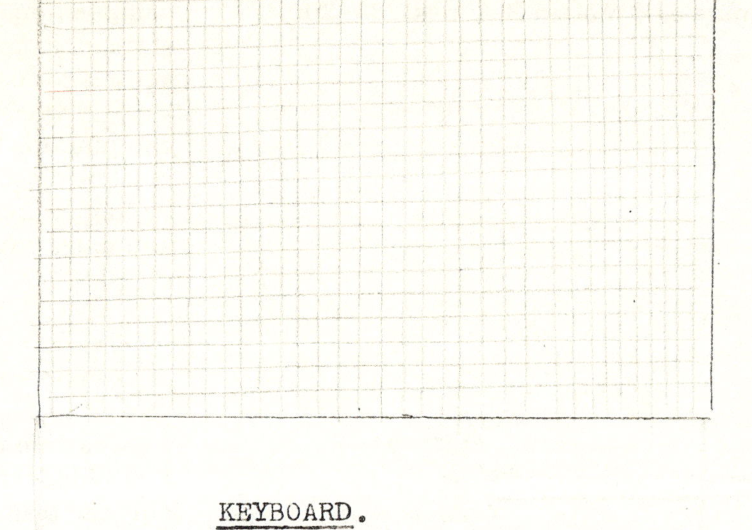

Insert paper in roll at top and press key and line forms on paper
Pressing color lever at same time will give desired color.

Charmion von Wiegand, sketch for "The Relationship Machine," August 3, 1941,
Collection of Khyongla Rato

18   Von Wiegand, letter to Piet Mondrian, May 29, 1941; the Armory Show (1913) is widely regarded as one of the most important exhibitions of European modern art ever to be held in the United States.

19   Von Wiegand, Diary, June 5, 1941.

20   Von Wiegand, letter to Piet Mondrian, September 7, 1941: Do you remember that I told you how I had an idea of bringing two men together--just a sudden notion--and it has seemed to click. And now the heavy political machinery is rolling into action and on the success of the campaign, which the two are working out, will depend what mayor we will have in NY. I have a great distaste for the mechanics of politics, but I am rather amused that the method of running a campaign came out of my desire to find the means to have a modern art exhibition. It seems I am no nearer the latter, but that other very concrete and actual things are happening because of that desire.

21   Von Wiegand, Diary, August 10, 1941: Last Sunday morning I woke up with a dream [...] I dreamed of a machine which would establish relationships, much like a typewriter. By means of it all painters, draughtsmen, designers, architects could more quickly find right relationships for their work and thus environment could be changed at once. I sat down and made a design and wrote nine pages about this discovery and how it could spread the idea of Mondrian throughout the world. It was not anything to take the place of creation but a mechanical means of spreading it much as the typewriter for the writer and radio for the musician. It was such a beautiful pipe dream while it lasted [...] And I felt that I had just about discovered the secret of the universe.

22   Von Wiegand, Diary, October 29, 1942.

23   Von Wiegand, Diary, August 10, 1941: When I told him, he said: "A Machine, I hope not for straight line art." I could see his face cloud over and his eyes flash for a moment. I knew he was furious at the very idea. I tried to explain and said maybe if he would look at it, he wouldn't mind. He said his eyes hurt and he had to work as long as daylight. "Oh I do everything wrong" I said, immensely hurt and feeling I was let down the elevator shaft.

postwar world. It was vital that they resist the destructive powers that had destroyed the modern art of Europe, she argued.[18] Mondrian did not share her enthusiasm, however, and dismissed the idea as "whistling in the storm."[19] Ultimately, Von Wiegand was not able to organize a second Armory Show, despite her best efforts to win politicians to her cause.[20]

On another occasion, Von Wiegand had a visionary dream of a machine. Her diary entry for August 10, 1941, describes how the dream left her with the feeling of having discovered the secret of the universe.[21] Eager to tell Mondrian of her discovery, she presented him with a nine-page script describing her vision of the machine. From today's perspective, digital drawing and painting software comes to mind and the device necessary to run it; for Von Wiegand, it was much like a typewriter. We would speak of a *painting machine* which operates according to the principles of Neo-Plasticism. With such a machine, Von Wiegand imagines, everyone would be capable of implementing Mondrian's theories into their own work, sharing their creations throughout the world. The device, which she named "The Relationship Machine," was of Portable Size, Based on the oppositions of LINE (Verticals and Horizontals) and COLOR (Color and Non-Color)--For the Establishment of a new Dynamic System of Proportion based on MONDRIAN's theory of NEO-PLASTICISM.[22] But Mondrian, wrote Von Wiegand, was furious at the very idea, leaving her with a sense of guilt, immensely hurt and feeling I was let down the elevator shaft.[23] He returned the text to her with numerous notes and some words of faint praise: "In the whole [there] are some good things you can use for later and the first two pages

24   Piet Mondrian, letter to Charmion von Wiegand, August 5, 1941: "Dear Charmion, Thank you for your letter. I am glad you agree with me about that machine. As long as 'Art' exists I think with Freeman that it is no good but will hinder to the true conception of Art. But I did not tear up the script and send it you back. In the whole are some good things you can use for later and the first two pages I like very much. With the little changes I made in it, it gives a good short idea of my work that you can use later. I don't know if you like to write a short preface by the edition of my writings, but in that case it would be a good introduction; the public could get a good idea of the content of the book."

25   Von Wiegand, letter to Piet Mondrian, July 2, 1942: `I can imagine a time in the future when a person working on a certain thought problem, can just press a button and tune in on a related personality working in the same way regardless of time or place--such a discovery would greatly accelerate progress. It would be a much more subtle kind of collective life than the external and mechanistic forms that one has so far conceived [...].`

26   Von Wiegand noted that Mondrian did not usually like journalists but had made an exception for her on the grounds that "you are a writer and an artist," Von Wiegand, Diary, June 12, 1941.

27   Von Wiegand, letter to Piet Mondrian, August 17, 1941.

28   Von Wiegand, Diary, August 24, 1941.

29   Piet Mondrian, letter to Charmion von Wiegand, August 26, 1941: "I just got your letter and was glad to hear you can see my point. You are quite right it is not 'in this time, for every one, just as neo-plastic it is not.' But it can already exist. (I mean the realisation of the separation we spoke of) just as n. pl. (neo plasticism) already exist. I don't know what to say more about this and send you my best greetings."

I like very much."[24] As the text about the machine that he was referring to here has not yet surfaced, presumably Von Wiegand destroyed it.

Around a year later, in early July 1942, Von Wiegand wrote to Mondrian about another futuristic vision of hers, this time of a technological feat that to us seems powerfully redolent of the Internet: `I can imagine a time in the future when a person working on a certain thought problem can just press a button and tune in on a related personality working in the same way regardless of time or place.`[25] Mondrian did not respond to this idea in any of his letters, and if Von Wiegand's diary is to be believed, her vision never came up in any of their discussions either.

The Rediscovery of Painting and Mondrian's Rejection

As far as Charmion von Wiegand's own art was concerned, Piet Mondrian knew very well that she was not just a journalist, but also an artist in her own right;[26] yet her art was never mentioned in the first few months of their acquaintance— possibly because Von Wiegand was focusing exclusively on her writing at the time. Besides, her editing skills were proving immensely useful to Mondrian, who had only a limited command of English. Numerous passages in Von Wiegand's letters and diary entries tell of their protracted discussions of how best to translate his very specific notions and concepts into English.

In the aforementioned letter of August 17, 1941, however, Von Wiegand asked Mondrian out of the blue whether he would teach her how to do his "technical work." Apparently he had previously told her of his intention to hire someone to relieve him of certain tasks.

30   I have been so busy working with Carl at night, and lots of chores and problems that I am tired out. **She was working with Carl Holty on a book about abstract art that was proving very time-consuming and that ultimately would never be published. Her troubles were compounded by the straightened financial circumstances that she and her husband were facing at the time, which she mentions in several places in her diary.**

31   Von Wiegand, letter to Piet Mondrian, June 11, 1942: What do you think happened to me right in the midst of all the annoying practical things? I burst right out in drawing. The other night when Richter was supposed to be coming here, he did not turn up, because he got tight at Sweeney's--it seems to have been quite a party--and I felt very disgruntled and [...] began to draw like mad. I filled the whole sketch book and it practically flowed over on the floor-- a whole flood of chaotic biomorphic forms turbulently moving on colored planes. I got up next morning and went on most of the day like mad and the result is that there are fifteen pastels--strange brilliant things--not at all what I would have made consciously or what you would approve of. But it just happened and it felt so wonderful and they look so happy. All of which has little or nothing to do with art, but Carl said yesterday that they were good and I should go right on. Richter, who just left here, said they were very "feminine" and pure feeling.

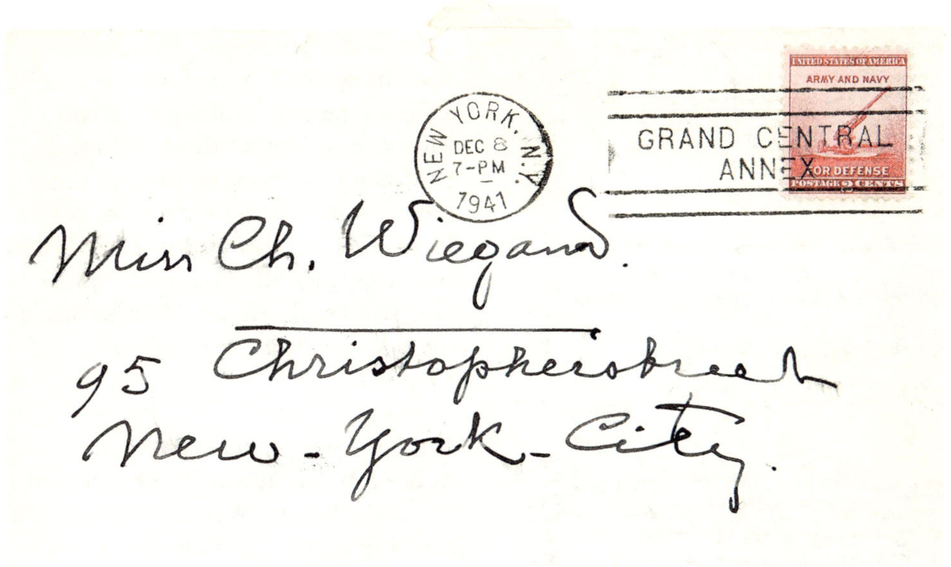

Envelope inscribed by Piet Mondrian, stamped December 8, 1941, Collection of Khyongla Rato

When you spoke of having someone to do your technical work, did you mean that you would teach me? she asked. **If so,** nothing would make me happier and you would not have to bother teaching me to paint, because it would be years before I reach that development where I would even try pure means--if I desire to paint at all. But I would like to learn to do all those things from you, which are after all so time consuming and could save your eyes for the more important work.[27]

However, as Von Wiegand confided to her diary, Mondrian declined her offer. Had he wished to give her lessons he would have told her so directly, he said.[28] While he appears to reopen the discussion in another letter,[29] the topic of Von Wiegand doing her own art again was no longer up for discussion—at least not in the conversations between them.

In a letter from June 11, 1942, Von Wiegand told Mondrian how her many chores and problems [30] **had driven her to take up drawing again. On one occasion, being** very disgruntled, **she had begun** to draw like mad. I filled the whole sketch book and it practically flowed over on the floor-- a whole flood of chaotic, biomorphic forms.[31] **After another day of the same manic behavior, she had** fifteen pastels--strange brilliant things, not at all what I would have made consciously or what you would approve of. But it just happened, and it felt so wonderful and they look so happy. All of which has little or nothing to do with art, but Carl [Holty] said yesterday that they were good and I should go right on. [Hans] Richter, who just left here, said

32   Von Wiegand, letter to Piet Mondrian, October 10, 1942.

33   Von Wiegand, Diary, October 29, 1942.

34   Ibid.

35   Ibid.

36   Von Wiegand, letter to Piet Mondrian, March 10, 1942: Imagine my surprise when Mr. Lion phoned from Holtzman's to Richter's tonight and said that Holtzman and you had spent last evening and today on the script. Just only this afternoon, Holty phoned to Holtzman from my house and I spoke with him and he never mentioned anything about the matter.

37   Von Wiegand, Diary, October 29, 1942: This is probably the last time I shall write any diary of my visits to Mondrian. I feel very heavy-hearted but I know our real friendship is at an end. The rest will be only an externality like with other people.

Letter by Piet Mondrian to Charmion von Wiegand, June, 4, 1941, recto, Collection of Khyongla Rato

they were very 'feminine' and pure feeling.

Mondrian seems not to have reacted to her account of this experience—at least there is no mention of any such response either in her diary or in their correspondence.

Another letter to Mondrian and a diary entry of October 1942 show that Von Wiegand was by then intent on going back to her own art and had even bought several tubes of paint. It's so exciting to own a few paints again and my hand itches to try them, she wrote, adding ruefully, but I have to work on the translation over the weekend.[32]

A few days later she told Mondrian that she had at last found a composition. It was so wonderful that moment when it came for the first time--like a wonderful rhythm for only a few minutes and I knew it was right.[33] Mondrian's response, however, was blunt and dismissive: "Don't tell me about it," he told her, "You are a writer and I don't want to know about your painting. You find your own way." The cold icy tone and the impatience of his words wounded her deeply.[34]

Yet, her diary records as dismayed as she was by Mondrian's rejection, Von Wiegand was also determined not to pay further heed to it. She tried to console herself by calling to mind Mondrian's own admonishment that the only way to understand the new aesthetic was to practice it oneself, since it was a path that was open to all. The real obstacle, she realized, was Mondrian's own ego, which simply can't stand it.[35]

But his rejection left her no peace, and eventually she could not help but reopen the subject in another letter of November 1942. The relationship with Mondrian had cooled markedly by then. Von Wiegand, for example, had

38   Von Wiegand, Diary, probably November 1942 or the first week of December 1942: While you deeply hurt me by your remarks and puzzled me most of all, by your attitude which seemed contradictory with your written ideas, perhaps the hurt was necessary. For suddenly I experienced the meaning of the plane, which I had only felt before dimly and instinctively but never really comprehended. And to the comprehension of things goes all our faculties, not merely our rational or even our instinctual drives. I had translated from your article that to really understand the new aesthetic, one must work in it. And another phrase: that the way lies open to all. And then you censured me severely that I was a writer and had no business to be painting. Nor do I blame you, for the decorative superficial things I was doing convinced you correctly that my understanding of the principles was only on the surface and in no sense profoundly understood.

But some people learn only by doing and how can one write about a thing if one does not experience it? I realized that on and off I had been painting for sixteen years. I came to it as an emotional release from an oppressive form of life and I never felt that I was professionally an artist. The first expression was personal, romantic, and expressionist; then came a period of realism in natural representation. I never liked this phase but it happened and I could not stop it. You saw only an impressionistic sketch that was twelve years old. But five years ago I began to work conscientiously from nature and with a deep feeling for the landscape and gradually the painting changed and became less realistic and this again was disturbing because I thought it was going backward. But what ever I did began to be simplified and to lose its depth illusion and because I did not understand it--this conflict between the natural representation and the effort toward greater abstraction, which was not conscious at all. I was discouraged.

And so coming to the city and changing environment, I could not find the way and so I ceased painting altogether for the city cannot be represented in terms of three dimensional illusion at all. Meeting with you I had felt a great change in my ideas but I could relate the change to the past and then thinking I had digested your ideas, I sought to express them. I never intended to paint again really and the need only appeared after you repudiated me and cut all communication--this is no complaint but a statement of fact--for I had to find some emotional outlet for myself in my hurt. As long as you were in communication with me, I had not the need, but I was sustained and nourished by your work and thought. But suddenly cut off, I sought you through working again at painting. [...]

The results were silly because I had not understood at all deeply and you felt that and were irritated by it. After all it was a colossal impudence to think one could make a jump that should take years in a few months and very childish too. I did work at it lately however more intensely with the same superficial decorative results. And so, I said, it is not for me, this abstraction, I will go back where I came from and took the landscape I had

learned several months earlier from a friend of a friend that Mondrian, no longer satisfied with her translations of his texts, had asked Harry Holtzman to review and in some cases rework them,[36] and by the autumn of 1942 she was convinced that our real friendship is at an end.[37]

The purpose of this new letter of November 1942 was therefore to tell Mondrian how deeply hurt she had been by his remarks. Most of all she was puzzled by what she saw as an attitude which seemed contradictory with your written ideas.[38] He himself had written that to really understand the new aesthetic, one must work in it [...] And then you censured me severely that I was a writer and had no business to be in painting. Perhaps the decorative superficial things I was doing convinced you correctly that my understanding of the principles was only on the surface and in no sense profoundly understood. But some people learn only by doing and how can one write about a thing if one does not experience it? I realized that on and off I had been painting for sixteen years. I came to it as an emotional release from an oppressive form of life and I never felt that I was professionally an artist.

Von Wiegand then went on to explain just how profoundly her encounter with him, Mondrian, had shaped her thinking and her ideas, and emphatically assured him that she had never intended to paint again really and the need only appeared after you repudiated me. That was what had engendered in her the desire to paint again, she explained, since I had to find some emotional outlet for myself in my hurt.

left unfinished over almost three years ago and began to paint. Being a winter scene, the background was white and the forms became simplified and the distance merged with a plane in the front and the colors were purified. And I felt suddenly, an advance had been made and I went back again to a pure abstract composition and suddenly it came for a few minutes like a rhythm and I felt it as a composition for the first time--primitive, perhaps, but still my own. And in that moment I experienced the meaning of the plane, emotionally but did not yet understand why [...].

And now a last personal remark. Why should you be so angry at anyone who seeks to understand the meaning of the plane? You yourself have said that plastic is anything that makes the image. If I seek the image with the color or with the word, what is the final difference? If I seek to emancipate the thought and therefore the word from Impressionism which is the last form of Naturalism, by studying the plastic image, which has made the greater advance, whom does it harm? If my gift is small, that is my misfortune, but as long as I do not adulterate the idea

As long as you were in communication with me, I had not the need, but I was sustained and nourished by your work and thought. But suddenly cut off, I sought you through working again at painting. [...] The results were silly because I had not understood at all deeply and you felt that and were irritated by it. After all it was a colossal impudence to think one could make a jump that should take years in a few months.

Von Wiegand went on to mention how, abandoning her first abstract experiments, she had taken out a three-year-old landscape and began working on it again, with the unintended consequence that it grew increasingly more abstract: Being a winter scene, the background was white and the forms became simplified and the distance merged with a plane in the front and the colors were purified. **She** felt suddenly, an advance had been made and I went back again to a pure abstract composition and suddenly it came for a few minutes like a rhythm and I felt it as a composition for the first time--primitive, perhaps, but still my own. **She then returned once again to Mondrian's brusque rejection:** Why should you be so angry at anyone who seeks to understand the meaning of the plane? [...] If I seek the image with the color or with the word, what is the final difference? [...] whom does it harm? If my gift is small, that is my misfortune, but as long as I do not adulterate the idea for a commercial or a personal reason, I do not stop the development [...] I do not write yet about the new art for I lack the language that must be

Sunday night.

Dear Mondrian:

Today I was so happy to hear you are getting better. I think of you constantly and will with my whole being that you will be strong and well. We <u>need</u> you so much,

Wednesday when you went to the hospital, I saw your picture. So luminous and living. I saw the new changes and it is the most wonderful picture in all the world.

Harry has been very kind and kept me informed about you. But they tell me I cannot come to see you. So this is just to say that I think of you, and Joe joins me in sending heartfelt wishes for a quick recovery. I long to see you - and to see you well again.

Devotedly
Charmion

Letter by Charmion von Wiegand to Piet Mondrian, undated, Collection of Khyongla Rato

for a commercial or a personal reason, I do not stop the
development. A pure idea may be born but it is spread
only through its corruption and adulteration that is its
popularization--whether that be Christianity, Communism
or Cubism. The idea is always changed in transit from the
world of reality into the world of appearance. I do not
write yet about the new art for I lack the language that
must be created for it--I can find it only through the
art itself. Perhaps I will never find it but I am impelled
to seek it.

39   Von Wiegand, Diary, August 27/28, 1941.

40   Von Wiegand, Diary, July 10, 1941.

41   Von Wiegand, Diary, June 5, 1941.

42   Von Wiegand, Diary, February 23, 1944.

43   See Von Wiegand, Diary, February 23 and April 26, 1944.

1944—JANUARY - - FEBRUARY—1944

SUNDAY **30** 30	
MONDAY **31** 31	
TUESDAY **1** 32	Mondrian died at about 5 a.m. this morning.
WEDNESDAY **2** 33	
THURSDAY **3** 34	
FRIDAY **4** 35	
SATURDAY **5** 6th WEEK 36	JANUARY and FEBRUARY

Calendar sheet with note by Charmion von Wiegand,
Collection of Khyongla Rato

created for it--I can find
it only through the art
itself. Perhaps I will never
find it but I am impelled
to seek it.

Piet Mondrian would not
read this letter, however, because
Charmion von Wiegand never
actually mailed it. It is preserved
among her papers, where it
is marked by hand, "never sent."

Very few letters have survived
and scarcely any diary entries
exist at all for the year 1943. The
impression we are given is that
what sounded the death knell
of Mondrian and Von Wiegand's
turbulent relationship was her
decision not to content herself
with only writing about *his* art,
translating *his* texts for him,
and helping him to exhibit and
to sell *his* works, but to go back
to producing art of her own.

Another reason for the cooling
off might well have been the
effusiveness of Von Wiegand's
affection for Mondrian—indeed,
her unabashed adoration of him.
For to her, he really was the
great saint of modern art,[39]
the Baptist of a new art,
of a new way of life,[40]
and the incarnation of the
Protestant Revolt.[41] In her
eyes, he embodied all I ever
dreamed of as a man, as
an artist and as a human
spirit.[42] The other artists
around Mondrian, above all Harry
Holtzman and Fritz Glarner,
had long viewed the initially very
close relationship between
Von Wiegand and Mondrian with
suspicion, and if Von Wiegand's
diary is to be believed, this was
also a factor in the eventual break-
up of their friendship.[43] In retro-
spect, there can be no doubt
that the intense dialogue between
Piet Mondrian and Charmion
von Wiegand that began in April
1941 affected her deeply and
continued to shape her life and
work long after Mondrian's death.

NANCY J. TROY

"MONDRIAN WAS MY GURU"

CHARMION VON WIEGAND AND PIET MONDRIAN IN THE 1940S AND 1950S

1   For granting me access to Von Wiegand's journal entries about Mondrian, I thank gallerist Michael Rosenfeld, New York, to whom I was introduced by Mondrian scholar and National Gallery of Art curator Harry Cooper.

2   Piet Mondrian, quoted in Charmion von Wiegand, "Mondrian: A Memoir of his New York Period," *Arts Yearbook* 4 (1961), 58.

3   Ibid.

4   Oral history interview with Charmion von Wiegand by Paul Cummings, October 9 and November 3, 1968. Archives of American Art, Smithsonian Institution, 35. For a detailed treatment of the authorship of this and other essays on which Von Wiegand collaborated, see Louis Veen, "Piet Mondrian's autobiographical writings (1941–43)," *Simiolus: Netherlands Quarterly for the History of Art* 37, no. 1 (2013–2014): 61–85.

5   Von Wiegand prepared a numbered list for Robert Motherwell in a typed letter mistakenly dated May 28, 1937 (the year was presumably 1947), George Wittenborn, Inc., Papers, Museum of Modern Art Archives, New York, IA.2.

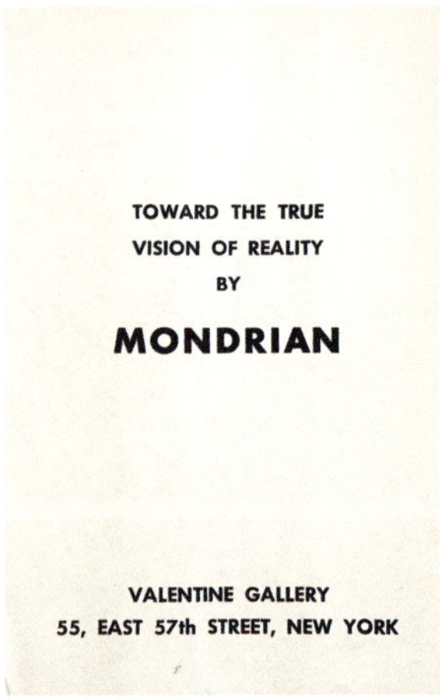

Cover of leaflet for the exhibition *Paintings and Drawings by Mondrian*, Valentine Gallery, New York (January 19–February 7, 1942)

The relationship that developed between Charmion von Wiegand and Piet Mondrian in the two and a half years that preceded his death on February 1, 1944, was significant for both of them in various ways. Von Wiegand herself narrated the story of their friendship in multiple essays and interviews, which, together with the unpublished journal she kept during that period, create an account of Mondrian's art and life in wartime New York that is valued for its sensitivity to the older, refugee artist and for its authenticity as a detailed, first-hand record of her interactions with the man, his ideas, and his paintings.[1] Their friendship blossomed during a period when Mondrian's work changed dramatically and enjoyed greater recognition than it had received at any earlier point in his career. For Von Wiegand, as for others in his inner circle of New York artworld acquaintances, the experience of Mondrian and his carefully constructed but nevertheless rapidly evolving work was key. And yet, even as the story of Von Wiegand's engagement with Mondrian during this period eventually coalesced as a valuable art historical resource for those interested in Mondrian's work, circumstances crucial to the story have remained obscure if not entirely overlooked. As a result, the nature and significance of Von Wiegand's own career as it emerged into public view during and especially after Mondrian's death have not been adequately acknowledged. It is therefore worth looking again at how her relationship with Mondrian both fostered and frustrated her recognition as an artist in her own right.

Commissioned to write what would become, upon its publication in 1943, the first substantial American essay devoted to Mondrian, Von Wiegand drew on her professional experience as a journalist and cultural critic, as well as years of engagement with painting, when she asked a mutual friend for an introduction, thereby initiating what would become a close friendship. Her journal entries not only carefully describe their interactions, but they also acknowledge Von Wiegand's intense personal attachment to Mondrian, who granted her extraordinary access to his creative process and to the theoretical underpinnings of his work, which she helped him to articulate in written form. Already during her initial visit to Mondrian's first Manhattan studio at 353 East 56th Street, Mondrian recognized Von Wiegand's potential as an articulate conduit for his ideas; he therefore gave her some handwritten notes that he hoped would help explain his abstract paintings and provide an aesthetic and theoretical context to support the article that she planned to write. When Von Wiegand, shortly thereafter, returned a typed version of those notes, having corrected the Dutch artist's less-than-perfect English, she revealed what for Mondrian proved to be valuable editorial skills that would provide a ground for their relationship going forward. "Very kind of you to copy off my writing," Mondrian told her, "I did not consider it an article. I have written it only to explain to you my art development, but it is perhaps useful to the public to a better understanding of Abstract Art."[2]

These notes, Von Wiegand later recalled, "formed the basis of Mondrian's article 'Toward a True Vision of Reality,' one of his classic essays. It was published as a brochure for his first exhibition."[3] In an interview recorded in 1968, she specified the fundamental role she had played in the composition of this essay: "I really wrote it because at that time his English was pretty bad. I mean it wasn't my ideas; it was entirely his, you know. He dictated the ideas but he couldn't yet formulate it so well in English. I don't know if I did it very well either. But I did the best I could."[4] In addition to working closely with Mondrian to edit and/or translate thirteen of his essays by the autumn of 1943,[5] Von Wiegand was invited to be present in Mondrian's studio while he developed

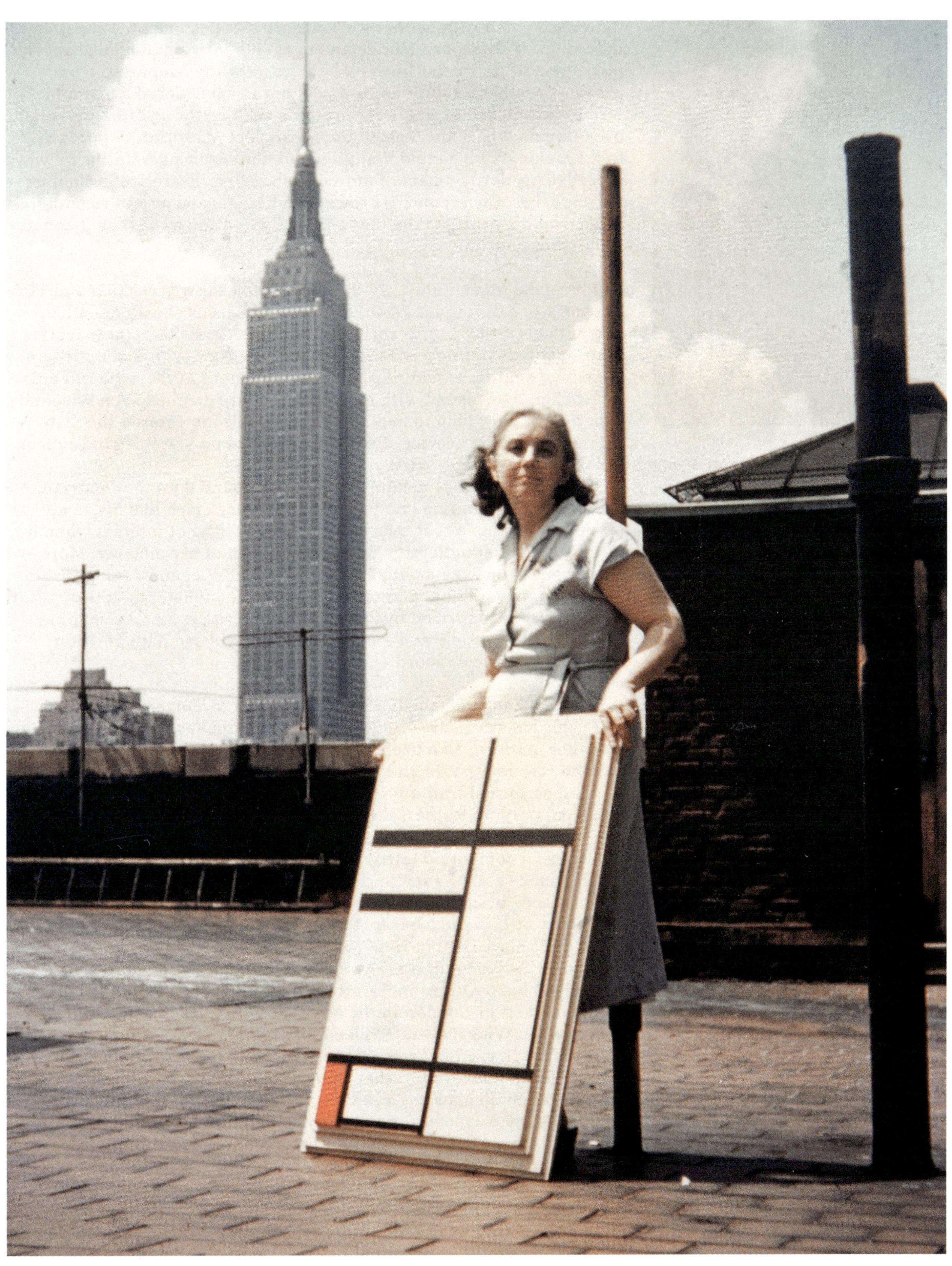

Charmion von Wiegand with Piet Mondrian's *Composition No. 1* (1931)
on the roof of her apartment building in New York, 1943

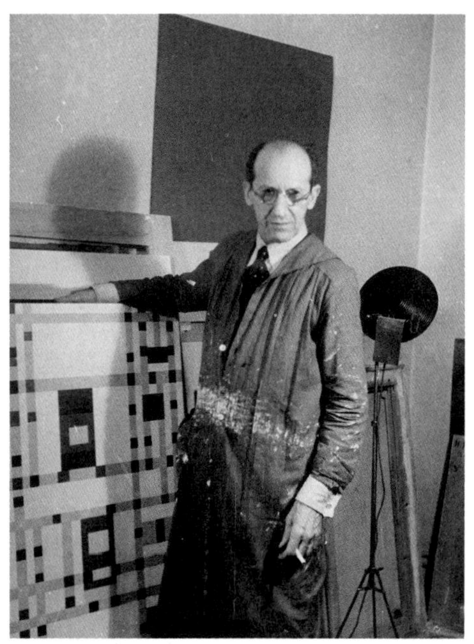

6 The commission came from *Living Age*, a magazine that ceased publication in August 1941, well before Von Wiegand completed her essay, which appeared as "The Meaning of Mondrian," *Journal of Aesthetics and Art Criticism* 2, no. 8 (Autumn 1943): 62–70.

7 Harry Cooper and Ron Spronk, *Mondrian: The Transatlantic Paintings* (Cambridge, MA: Harvard University Art Museums; New Haven, CT: Yale University Press, 2001); and Yve-Alain Bois, "Piet Mondrian, *New York City*," trans. Amy Reiter-McIntosh, *Critical Inquiry* 14 (Winter 1988): 244–277, esp. 274.

Piet Mondrian with *Broadway Boogie Woogie* (1942–1943) in his studio, 353 East 56th Street in New York, early 1943

individual compositions that were destined to become paintings; indeed, more than once Mondrian engaged her in a dialogue about the placement of particular lines and colors, how they departed from previous aesthetic solutions, and whether he considered a given picture to be finished or not. Deliberations such as these, often revisited over extended periods, formed the bedrock of Mondrian's approach to art making and, he told Von Wiegand, the resulting paintings always preceded his development of any corresponding theoretical principles—not the other way around. He thus gave her unusual access to both aspects of his practice: the theoretical elaboration as well as the material expression.

Von Wiegand was not the only close friend to bear witness to Mondrian's life and work during his New York years. Nor was she alone in helping him with his writing or in choosing, after his death, to paint in a style that—justifiably or not—was invariably identified with his. But there are some significant features of her engagement in the artworld at the time of her involvement with Mondrian that are unique to Von Wiegand's experience. They help to explain how this episode entered the historical record and the bearing it subsequently had on Von Wiegand's recognition as a practicing artist.

That she always acknowledged a profound debt to Mondrian, even when her paintings no longer looked very much like his, is an oft-repeated truism that tells us surprisingly little of interest when it comes to understanding the critical reception of her pictures. More significant is the way in which aspects of Von Wiegand's relationship to Mondrian went unacknowledged while the stylistic debt was consistently reconfirmed by journalists and critics, thereby shaping Von Wiegand's profile and locking her into a subordinate position in the art historical record.

A review of some facts will help set the stage for understanding how this came about. As already noted, Von Wiegand encountered Mondrian from her platform as a professional journalist. Although she had painted for many years and was friendly with numerous visual artists, she had no formal training, nor did she consider painting to be her principal pursuit. Rather, she was primarily a writer and deeply engaged art critic whose identity was shaped in part by her cultural politics as a committed leftist who regularly contributed to such publications as *Art Front* and the *New Masses*. In addition, she took on free-lance assignments, one of which prompted her to ask painter Carl Holty to introduce her to Mondrian.[6]

After his arrival in New York as a refugee from war-torn Europe in October 1940, Mondrian devoted a great deal of time and energy not only to his writings but also to reworking paintings that he had begun in Paris or London in the late 1930s.[7] An American friend—quite possibly Von Wiegand—introduced him to colored adhesive tapes that he thenceforth used in composing his pictures.[8] The tapes facilitated his inclusion of colored (rather than his customary black) linear elements that challenged the relative repose of the austere yet sensuous style of geometric abstraction which he had developed during the 1920s and early 1930s. "The tapes were a laborsaving device he liked," Von Wiegand noted in a memoir of Mondrian published in 1961:

> [. . .] he could try out a line, then quickly remove it, or shift its position repeatedly without losing time or soiling the canvas. One of the large American companies manufactured tapes of different widths in pure primary colors [red, yellow, and blue] as well as in black and gray. They seemed made to order for his work, but because of the wartime paper shortage their manufacture was

8   On the colored adhesive tapes, see Nancy J. Troy, *The Afterlife of Piet Mondrian* (Chicago: University of Chicago Press, 2013), 240n34; and Ysbrand Hummelen, "The role of the tapes in creating *Victory Boogie Woogie*," in *Inside Out Victory Boogie Woogie: A Material History of Mondrian's Masterpiece*, ed. Maarten van Bommel, Hans Janssen, and Ron Spronk (Amsterdam: Amsterdam University Press, 2012), 225–244.

9   Von Wiegand, "Mondrian: A Memoir," 62.

10   *Broadway Boogie Woogie* was first exhibited publicly by New York dealer Valentine Dudensing in a show shared by Mondrian and sculptor Maria Martins, March 22–April 10, 1943. At the close of the exhibition, the painting was acquired by the Museum of Modern Art through an anonymous donation (funded by Martins).

discontinued. I used to look for these rolls of colored tape in art and stationery shops, some of which still had them in stock. Finding a large roll of bright red tape, enough to last months, was an occasion for rejoicing.[9]

During this period, Mondrian intensified his longstanding engagement with jazz music, especially the syncopated rhythms of boogie-woogie, to which he was introduced almost immediately upon his arrival in New York. He readily acknowledged boogie-woogie as the inspiration for the way he handled the visual rhythms of his latest paintings, particularly when he broke up the expanse of interwoven lines of primary colors that his use of colored tapes had facilitated: for example, in *New York City* of 1942. Von Wiegand herself witnessed the creation of this and other paintings, including Mondrian's breakthrough *Broadway Boogie Woogie*, completed in 1943, and his last, unfinished diamond-shaped *Victory Boogie Woogie*—two canvases that had a profound impact not only on Von Wiegand but also on numerous American artists who would have seen them in a memorial retrospective, *Piet Mondrian*, mounted by the Museum of Modern Art (MoMA) between March 21 and May 13, 1945.[10] Of course Von Wiegand had already seen and discussed both pictures with Mondrian on multiple occasions while he was working on them in his studio. Her *Sketch of*

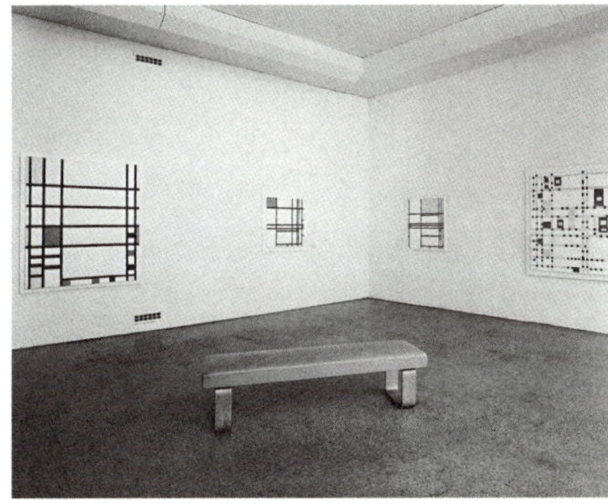

Invitation card for the exhibition *Paintings and Drawings by Mondrian*, Valentine Gallery, New York (January 19–February 7, 1942)

View of the exhibition *Piet Mondrian*, Museum of Modern Art, New York (March 21–May 13, 1945)

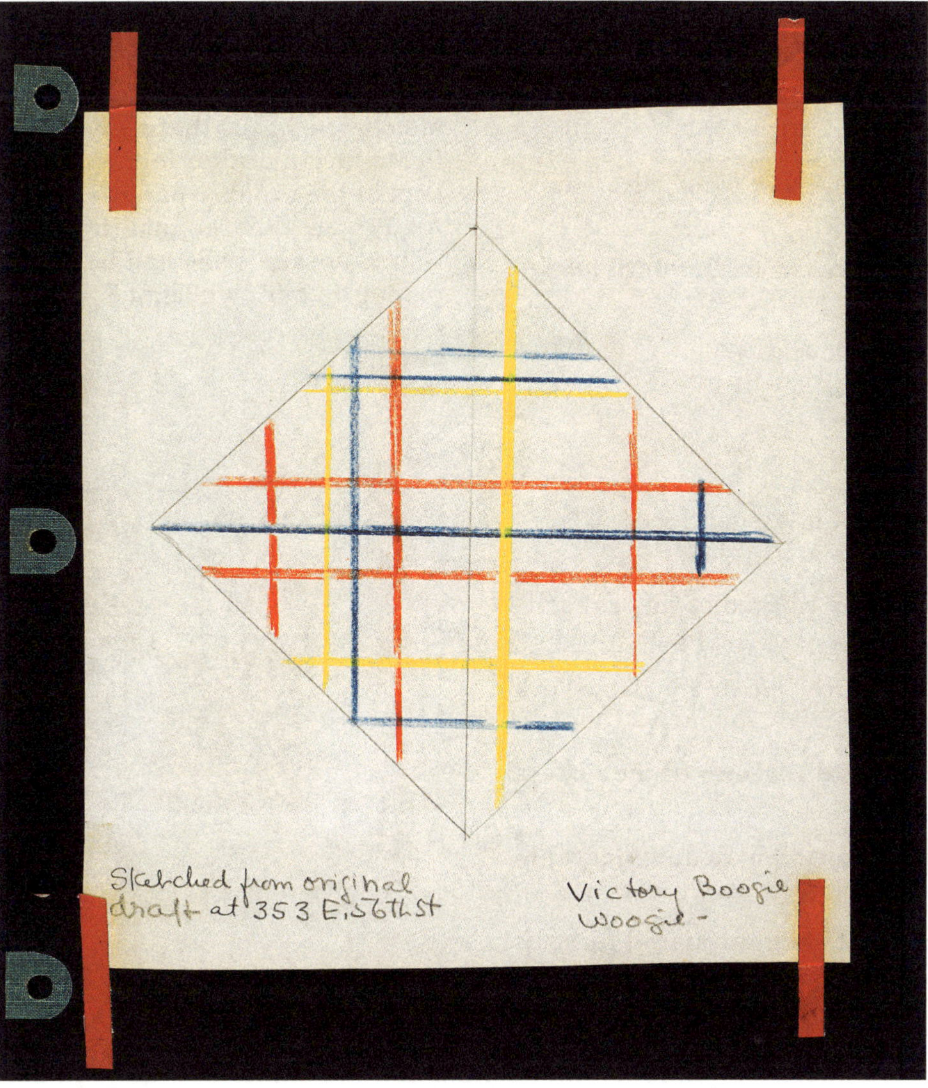

Charmion von Wiegand, *Sketch of Victory Boogie-Woogie*, 1942 or later, pencil and colored pencil on paper taped on colored paper, 20 × 21.6 cm, Museum of Modern Art, New York (Von Wiegand mistakenly inscribed the sketch with the image upside down)

11   Margit Rowell, "Interview with Charmion von Wiegand, June 20, 1971," in *Piet Mondrian, 1872–1944: Centennial Exhibition* (New York: Solomon R. Guggenheim Foundation, 1971), 83.

12   Von Wiegand, interview by Cummings, 43. Not until several years after Mondrian's death did Von Wiegand become active in the AAA, of which she was president from 1951 until 1953 (see below, p. 87).

13   Von Wiegand indicated that she worked in this capacity for Audrey McMahon, New York Regional Director of the Federal Art Project, in an autobiographical statement prepared for artist and art critic Michel Seuphor. Seuphor Archive, Letterenhuis, Antwerp, 187352/2b.

Victory Boogie-Woogie (fig. p. 71)—drawn sometime after a visit on June 13, 1942, while its composition was still defined by long lines of colored tape—constitutes a precious historical record of the work in an early state that Mondrian chided her for making.[11]

Welcomed as an elder statesman of European abstraction, Mondrian enjoyed a vibrant social life in New York that encompassed curators, dealers, collectors, and artists, including a group of younger painters who were eventually identified as his followers because in their own work they offered variations on the signature style of painting that he had developed during the 1920s and 1930s, and in some cases were especially impressed by the boogie-woogie pictures he created in New York. Among these figures were several American artists—Burgoyne Diller, Ilya Bolotowsky, and Harry Holtzman—who had been supported during the mid- and late 1930s by the Federal Art Project, a government sponsored program that enabled otherwise unemployed painters to be paid for their labor as artists when the regular art market dried up as a result of the Great Depression. In addition, these three, together with another Mondrian disciple, Fritz Glarner, were involved early on in an exhibiting group that coalesced in 1936–1937 called the American Abstract Artists (AAA). Mondrian accepted an invitation to become a member of the AAA in January 1941, and he urged Von Wiegand to join so that—he said to her, perhaps not entirely in jest—she could tell him what went on at the organization's meetings, which he never attended.[12] Von Wiegand demurred, acknowledging that she was not making abstract art at the time, but she did sign on as an Associate Member, a status that signaled her second-class citizenship compared to Mondrian's other followers who from early on were prominent members of the group. Similarly, Von Wiegand's experience at the Federal Art Project differed qualitatively from those of Diller, Bolotowsky, and Holtzman, since she had been hired to write about painting—not as a painter in her own right.[13]

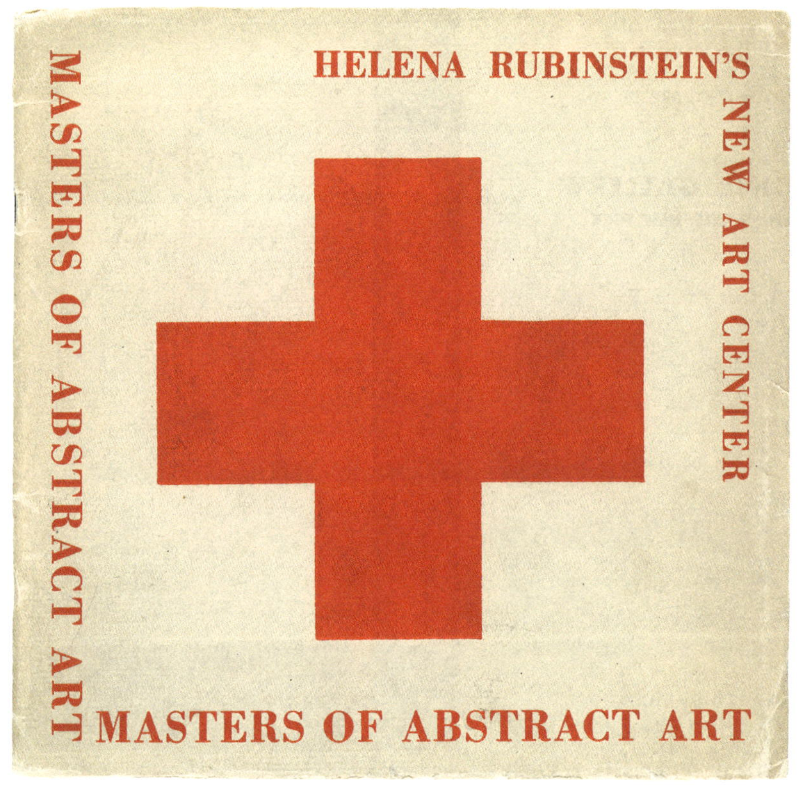

Cover designed by Herbert Bayer of the catalog to the exhibition *Masters of Abstract Art*, Helena Rubinstein's New Art Center, New York (April 1–May 15, 1942)

Continue on p. 85

73

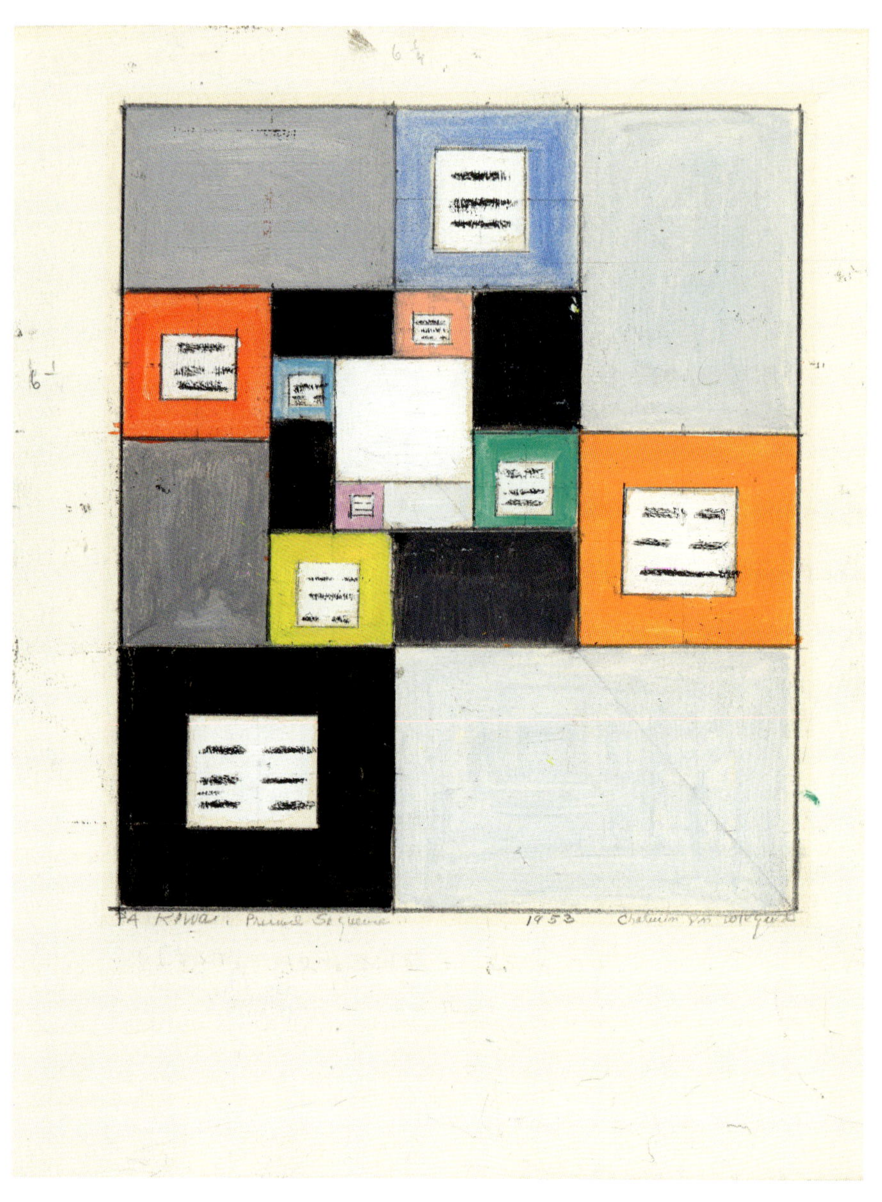

I Ching Studies: #Pa K'Wa, Primal Sequence, 1953
oil, gouache, and pencil on paper, 27.6 × 20.6 cm
Estate of Charmion von Wiegand, Courtesy of
Michael Rosenfeld Gallery LLC, New York

Cat. 17   74

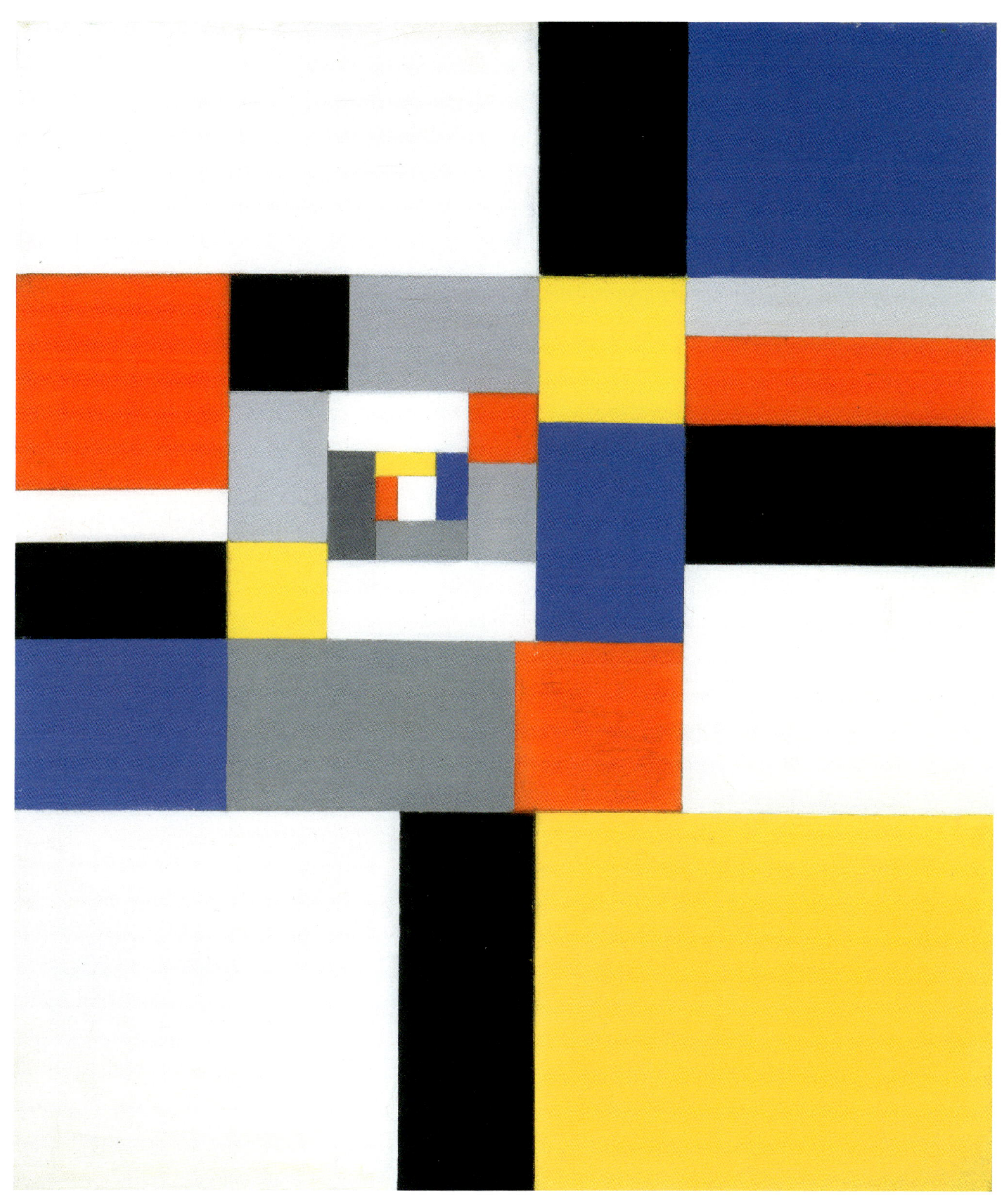

The Sign of Keeping Still, 1953
oil on canvas, 76.2 × 63.5 cm
The Newark Museum of Art,
Gift of Mr. and Mrs. Robert Miller, 1956

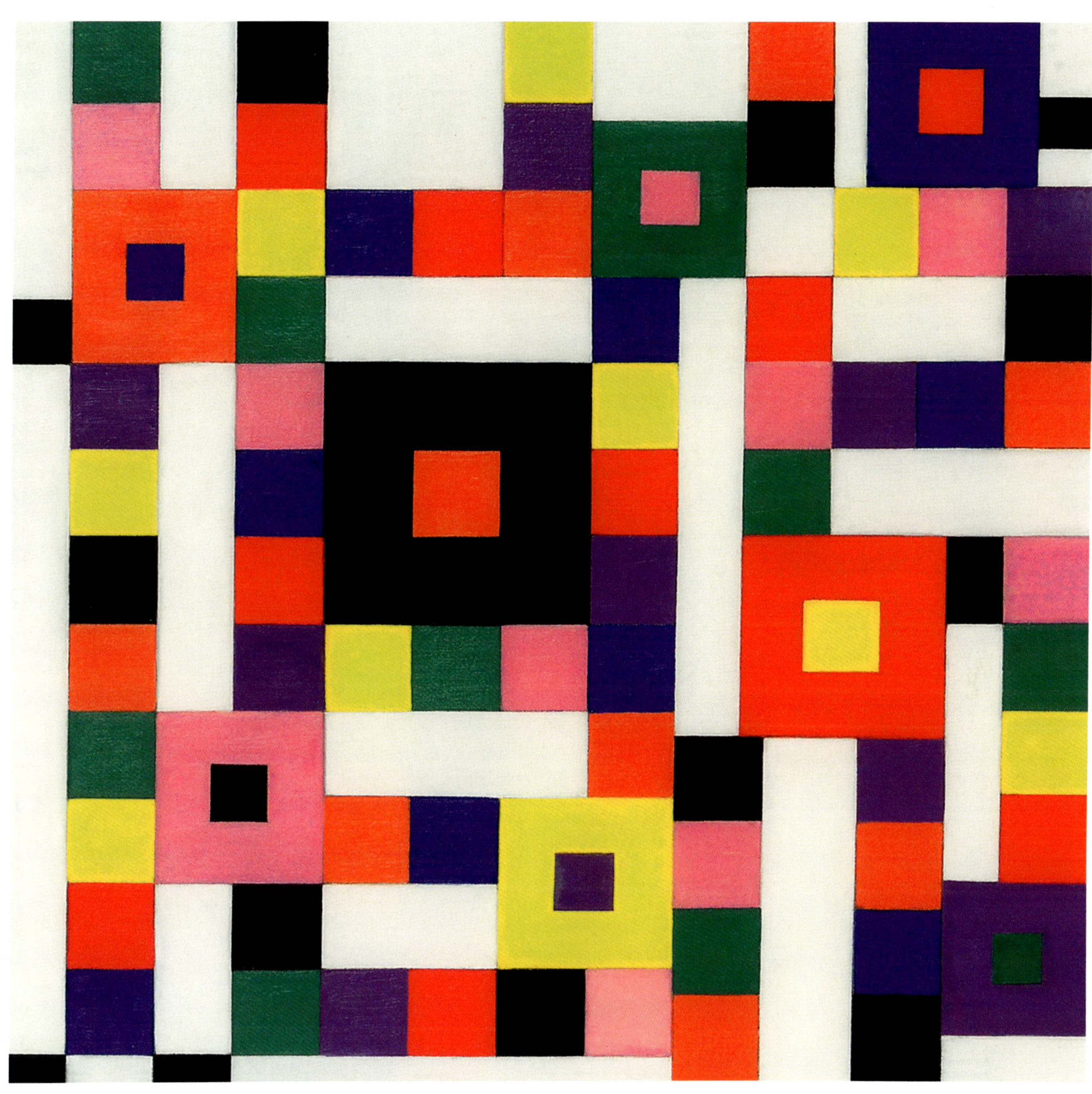

The Great Field of Action or the 64 Hexagrams, 1953
oil on canvas, 70.5 × 70 cm
Collection Walker Art Center, Minneapolis,
Gift of Mr. and Mrs. Howard Wise, New York, 1974

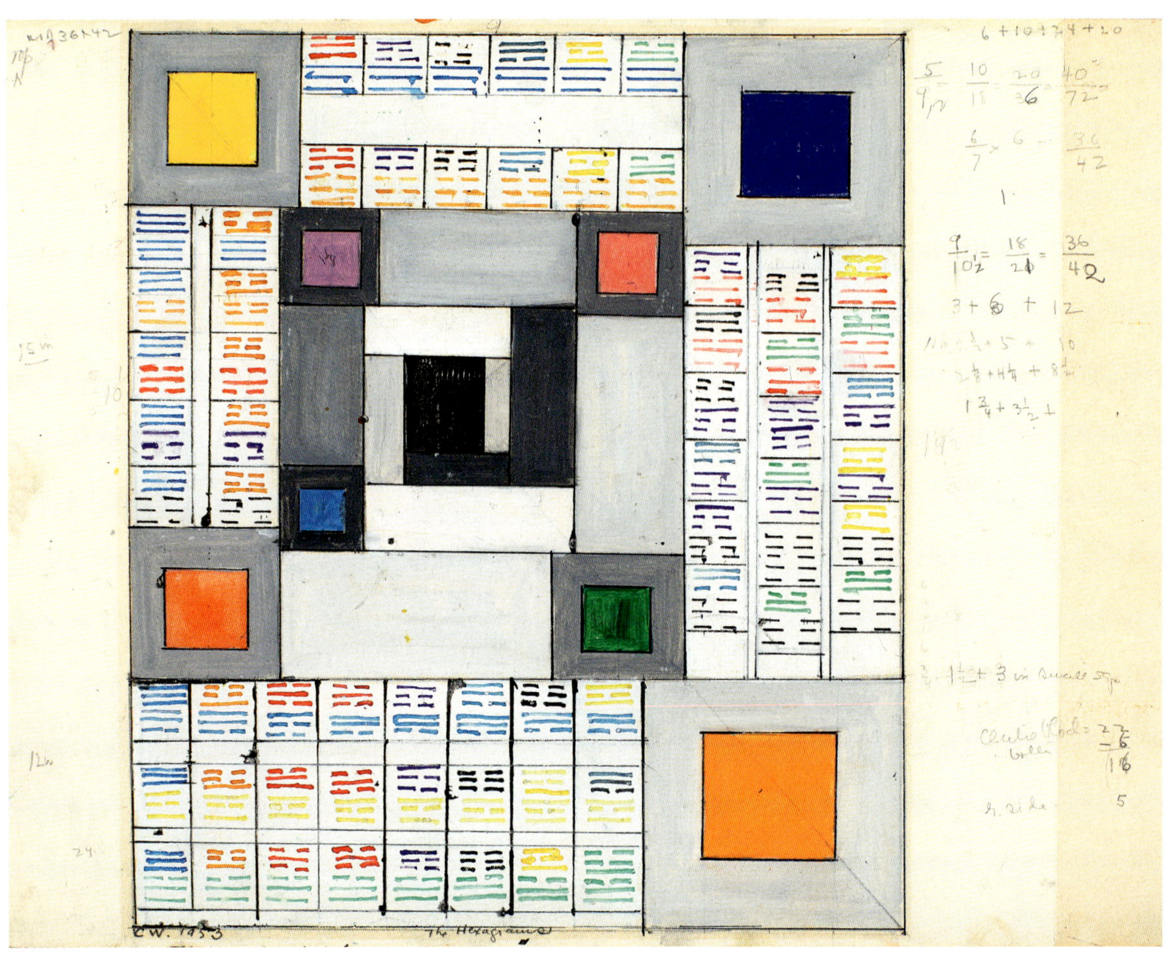

I Ching Studies: #8 The 64 Hexagrams, 1953
gouache and ink on paper, 27.6 × 34.3 cm
Estate of Charmion von Wiegand, Courtesy of
Michael Rosenfeld Gallery LLC, New York

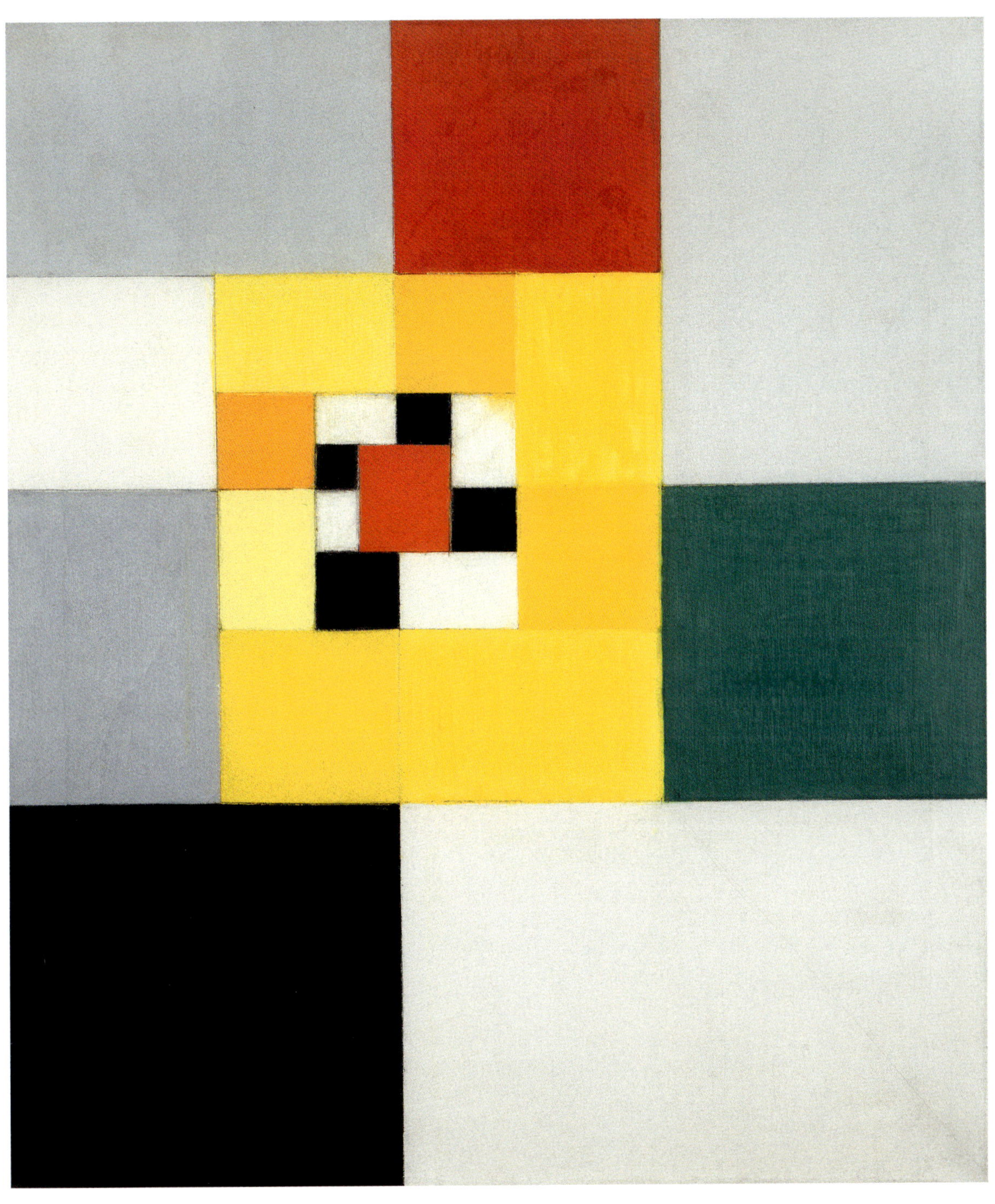

The Ancestral Altar from I Ching, 1954
oil and pencil on canvas, 76.2 × 63.5 cm
Brooklyn Museum, Purchased with funds given by Marlene and
Edward Shufro, Frank L. Babbott Fund, and Dick S. Ramsay Fund

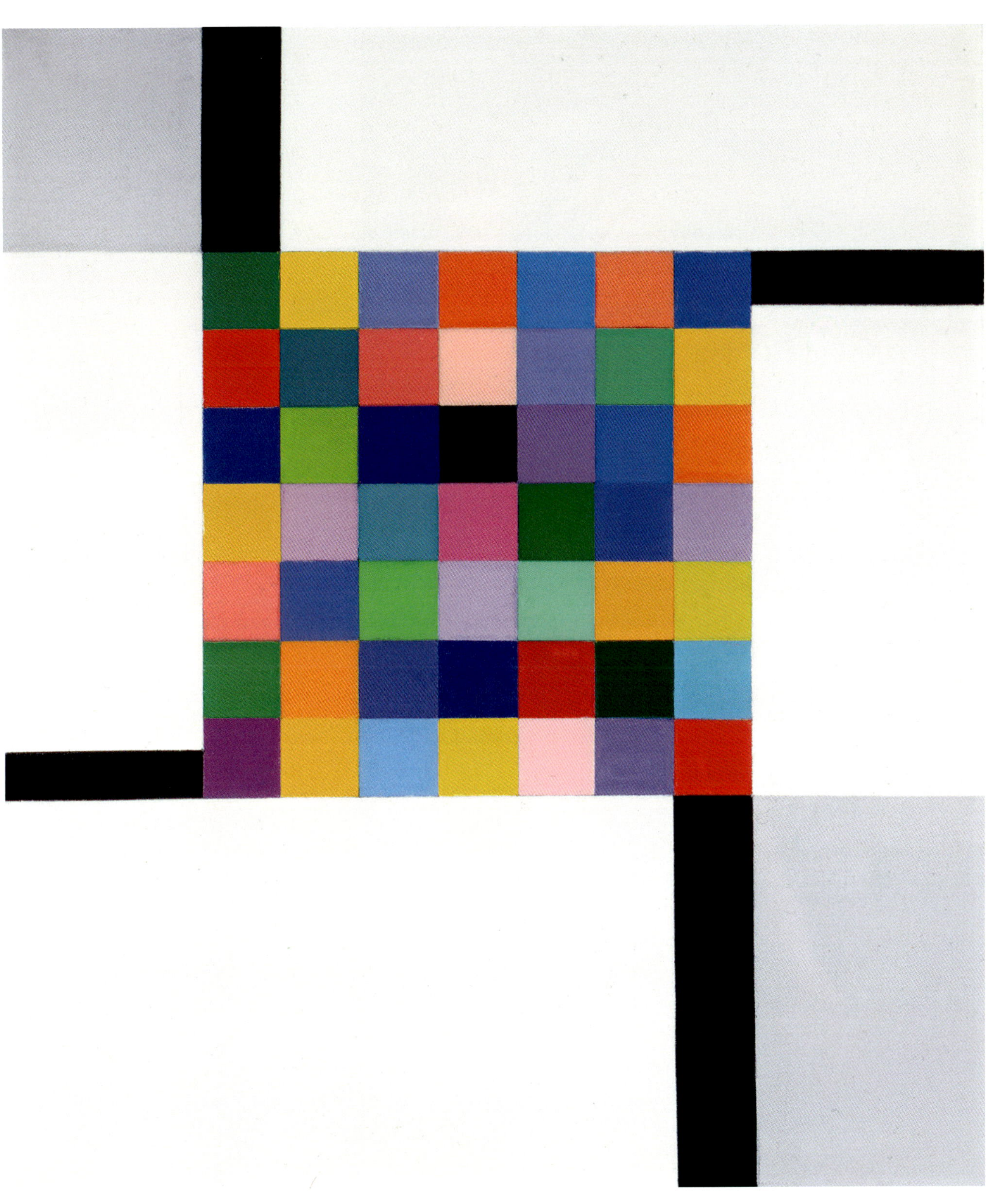

The Wheel of the Seasons, 1957
oil on canvas, 99.1 × 82.6 cm
Collection Albright-Knox Art Gallery, Buffalo, New York,
Charles Clifton Fund, 1981

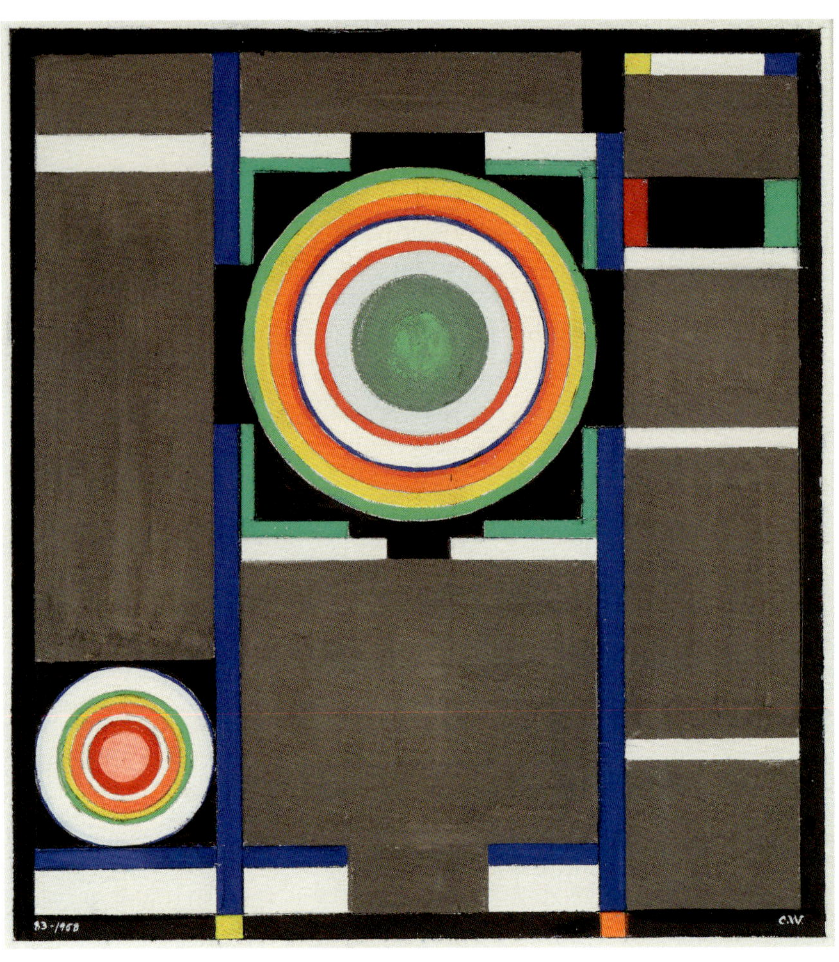

The Wheel of the Law, #83, 1958
gouache and pencil on paper, 38.6 × 34.3 cm
The Newark Museum of Art,
Gift of Mr. and Mrs. Alan Loesberg, 1983

Cat. 23   82

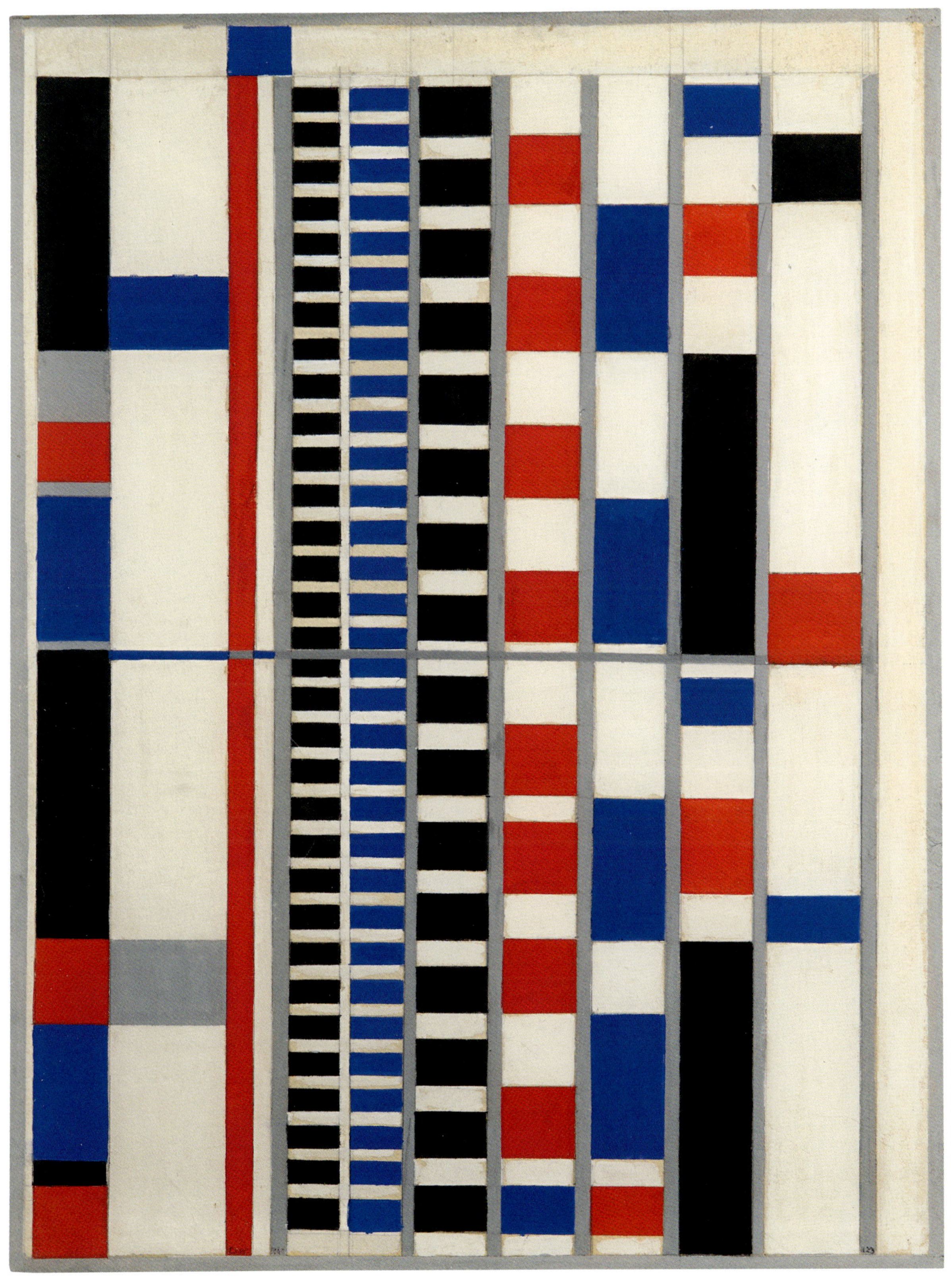

Study for Chinese Horoscope, 1960
gouache on paper, 66 × 45.7 cm
Collection of Nancy and Fred Poses, New York,
Courtesy of Meredith Palmer Gallery, Ltd.

Cat. 24   83

14   See Piet Mondrian, *Plastic
Art and Pure Plastic Art, 1937,
and Other Essays, 1941–1943*.
The Documents of Modern Art
(New York: Wittenborn, 1945), 6.
Holtzman made no effort to
correct the record when, more
than four decades later, he
published Mondrian's collected
writings: Piet Mondrian,
*The New Art—The New Life:
The Collected Writings of Piet
Mondrian*, ed. Harry Holtzman
and Martin S. James (Boston:
G. K. Hall, 1986).

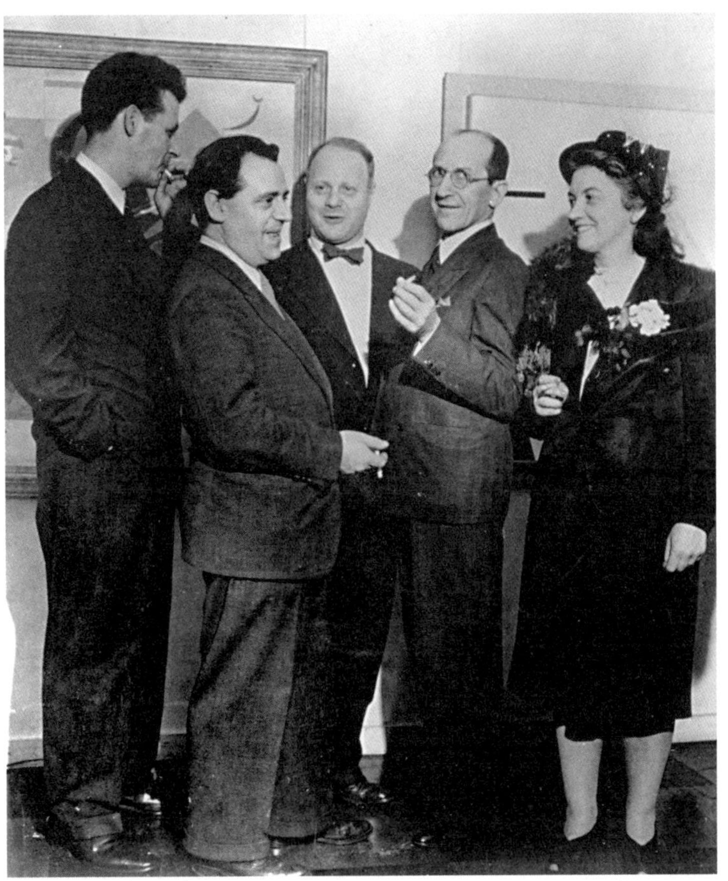

Opening of the exhibition *Masters
of Abstract Art*, Helena Rubinstein's
New Art Center, New York, April 1, 1942,
from left to right: Burgoyne Diller,
Fritz Glarner, Carl Holty, Piet Mondrian,
and Charmion von Wiegand

Moreover, when she co-organized *Masters of Abstract Art*, an important exhibition of vanguard works by modern and contemporary artists at Helena Rubinstein's New Art Center in 1942, her contributions were neither acknowledged nor remunerated. (See the catalog's frontispiece which lists Stephan C. Lion as solely responsible for assembling the exhibition.) A photograph taken by Lisette Model at the opening shows Von Wiegand together with Mondrian, Diller, Glarner, and Holty and is often included in publications devoted to Mondrian and his American followers. However, Von Wiegand was there in her administrative capacity as co-curator and editor, not as a practicing artist. With these circumstances in mind, we can justifiably conclude that, as much as Von Wiegand was an insider in Mondrian's New York world, she nevertheless remained, in crucial respects, an outsider to this predominantly male group of Mondrian-affiliated artists.

The ultimate insider among the followers of Mondrian was Harry Holtzman, who met Mondrian in Paris in 1935 and later was instrumental in sponsoring his immigration to New York. In appreciation, Mondrian named Holtzman as his sole heir in 1942. From that platform, after Mondrian's death, Holtzman was better positioned than Von Wiegand to influence the historical narrative of Mondrian's experiences in New York, about which he was frequently invited to comment. And even when no comment was involved, he nevertheless shaped the way the story would be told, often occluding the role Von Wiegand had played. For example, in 1945, to coincide with the memorial exhibition of Mondrian's work at MoMA, Holtzman brought out a book of essays by Mondrian in English, *Plastic Art and Pure Plastic Art, 1937, and Other Essays, 1941–1943*. Although Von Wiegand had translated and/or edited many of the essays it contained, she received no credit for that effort: her name was not mentioned in Holtzman's forward or anywhere else in the volume.[14] Sorely disappointed, she wrote to her father: [. . .] the

15   Charmion von Wiegand
to Karl von Wiegand,
May 4, 1945, Karl von Wiegand
Papers, Hoover Institute,
quoted in Jennifer Newton Hersh,
"Abstraction, Spiritualism,
and Social Justice: The Art and
Writing of Charmion von Wiegand"
(PhD dissertation, City University
of New York, 1998), 260.

16   Harry Holtzman, "Piet
Mondrian, 1872–1944: Some Notes
on Mondrian's Method, The
Late Drawings," in *Mondrian:
The Process Works* (New York:
Pace Gallery, 1970), 3.

17   Holtzman was often out
of town for prolonged periods;
he and his wife summered in
Massachusetts. In 1942, he was
living in Kansas, according to the
Masters of Abstract Art catalog; and, he later told an inter-
viewer, he spent the winter of
1943 in Colorado. See Virginia
Pitts Rembert, "Mondrian,
America, and American Painting"
(PhD dissertation, Columbia
University, 1970), 110n108.

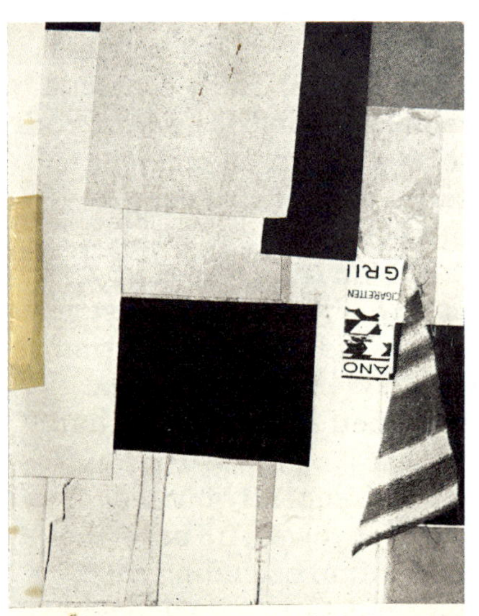

Cover of the catalog to the exhibition
Kurt Schwitters, The Pinacotheca,
New York (January 19–February 1948)

essays and translations I worked on with Mondrian have now been published by the painter [Harry Holtzman], who inherited his estate, and without giving me the slightest credit for months of labor. [...] My lawyer wanted me to sue, but it would have made an unpleasant situation and I might have been criticized. There was nothing to get out of a suit but a headache and annoyance.[15]

The treatment she received (or lack thereof) in the forward by Robert Motherwell, who edited the series in which the volume of essays by Mondrian appeared, was no better. Motherwell noted how slight was the existing literature on Mondrian, listing publications by James Johnson Sweeney, Alfred Barr, Jr., A. E. Gallatin, and László Moholy-Nagy—but not Von Wiegand's more sustained engagement with Mondrian's work in her 1943 essay.

Over the years that followed, and until his death in 1987, Holtzman repeatedly claimed that "Mondrian and I were often together daily in each other's studios, always discussing art and ideas or working on his writings."[16] This statement probably exaggerates the frequency of their interaction,[17] but, more to the point, by ignoring Von Wiegand's substantial collaboration on Mondrian's essays, Holtzman effectively wrote her out of his widely circulated story of Mondrian's life in New York.

Of course, Von Wiegand had her own story to tell and she too was consulted—though not nearly so frequently as Holtzman was—about her relationship to Mondrian and her experience of his work. In 1961, she published a memoir of his New York years, drawing in part on her journal entries, and ten years later these also featured in an interview conducted by Margit Rowell that was published on the occasion of the Solomon R. Guggenheim Museum's centennial exhibition of Mondrian's work. But even earlier, in the 1950s, Von Wiegand sought opportunities to share information about her editorial role and her familiarity with Mondrian's art and ideas, not only with Motherwell but also with Michel Seuphor, a Belgian writer, artist, and friend of Mondrian in Paris who would author the first monograph devoted to the artist.[18] However, these behind-the-scenes attempts to establish the substance of her contributions had no apparent impact; they never surfaced in any publications of the period.

Given the depth of her admiration for Mondrian as a person and as an artist, it is not surprising that Von Wiegand was devastated by his death. After 1944, she gradually returned to her own art practice by making hundreds of automatic drawings and eventually by creating small gouaches and collages (cat. 12) that demonstrate her interest not solely in Mondrian's work but in a variety of abstract styles that she and others identified with such artists as Hans Arp, Wassily Kandinsky, Joan Miró, and Kurt Schwitters. Many of those artists also appeared in one-person and group exhibitions she organized in the mid- and late 1940s for dealer Rose Fried's Pinacotheca Gallery (fig. left), where Von Wiegand's curatorial expertise continued to play out in tandem with the development of her art practice. Especially noteworthy shows include *The White Plane* (1947), focusing on Kandinsky, Malevich, and Mondrian; a one-person exhibition of collages by Schwitters; and a show of so-called Relational Paintings in which Fritz Glarner revealed his own formal debts to Mondrian's work. In 1947, Fried surprised Von Wiegand when she offered to show her paintings (Von Wiegand initially protested that she was not ready for such attention, but Fried persisted and the eventual exhibition was installed by Burgoyne Diller),

18   Michel Seuphor, *Piet Mondrian: Life and Work* (New York: H.N. Abrams, 1957).

19   Michael Auping, "Fields, Planes, Systems: Geometric Abstract Painting in America since 1945," in *Abstraction-Geometry-Painting: Selected Geometric Abstract Painting in America since 1945* (Buffalo, NY: Albright-Knox Art Gallery, 1989), 35.

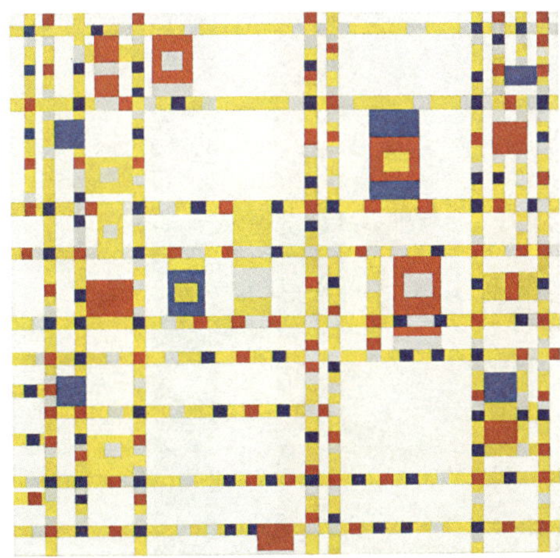

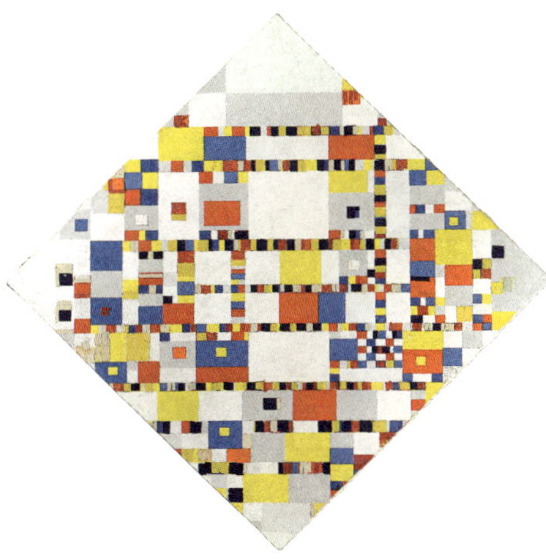

Piet Mondrian, *Broadway Boogie Woogie*, 1942–1943, oil on canvas, 50 × 50 cm, Museum of Modern Art, New York, Given anonymously

Piet Mondrian, *Victory Boogie Woogie*, 1942–1944, oil, tape, charcoal, and pencil on canvas, 178.4 × 178.4 cm, Kunstmuseum Den Haag, long-term loan Cultural Heritage Agency of the Netherlands/Ministry of Education, Culture, and Science

which was followed the next year by a show of her collages. Despite the attention to her work that these two early exhibitions provided, Von Wiegand's status as an artist was in some respects still liminal: lacking a dedicated studio space, she had to make do with a small guest bedroom in the apartment she shared with her husband, a situation that helps to account for the intimate scale of her art from this period.

While many of the works Von Wiegand produced in the mid- to late 1940s demonstrate a willingness to move beyond Mondrian, she also returned to his example, creating a series of pictures, some with urban themes (see *City Lights* [1947; cat. 10] and *City Rhythm*) inspired by the vibrancy of his late paintings which had been conceived in response to the lively urban environment he had discovered in New York. In her City pictures, as well as a number of other works that are reminiscent of *Broadway Boogie Woogie* (fig. left above) and *Victory Boogie Woogie* (fig. left below), Von Wiegand distributed small, sometimes slightly irregular rectangular planes of color more or less evenly across the picture surface to achieve compositions that share Mondrian's commitment to the limited means of flat planes deployed in a grid-like arrangement. These works are pervaded by the spirit of Mondrian's style without being slavishly dependent upon it.

Von Wiegand's profile as an accomplished artist was beginning to take shape by 1947 when she rejoined the American Abstract Artists as a full member. Thereafter she regularly participated in the group's annual exhibitions and eventually acted as its president for two years, beginning in 1951. Her administrative skills thus continued to complement her aesthetic achievements. But as her work began to circulate more widely in AAA shows, some of which traveled to venues outside New York, the potential for increased visibility and sales unfortunately coincided with a downturn in the prestige of the organization, whose close association with Mondrian's influential work began to be seen as a problem rather than a plus.

Even though Von Wiegand was never a slavish follower of Mondrian, she did produce many geometric abstract works, and several examples display the restricted palette characteristic of his signature paintings. It is therefore hardly surprising to find that she shared the fate of other AAA artists—Diller and Glarner, for example—who more consistently followed in Mondrian's wake: neglect in the face of an emerging art historical canon that, by mid-century, was otherwise oriented. As Michael Auping has explained:

> Historically, the contributions of the AAA artists have tended to be buried between the breakthrough achievements of Mondrian and the emergence of Abstract Expressionism, which we often mistakenly think of as "the beginning" [of important post-war painting in America]. These early pioneers of American abstraction inhabited a kind of aesthetic purgatory, a transitional position that involved extending the theoretical direction of Mondrian while attempting to forge a geometric approach to abstraction that was particularly American.[19]

While the original momentum of the American Abstract Artists was losing steam, there were a number of abstract painters—Ad Reinhardt and Mark Tobey come readily to mind—who, like Von Wiegand, began to manifest an ever-deepening interest in non-Western art, the art of India, China, and eventually of Tibet, which resonated with Von Wiegand's lifelong engagement with Theosophy and related spiritual traditions. These she linked to Mondrian (he had also been a Theosophist)— "Mondrian was my Guru," she told Guggenheim Museum curator Margit Rowell in 1970—a reference to his importance in many aspects of her

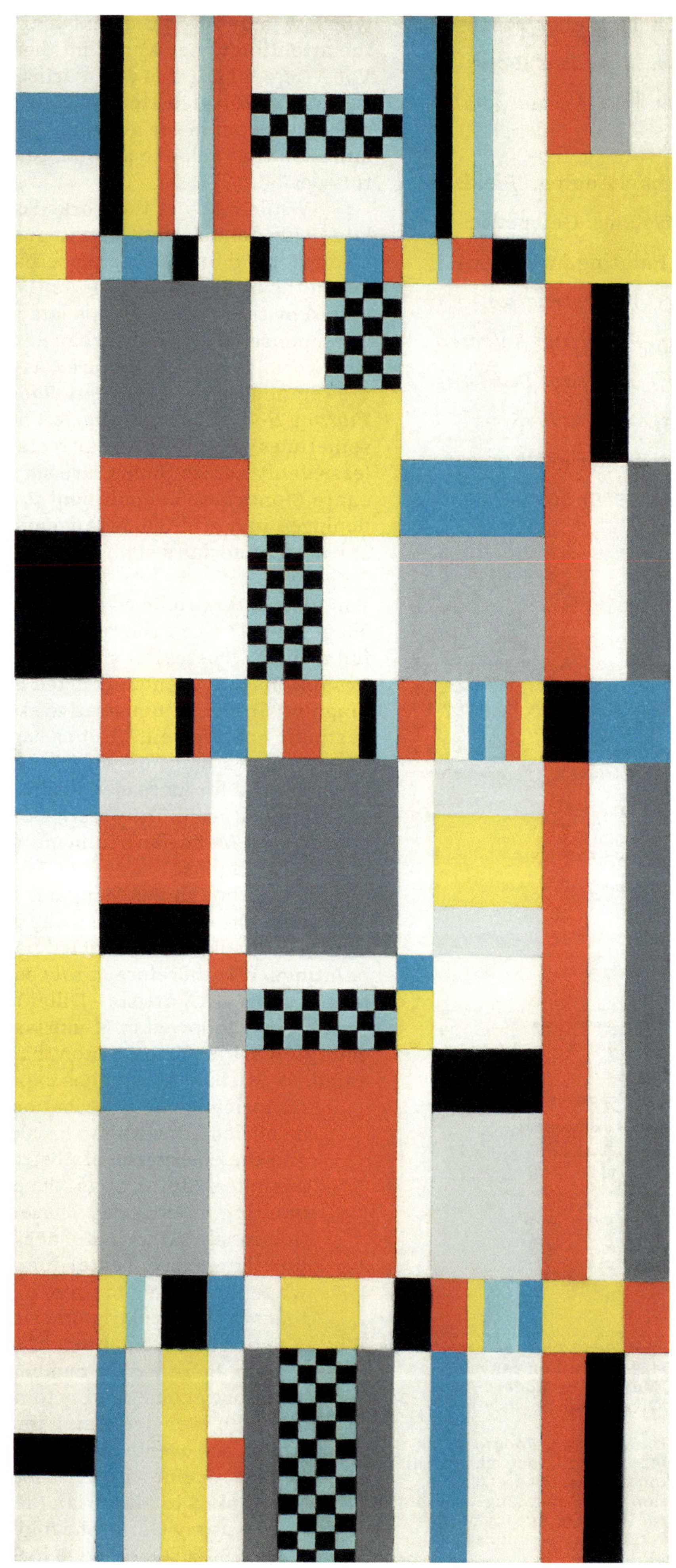

Charmion von Wiegand, *The Ka Door*,
1949–1952, oil on canvas, 107 × 46 cm,
Estate of Charmion von Wiegand,
Courtesy of Michael Rosenfeld
Gallery LLC, New York

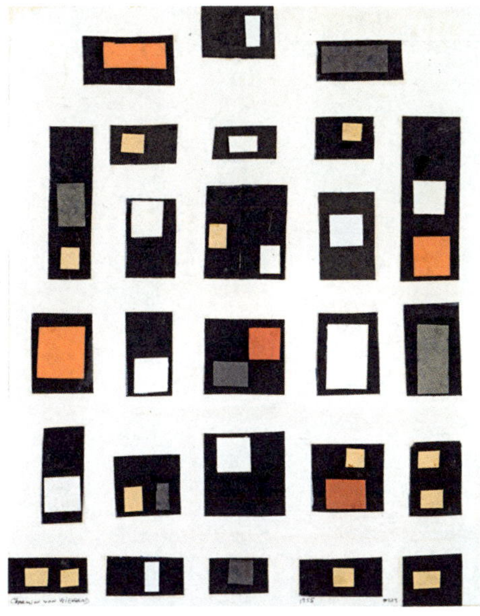

20 Rowell, "Interview with

Charmion von Wiegand," 78.

21 Owen McNally, "A Mondrian

Influence, but Wiegand an

Original," *Hartford Courant*,

November 21, 1993, https://www.

courant.com/news/connecticut/

hc-xpm-1993-11-21-0000001661-

story.html.

22 Ibid.

Charmion von Wiegand, *Collage #127: Magic Squares*, 1955, collage and gouache on paper, 34.6 × 27.9 cm, Private Collection, New York

life and art, if not always to her spiritual development.[20] Thus, even as she continued to acknowledge Mondrian, she was exploring alternative directions, particularly the study of Buddhism as a religion, a philosophy of life, and as a new focus of her art practice. The development in this direction appears to have been almost seamless, as paintings such as *Power Plant II* (fig. below) and *Radiating Plane* (cat. 13) display numerous similarities with Mondrian's *Broadway Boogie Woogie*, while they also demonstrate an affinity with *The Ka Door* (fig. facing page), an early example of painting by Von Wiegand that was inspired by a non-Western spiritual theme.

For a variety of reasons Von Wiegand's output in the 1950s and after continued to be relatively modest, and while the works most reminiscent of Mondrian are represented in the collections of prominent art museums, the early and late periods of her career are relatively neglected and rarely shown; indeed, her oeuvre has not often been seen or studied as a coherent whole. When eighty paintings and collages were presented in a comprehensive exhibition in Hartford, Connecticut, in 1993, Owen McNally, who reviewed the show for the *Hartford Courant*, could justifiably wonder, "So why just 10 years after her death isn't she a better-known figure?"[21]

While the answer to this question is multifaceted, as the discussion above has shown, part of the explanation surely has to do with the fact that Mondrian was always an inescapable presence, shaping and in some ways overshadowing her reception, if not the visual features of her work. McNally was no different from many other critics over the years in noting at the outset of his review, "Von Wiegand's abstract style was heavily influenced by Dutch painter Piet Mondrian."[22] While true enough, this assessment does not do justice to the complex nature of the role Mondrian played in Von Wiegand's life, or she in his; nor does it encourage a nuanced appreciation for Von Wiegand's unusually variegated talents—editorial, curatorial, and administrative, to name only a few—which helped to shape her multifaceted career even as they complicated and sometimes obscured her reception as a female visual artist.

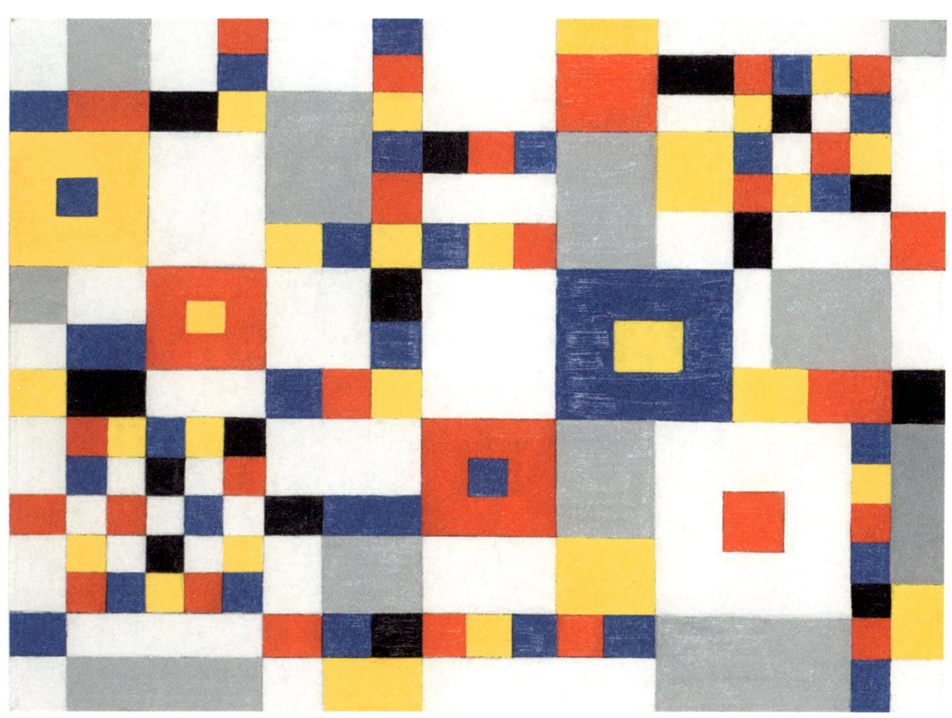

Charmion von Wiegand, *Power Plant II*, 1949, oil on canvas, 50.9 × 61 cm, The Cleveland Museum of Art, Cleveland, OH, Dorothea Wright Hamilton Fund

HAEMA SIVANESAN

CHARMION VON WIEGAND'S VISION OF MODERN BUDDHISM

1   Oral history interview with
Charmion von Wiegand by
Paul Cummings, October 9 and
November 3, 1968. Archives
of American Art, Smithsonian
Institution, 22.

2   See Jennifer Newton Hersh,
"Abstraction, Spiritualism and
Social Justice: The Art and Writing of Charmion von Wiegand"
(PhD dissertation, City University
of New York, 1998), 357ff.

3   Hersh, 366; also,
Von Wiegand, interview by
Cummings, 68.

Asian Ideas and Modern Art

In 1952, Charmion von Wiegand prepared for a one-person exhibition of new paintings at the Eleanor Saidenberg Gallery, New York (April 22–May 24, 1952). A painting titled *The Golden Flower* (1951–1952; fig. left) was one of the first paintings to depart from the gridded, orthogonal compositions that were essential to Piet Mondrian's ideas of plasticity in painting. This painting was a syncretic image composed of a field of interlocking and chromatic yellow and blue squares, organized around the axes of a Latin cross. At the intersection of the cross was the design of a lotus within a six-pointed star (hexagram): the "mandala-like" golden flower of the painting's title. The painting referred to a book titled *The Secret of the Golden Flower*, a Taoist text full of imagery and allusion, concerned with the cultivation of the higher self via meditational practices termed as a "turning around of the light." Unlike previous works, *The Golden Flower* was highly personal and symbolistic, evoking the ideas and aspirational qualities of the Taoist text. The artist's palette of complementary blues and yellows conveyed a quality of transcendent light. Von Wiegand reflected on the unconscious surfacing of Asian motifs in her artwork and her shift away from strict Neo-Plasticism: "I put a circle in the midst of all the very geometric planes with the squares [. . .] the circle enlarged and drove out the square."[1]

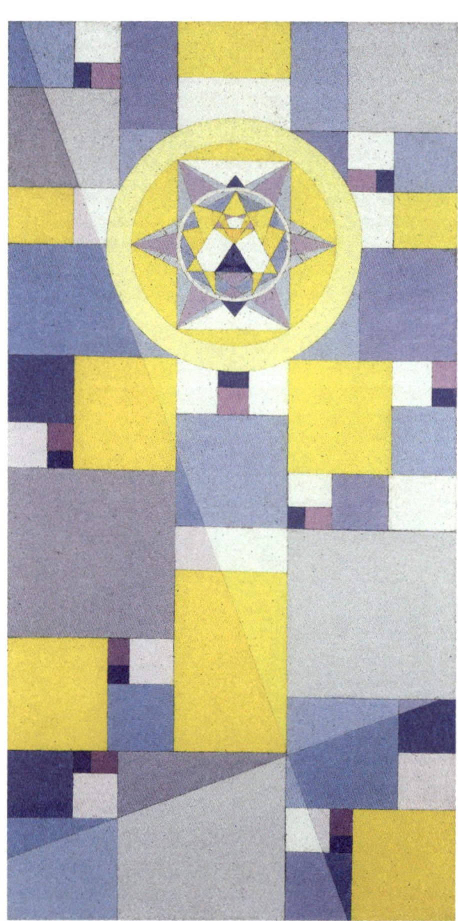

Charmion von Wiegand, *The Golden Flower*, 1951–1952, oil on canvas, 101.6 × 50.8 cm, Private Collection, New York

Invitation card to the exhibition *Charmion von Wiegand*, Saidenberg Gallery, New York (April 22–May 24, 1952)

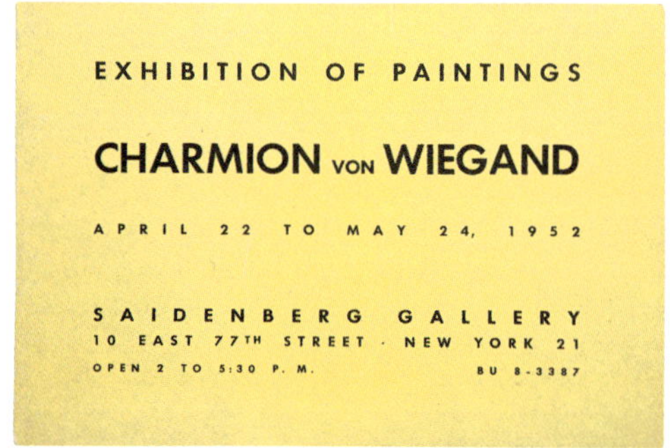

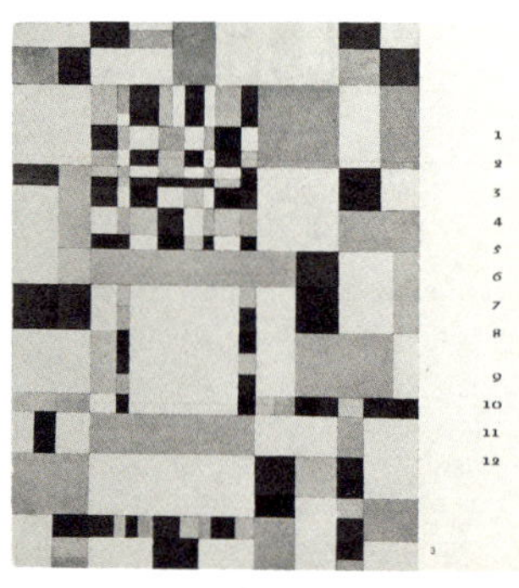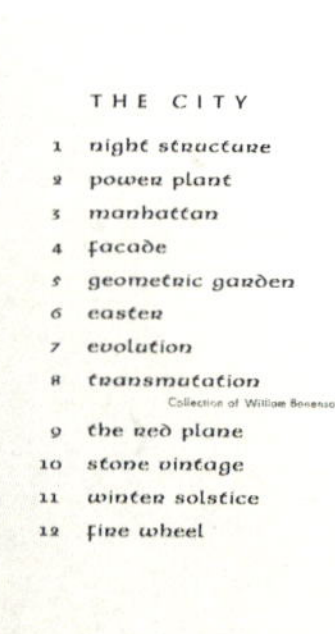

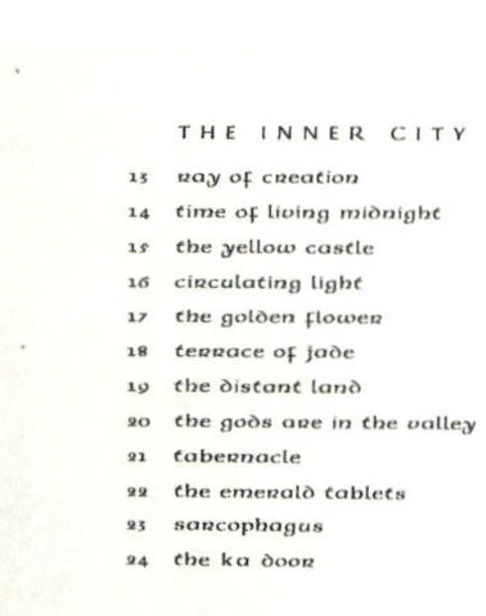

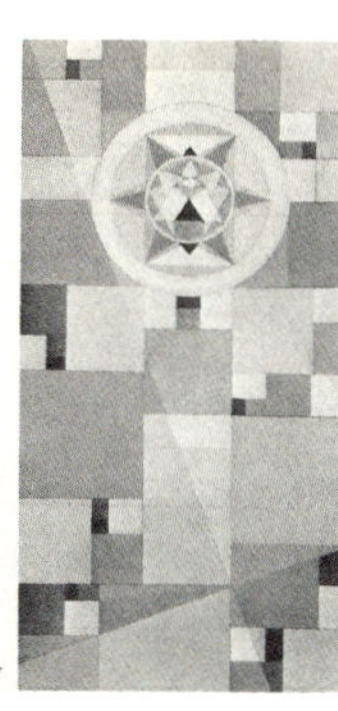

The period of the 1950s reflected Von Wiegand's steady search for spiritual and metaphysical models. She and many of her contemporaries regarded Asian art as the stylistic paradigm of modernism, where spirituality was considered a central value.[2] Von Wiegand was drawn to the study of Asia as an antidote to the culture of materialism and individualism increasingly characterizing modern art in New York. She regarded painting as a site of spiritual inquiry and expression. Accordingly, her search for spiritual fulfilment was recorded by way of her artistic production, where the study of Asia and the search for spiritual meaning were intertwined.

In 1951, Von Wiegand attended a lecture given by the scholar of Zen Buddhism, Daisetz Teitaro Suzuki at the Church Peace Union, New York; and she later attended his lectures at Columbia University

4   Von Wiegand's close friend Mark Tobey was, in 1934, possibly the first American artist to spend an extended period of time at a Zen monastery, an experience that had a singular and lasting impact on his painting. Tobey gifted and referred a number of books on Zen to Von Wiegand. For example, a copy of Alan Watts's book *The Spirit of Zen: A Way of Life, Work and Art in the Far East* (New York: Grove, 1957) is in Von Wiegand's estate. It is inscribed to Von Wiegand from Mark Tobey and dated 1958. Tobey possibly also made the suggestion to Von Wiegand to attend Suzuki's lectures at Columbia University, as he had done with the composer John Cage. See Debra Bricker Balken, *Mark Tobey: Threading Light* (New York: Skira Rizzoli, 2017), 172.

5   Von Wiegand, letter to Mark Tobey, May 21, 1957, Mark Tobey Papers, Archives of American Art, Smithsonian Institution, reel 3200.

6   See Aliza Edelman, "Departing the Plane: Charmion von Wiegand's Otherworldly Abstractions of the 1950s," in *American Women Artists, 1935–1970: Gender, Culture, and Politics*, ed. Helen Langa and Paula Wisotzski (London: Routledge, 2016), 201.

(1952–1953).[3] She read widely on Zen,[4] but its practical application appeared opaque to her. She would write to her friend, the artist Mark Tobey, You wrote me about the book, Zen and the Art of Archery. I read it with great delight when it first came out. After all it gets to the crux of the matter. But how to attain it?[5]

Subsequently, the artist Ibram Lassaw gave her the book *The Secret of the Golden Flower*, which inspired numerous works in her Saidenberg Gallery exhibition. She quoted from the book in the exhibition checklist: "In the midst of primal becoming, the radiance of the light is the determining thing. In the physical world it is the sun; in the man the eye."[6]

Then, her husband, the writer Joseph Freeman, gave her *The Book of Changes*, another Taoist text that was to impact Von Wiegand's work in significant ways, introducing her to ideas including the divination concepts of the *I Ching*, ideas of non-duality, and the universal law of change, which situates the individual in relation to the cycles of the cosmos. Her exploration of the concept of cosmic cycles is illustrated in paintings such as *The Wheel of the Seasons* (1957; cat. 22) and *The Wheel of the Law, #83* (1958; cat. 23), both of which also correlate with the Theosophical concept of the "Doctrine of Cycles," referring

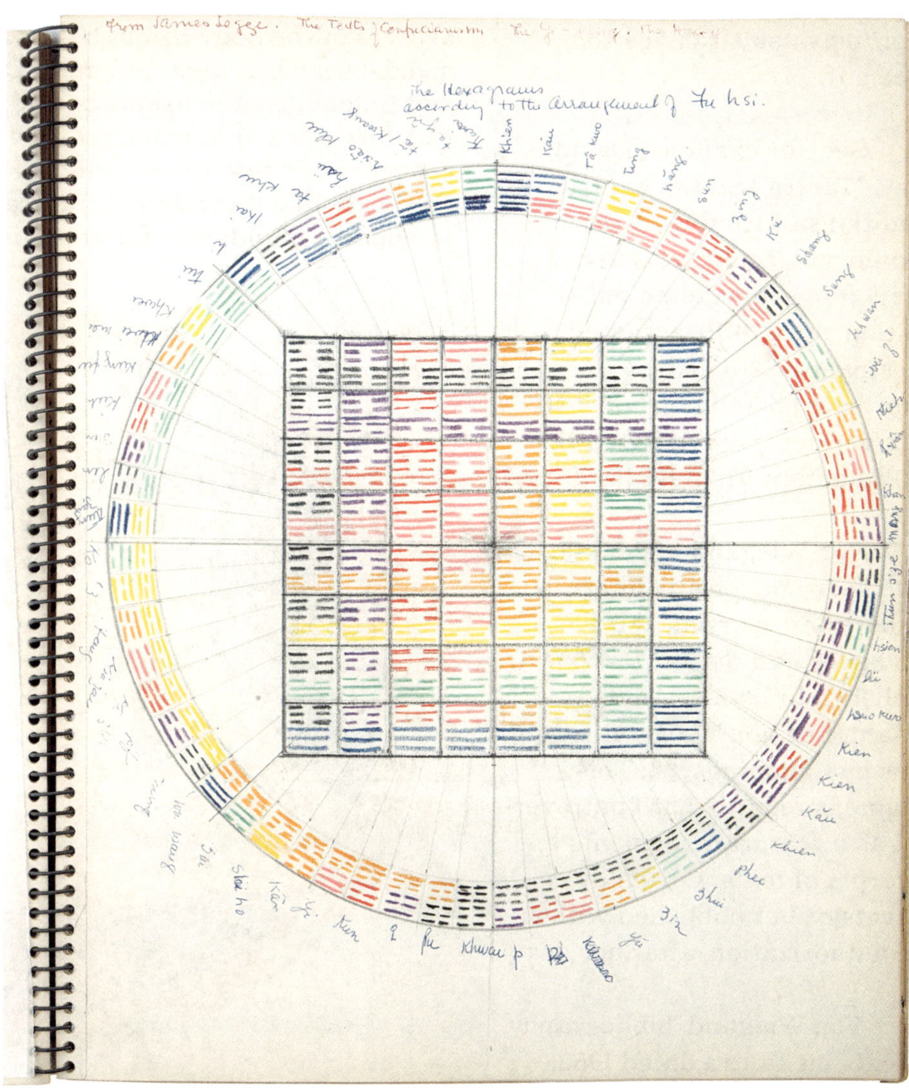

Charmion von Wiegand, study *The Hexagrams According to the Arrangement of Fu Hsi*, undated, pencil, colored pencil, and ink, Collection of Khyongla Rato

7   Freeman, Joseph, "The Wheel," January 5–9, 1959 (unpublished), Joseph Freeman Papers, Box 142, Folder 1, Hoover Institution Archives, Stanford University, California.

8   See Von Wiegand, interview by Cummings, 28; Helena Petrovna Blavatsky, *The Secret Doctrine*, 2 vols. (Pasadena: Theosophical Society, 1888), vol. 3 published post-humously (Adyar, India: Theosophical Society, 1897).

9   Possibly the *Kalachakra Tantra*. See Leslie Price, "Madame Blavatsky, Buddhism and Tibet" (paper presented at the Theosophical History Conference, London, 2003), accessed December 17, 2019, http://blavatskyarchives.com/price.pdf.

10   See, for example, David B. Gray, "Tantra and the Tantric Traditions of Hinduism and Buddhism," *Oxford Research Encyclopedias*, online publication, April 2016, accessed December 19, 2019, https://oxfordre.com/religion/view/10.1093/acrefore/9780199340378.001.0001/acrefore-9780199340378-e-59.

11   Von Wiegand appears to have been specifically interested in the "controversial" third volume of *The Secret Doctrine* published in 1897 by Annie Besant. See Von Wiegand, interview by Cummings, 28. This volume is regarded as controversial as it features fragments and excerpts of texts written by Blavatsky, but published without her authorization, after her death.

12   Von Wiegand, bibliography of texts on Tantra dated 1953, hand-written notes in the estate of the artist, Collection of Khyongla Rato.

to the universality of the "law of periodicity," and considered one of three fundamental propositions of Theosophy. These paintings, moreover, relate to an essay by Freeman titled "The Wheel" (January 5–9, 1959), which reads as a breathless, stream of consciousness reflection on the "Doctrine of Cycles" as a critique of the modern age, expressing a disenchantment with the post-war social and political reality in the United States.[7]

Theosophy and Tantra

By 1952, Von Wiegand and Freeman had met and become great friends with Louis James, the President of the Theosophical Society in New York. They regularly attended lectures, and James lent Von Wiegand a copy of Madame Blavatsky's famous text on occultism titled, *The Secret Doctrine* (1888).[8] It encompasses an Orientalized reading of certain Tantric texts,[9] conflating Tibetan Buddhist teachings with Vedic/Hindu concepts, and ideas drawn from *philosophia perennis*, in an attempt to reconcile ancient wisdom with modern science. In Hindu and Buddhist traditions, the Tantras refer to a category of ritual practice centered on the practical use of subtle forces and energies within the human body as a vehicle and means of integrating with the deity and fostering higher states of consciousness. Tantra emphasizes the union of masculine (consciousness) and feminine (energy) aspects of the body through practices including initiation, mantra, mandala, mudra, yoga, and meditation. Nineteenth-century Theosophists and Indophiles mistakenly considered the Tantras as being set apart from orthodox Hinduism and Buddhism and therefore considered its concepts and practices occult.[10] However, Blavatsky's endorsement of an Orientalized version of Tantra as found in *The Secret Doctrine* provided a foundation for Von Wiegand's initial study.[11]

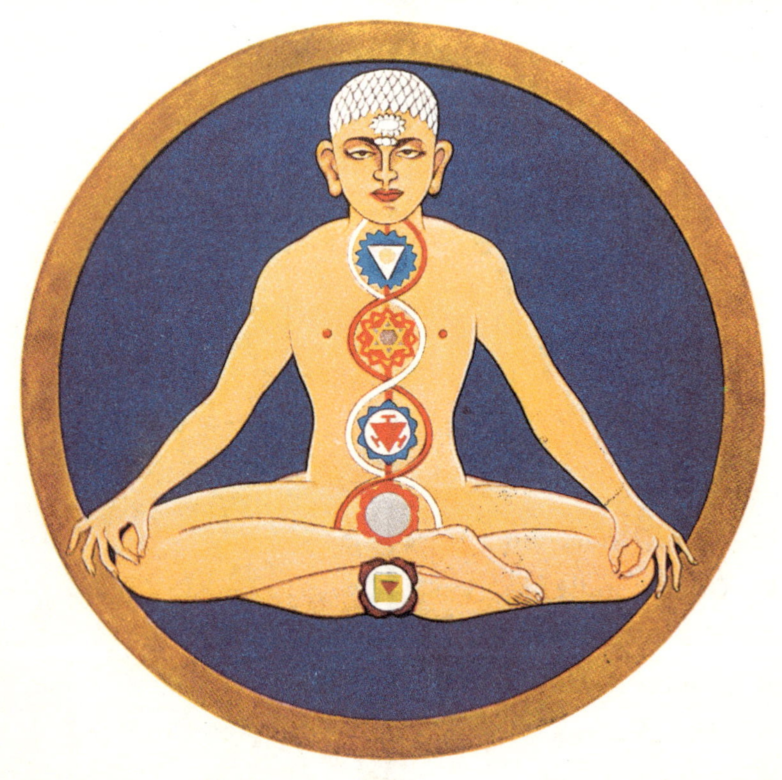

"Lotus centers in man," illustration in *The Serpent Power: The Secrets of Tantric and Shaktic Yoga* by Arthur Avalon [Sir John Woodroffe], first published in 1919

13   John Woodroffe, *The Serpent Power* (London: Luzac, 1919) a translation and commentary on two Sanskrit texts, *Ṣaṭcakranirūpaṇa* and *Pādukāpancaka*.

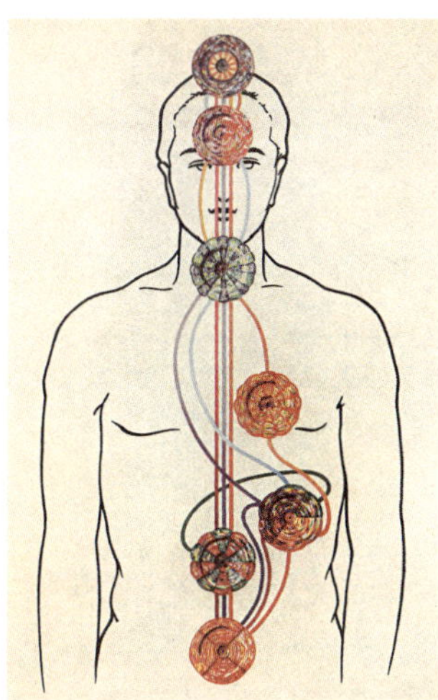

14   Charles Webster Leadbeater, *The Chakras* (Adyar, India: Theosophical Publishing House, 1927). Kurt Leland has written about Leadbeater's concept of the chakras as the inception of a Western system; see Kurt Leland, *Rainbow Body: A History of the Western Chakra System from Blavatsky to Brennan* (Lake Worth, FL: Ibis, 2016). Karl Baier, "Theosophical Orientalism and the Structures of Intercultural Transfer: Annotations on the Appropriation of the *Cakras* in Early Theosophy" contributes to a deeper scholarly discussion of Theosophy and its relationship to Tantra; available at https://www.academia.edu/14024830/Theosophical_Orientalism_and_the_Structures_of_Intercultural_Transfer_Annotations_on_the_Appropriation_of_the_Cakras_in_Early_Theosophy, accessed September 25, 2019.

"Sources of Vitality," illustration in *The Chakras: The Original Monograph Based on Clairvoyant Investigations* by Charles Webster Leadbeater, first published in 1927

What furthered Von Wiegand's interest in Theosophical Tantra were the beautiful and compelling illustrations of cosmograms, chakras, mandalas, and esoteric diagrams that accompanied many early texts published for Western readers. For example, from Von Wiegand's personal bibliographies on Tantra, it is clear that she was familiar with the writings of Sir John Woodroffe, who published his works under the pen name Arthur Avalon.[12] *The Serpent Power* (1919), Woodroffe's translation of two sixteenth-century Sanskrit texts, introduced the Western world to the now sensationalized concept of the kundalini.[13] The frontispiece of this book featured a diagram of a man seated in a crosslegged meditation posture, depicting the esoteric anatomy of the six-chakra system of the yogic body (fig. facing page), and several full-page color plates depicting the esoteric diagram (yantra) of each chakra . Through her close connections with the Theosophical Society, Von Wiegand was no doubt also familiar with Charles Webster Leadbeater's book, *The Chakras* (1927), a westernized interpretation of a seven-chakra system, which featured numerous, fascinating, color plates of whirling chakras and their associated yantras (fig. left).[14] Drawing on these texts and their accompanying technical diagrams as inspiration, Von Wiegand produced the meticulously drawn and intimately scaled, jewel-like painting, *Region of the Unstructured Sound* (1955–1961; fig. below), which revealed her rich exploration of

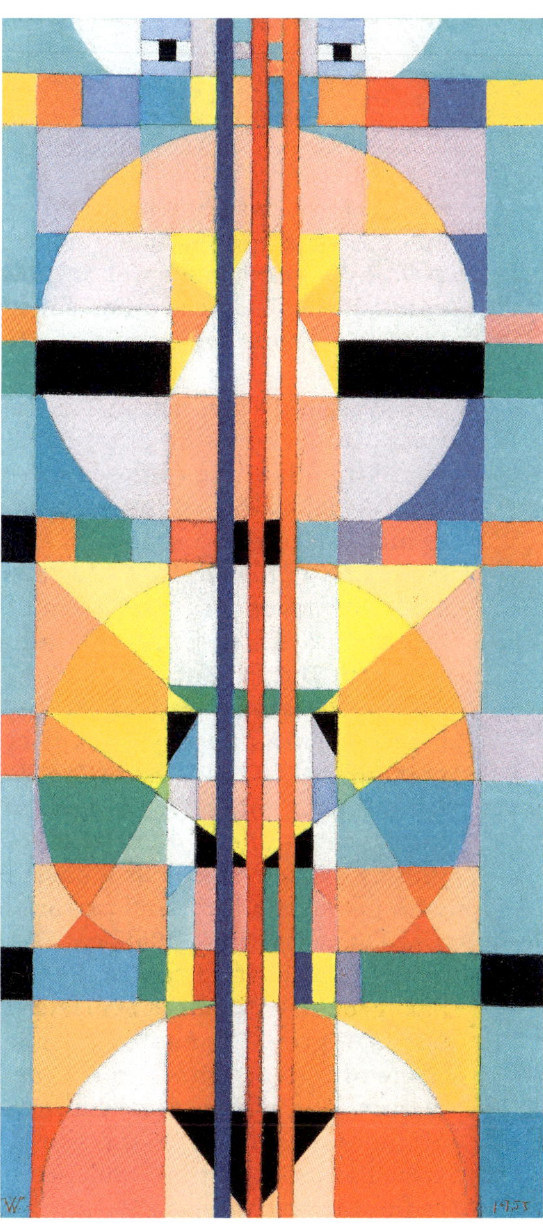

Charmion von Wiegand, *Region of the Unstructured Sound*, 1955–1961, oil on canvas, 55.9 × 25.4 cm, Michael Rosenfeld Gallery LLC, New York

15   See Blavatsky, "Sound and Colour" in *The Secret Doctrine*, vol. 3, 451, accessed December 19, 2019, http://blavatskyarchives.com/theosophypdfs/blavatsky_the_secret_doctrine_3rd_volume_1897.pdf.

16   In 1957, Von Wiegand wrote in a letter to Mark Tobey, I started taking Yogi exercises and so far have had 4 lessons. A friend, an abstract painter, Jean [Jeanne] Miles, persuaded me. Our teacher is Yogi Vithaldis, who is the teacher of Yehudi Menuhin, the violinist. It's pure Hatha-yogi and it has made me realise how unhealthy a life we lead in N Y. Von Wiegand, letter to Mark Tobey, May 21, 1957, Mark Tobey Papers, Archives of American Art, Smithsonian Institution, reel 3200. Stephen Westfall has noted that in 1952, Von Wiegand attended a lecture by the Theosophist Ernest Wood titled "The Practice of Patanjali's Eight Steps of Yoga." See Stephen Westfall, "Abstraction and Invisible Realms," in *Charmion von Wiegand: An Artist's Path from Mondrian to Mantra* (New York: Michael Rosenfeld Gallery, 2007), 16. Yogi Vithaldas's book, *Yoga Psychotherapy* (New York: Crown Publishers, 1956) is also found in Von Wiegand's personal library at the estate of the artist.

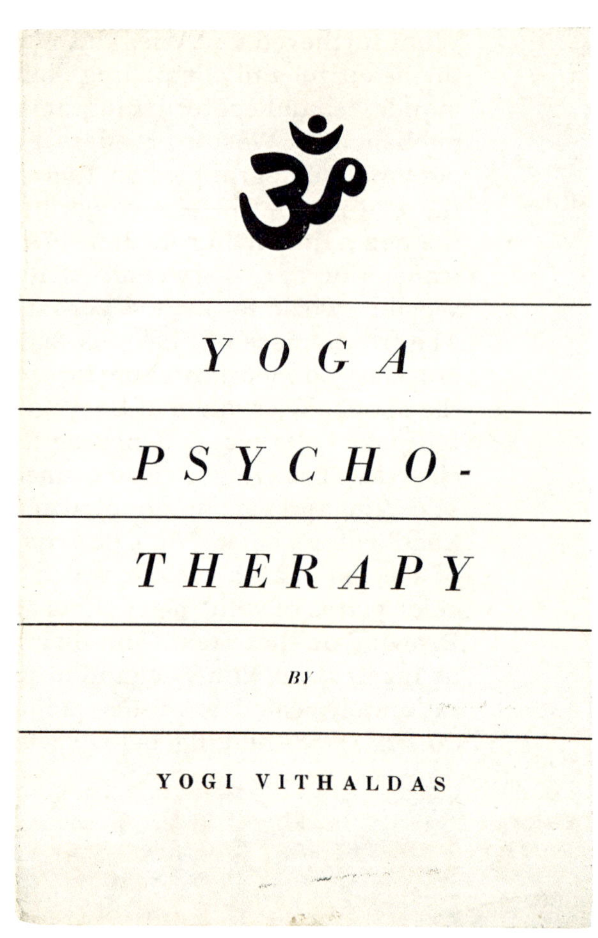

Cover of Charmion von Wiegand's copy of *Yoga Psychotherapy* by Yogi Vithaldas (New York: Crown Publishers, 1956)

Blavatsky's ideas of sound and prismatic color as it was thought to inhere in the body.[15] This painting reveals, on the one hand, the depth of Von Wiegand's research interest into this esoteric subject matter and her talent, on the other, for translating technical and esoteric concepts into artworks of exceptional liveliness and sophistication.

Von Wiegand's interest in Tantra developed further in 1957, when she was introduced to the practice of yoga, attending classes given by Yogi Vithaldas, one of the first teachers of modern yoga in the West.[16] Yogi Vithaldas promoted yoga as a system of health, making efforts to include women and foreigners in his circle, and promoting the idea that Indian philosophy could coexist with Western science and medicine. The seven-chakra system of the body is central to the core texts and meditative exercises of Hatha Yoga, which comprises a branch of Hindu Tantra. Between 1957 and 1962, the esoteric anatomy of the chakras became a significant theme in Von Wiegand's paintings, well before chakra imagery and the concept of *Tantra art* had become popularized in the West.[17] Von Wiegand found novel ways to express the ultimate goal of yogic meditation, being *samadhi* or the dissolution of self and ego into a state of pure consciousness, using the iconography of the chakras as a basis for intricate and lively experiments with geometric form and prismatic color. For example, a painting titled *The Chakras* (1958–1968; cat. 32) depicts each node of this esoteric anatomy as a ritual yantra. The image is made expansive by a tripartite background of squares overlaid on a pattern of alternating vertical bands of grey. The energy channels of the body *(nadi)* are depicted as a line of red *(pingala)* and a line of blue *(ida)* to either side of the picture. The subtle-most chakra *(sahasrara chakra)* above the crown of the head, relating to the site of pure consciousness, is depicted as scintillating confetti of multi-colored squares, conveying a concept of radiant transcendence.

17   An acclaimed exhibition in 1971 titled *Tantra* at the Hayward Gallery, London, curated by artist and art historian, Philip Rawson, and collector and essayist, Ajit Mookerjee, introduced and popularized the concept of "tantric art" internationally. Subsequently, an exhibition titled *Neo-Tantra: Contemporary Indian Painting Inspired by Tradition*, curated by Edith Tonelli, opened at UCLA's Frederick S. Wight Gallery in 1985.

18   Von Wiegand is likely to have come across a ground plan of the Potala Palace in L. Austine Waddell, *Lhasa and Its Mysteries* (London: John Murray, 1905), which is noted in her personal bibliography dated 1953, hand-written notes in the estate of the artist.

19   Von Wiegand, letter to Mark Tobey, December 19, 1956, Mark Tobey Papers, Archives of American Art, Smithsonian Institution, reel 3200.

Charmion von Wiegand, *Sanctuary of the Four Directions*, 1959–1960, oil on canvas, 91.5 × 81.3 cm, Museum of Modern Art, New York, The Riklis Collection of McCrory Corporation

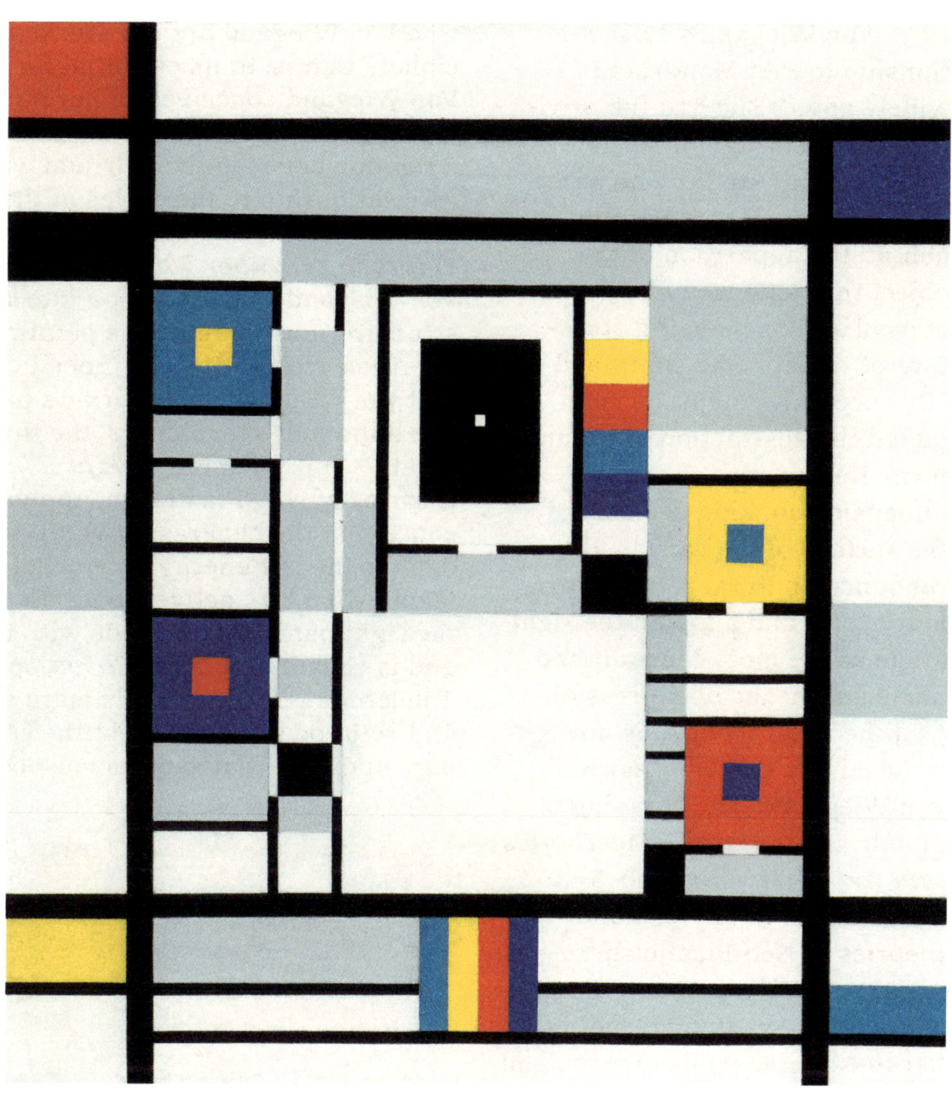

During the same period, Von Wiegand painted a major work titled *Sanctuary of the Four Directions* (1959–1960; fig. above) that appears to be loosely based on the ground plan of the Potala Palace (Lhasa, Tibet), the traditional seat of the Dalai Lama.[18] The compositional structure of this painting is related to previous works, *The Wheel of the Seasons* (cat. 22) and *The Wheel of the Law, #83* (cat. 23), but it is also the culmination of a set of smaller studies based on the ground plans of various Indian and Central Asian temples. Unlike the prismatic colors of the wheel paintings, however, this painting appears to return to Mondrian's palette of primary colors to explore ideas of sacred space and geometry. By making these paintings, Von Wiegand began to perceive an interrelation between geometric space, as suggested by architecture; bodily space, as evoked by her investigations into the concept of the chakras; and space as an infinite macrocosm. Whereas Mondrian's concept of Neo-Plasticism grappled with the nature of "exterior realities," of landscapes, cityscapes, the natural object, and so on, by the late 1950s, Von Wiegand began exploring painting as a means of representing interior experience and higher states of consciousness. Von Wiegand once remarked in a letter to Mark Tobey, `I would like to get inside a mandala and stay for a while`.[19] The paintings of this period would appear to demonstrate the significance of that remark, which, while not being mandalas in the true sense (as ritual or consecrated devices for meditative practice), are ultimately concerned with exploring the formal, geometric, and painterly means by which the esoteric nature of the world could be grasped. In this respect, there is a further comparison with Mondrian,

20   Von Wiegand's close relationship to Piet Mondrian is
widely noted. She had the privi-
lege of observing him as he
worked in his studio. She wrote
of Mondrian, "It was the thing
behind the apparition of the
object that intrigued him [...] the
eternal and unchanging structure of reality." She continued,
"By successive steps, he completed the abstraction of natural
form. He excluded the third
dimension, making use only of
the surface of the canvas. He
renounced natural color for primary color and adopted the right
angle as the most constant and
universal means of expression
[...] the natural object is now
reduced to a cipher." Charmion
von Wiegand, "The Meaning of
Mondrian," *Journal of Aesthetics
and Art Criticism* 2, no. 8
(Autumn, 1943): 62–70. Mondrian's
theories of Neo-Plasticism re-
vived Von Wiegand's interest in
Theosophy, eventually leading
her to examine its deeper roots in
Tantrism and Tibetan Buddhism.

21   According to art historian,
Robert Welsh, Mondrian's tripartite painting *Evolution* depicts
the three stages of Theosophical
enlightenment described as
ignorance, knowledge, and
consciousness. Mondrian drew
on symbolist language and color
symbolism, incorporating the
six-pointed star, the seal of
the Theosophical Society, in the
painting. Robert Welsh,
"Mondrian and Theosophy," 1971,
accessed September 28, 2019,
https://www.theosophyforward.
com/index.php/theosophy-and-
the-society-in-the-public-eye/
643-mondrian-and-theosophy-
part-one.html.

Charmion von Wiegand, sketch of
Helena Petrovna Blavatsky,
The Secret Doctrine, undated,
Collection of Khyongla Rato

who Von Wiegand argued, worked to "reduce the natural object to a
cipher," that is, to its essential form, through painting.[20] Similarly,
Von Wiegand conceived of her paintings as *conceptual mandalas* or
ciphers of a type, as mediums or devices expressing the essence of
a relation between the spiritual world, the condition of the body, and
its relationship to the cycles of the universe.

Triptych, Number 700 (1961; fig. pp. 6/7) stands as the culmination of
Von Wiegand's investigation into Theosophical Tantric ideas. In form,
structure, and content, this painting recalls Mondrian's tripartite painting *Evolution* (1911), and indeed the painting appears as a tribute to
that work. But while Mondrian's painting took an expressive and figurative approach to exploring "the three stages of Theosophical enlightenment,"[21] Von Wiegand's *Triptych* also draws on Mondrian's later
theories of Neo-Plasticism, applying them to interpret a Theosophical
concept of the chakras. In Von Wiegand's *Triptych*, the center panel
depicts the left energy channel of the body *(ida)*, which is considered
female *(Shakti)*, active, energetic, and corresponding with the moon;
the right panel corresponds with the right energy channel *(pingala)*
and is considered male *(Shiva)*, passive, and associated with the sun.
The left panel merges the square and circle geometries of the center
and right panels to suggest the condition of *samadhi*, the state of
pure undifferentiated consciousness. *Triptych, Number 700* is a deeply

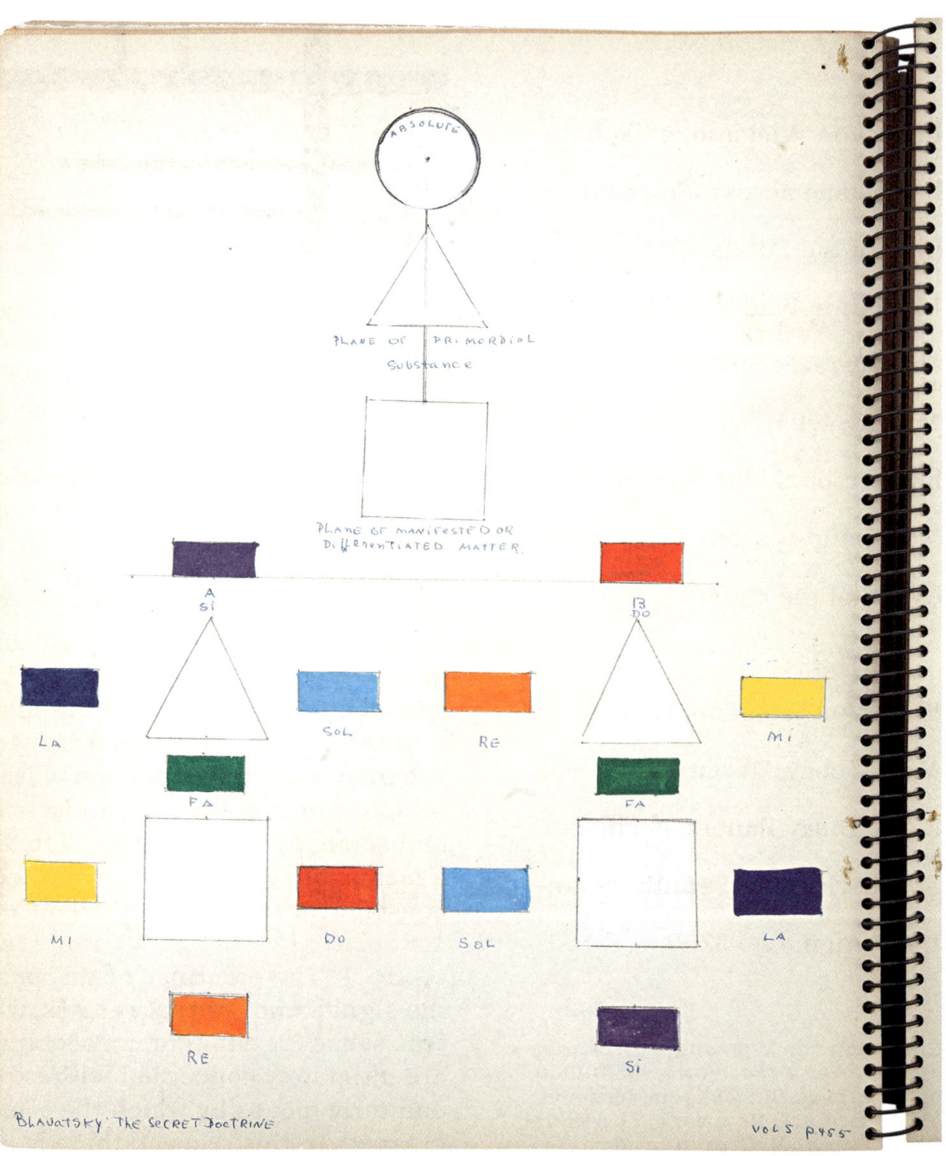

considered, ambitious, and confident work that is a high point in Von Wiegand's oeuvre. It was shown in the Whitney Museum of American Art's *Geometrical Abstraction in America* exhibition in 1962. Von Wiegand commented on the work's inclusion: `Good to see one's work objectively and was surprised how far I had navigated from Neo-Plasticism.`[22] Yet the painting represents an important synthesis of Von Wiegand's study of both Neo-Plasticism *and* Theosophical Tantra, revealing the extent to which the artist was producing work in conversation with Mondrian, even long after his death.

From Theory to Practice: Vajrayana

In the early 1960s, Von Wiegand began making small, naïve gouache paintings of Tibetan altars. Two of these paintings were gifted to Mark Tobey. Until this point, Von Wiegand's understanding of Asian religions came largely by way of books, lectures, and talks by Western interpreters and authors, primarily in English. These paintings indicate the beginnings of her shift away from a Theosophically influenced interest in Asian philosophies and concepts, to her growing involvement with Tibetan Buddhism as it began to take root in the United States. The artist began to meet descendants of the Russian group that first inspired Madame Blavatsky's interest in Buddhism,[23] members of the Mongolian Kalmyk community who arrived in New Jersey in the 1950s as refugees fleeing what was then the Soviet Union. By 1962, Von Wiegand was known to the Tibetan refugee community and by 1966 had met the representative of His Holiness the 14th Dalai Lama in New York. These relationships gained her an invitation to a Buddhist monastery in Freehold, New Jersey. Von Wiegand remarked on her experience of the monastery: "I was spell-bound—knocked out by the color. That is why my pictures changed."[24]

Around 1963, the subject matter of her paintings began to shift from Tantric-inspired themes in prismatic colors, to paintings based on the symbols and accoutrements of Tibetan Buddhist practice. A painting titled *To the Winter Goddess* (1963; cat. 34) signals this shift, drawing on bold Tibetan Buddhist colors (blue, white, yellow, green, and red) and a strong, geometric composition comprised of circles and triangles to depict a golden pathway leading to an ornate altar table adorned with offerings *(torma)*. The painting is organized around a downward pointing triangle at the center of the picture, being the yantra of the goddess. The rainbow circle at the top of the picture alludes to the concept of the rainbow body *(jalu)*, referring to a non-material body of light produced by highly adept Buddhist practitioners who have transcended the physical body at the time of death,[25] the imagery of which is commonly found in Tibetan thangkas. This painting incorporates esoteric symbolism as a central compositional device to express the experiential power and deeper meaning of the altar by visual means. Tibetan Buddhist symbols such as the vajra, the arrow, and Mount Meru, abstracted into bold, colorful forms, also become important themes in Von Wiegand's paintings of this period, suggesting her increasing commitment to Tibetan Buddhism as a student in the Gelugpa tradition.

1967 was a watershed year for the artist: it was the year that she met her Buddhist teacher, Khyongla Rato Rinpoche, assisting him to write his autobiography,[26] and the year that she accepted an invitation to organize one of the first exhibitions of Tibetan art in North America, produced by the American Federation of Arts.[27] This exhibition,

22   Von Wiegand, letter to Mark Tobey, April 19, 1962, Mark Tobey Papers, Archives of American Art, Smithsonian Institution, reel 3200.

23   See Virginia Pitts Rembert, "Charmion von Wiegand's Way Beyond Mondrian," *Woman's Art Journal* 4, no. 2 (Autumn 1983–Winter 1984): 32.

24   Von Wiegand quoted in Pitts Rembert, 32.

25   See Ian A. Baker, *Tibetan Yoga*, (Rochester, VT: Inner Traditions, 2019), 203–208.

26   Khyongla Rato, *My Life and Lives: The Story of a Tibetan Incarnation* (New York: Rato, 1977).

27   Von Wiegand wrote to Tobey, `I have been meeting a lot of new people and peeking into a new world, in which I have not got my bearings. It is a sure sign there is a new change coming in painting but it has not put out any leaves as yet.` Von Wiegand, letter to Mark Tobey, December 11, 1967, Mark Tobey Papers, Archives of American Art, Smithsonian Institution, reel 3200.

28   This exhibition opened shortly after the first major international exhibition of Tibetan art, also titled *The Art of Tibet*, curated by Pratapaditya Pal (Museum of Fine Arts, Boston) and Eleanor Olson (Newark Museum, New Jersey) at Asia House, Asia Society, New York, in 1969, touring to Washington, D.C., and Seattle. Von Wiegand responded to this exhibition with an expanded review titled "The Adamantine Way," *Art News* 68, (April 1969): 38–41, continued 72B–75E.

29   Charmion von Wiegand, *The Art of Tibet* (New York: American Federation for the Arts, 1969), n.p.

30   A photograph providing a document of Von Wiegand's shrine is found in her estate (fig. p. 154).

titled *The Art of Tibet* (1969),[28] took the logic of the altar as its organizing principle to convey the context and purpose of Tibetan artistic production. She wrote in the catalog essay for this exhibition:

> Tibetan art evinces a great sensibility, particularly in the use of color, at once powerful and subtle. [. . .] The Tibetans worship daily at their household altars, going to the temples for the days of high ceremonials. Thus every home from the farmer's cottage and the nomad's tent to the noble's palace and the monk's private room or meditational retreat has its shrine [. . .] Books, images, Tangkas and ritual objects are the proper furnishings of a shrine.[29]

Von Wiegand maintained an elaborate Tibetan altar in her home, an indication of her sincere dedication to a personal Buddhist practice. Of particular note is the inclusion of one of Mondrian's *Chrysanthemum* paintings on this altar, reading as both an offering and a recognition of his significance to her as a "guru" or teacher.[30] From a Tibetan Buddhist point of view, the altar is a profound symbol of faith and the expression of ultimate beauty; it is the highest goal of artistic production. Accordingly, some of her last paintings, for example, *To the Adi Buddha* (ca. 1968–1970; cat. 39) and *Invocation to the Adi Buddha* (1968–1970), develop upon, and refine, earlier paintings on the theme of the altar to convey a concept of spiritual clarity or awakening.

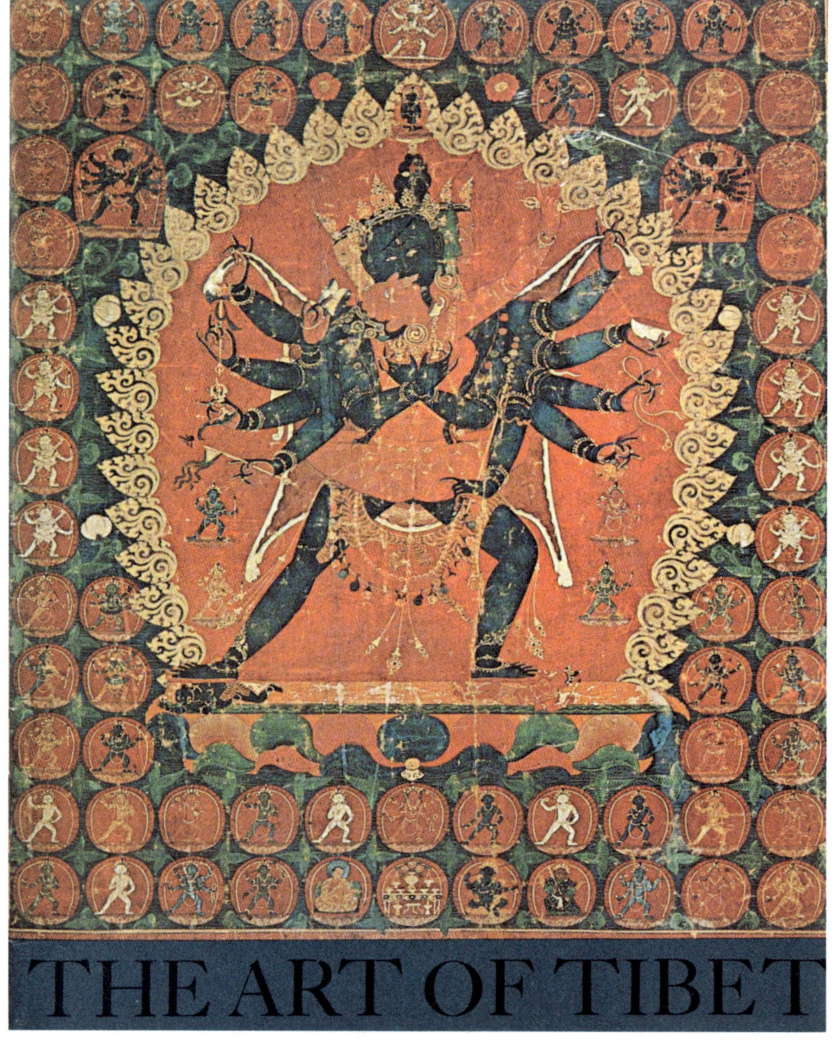

Cover of the catalog to the exhibition *The Art of Tibet* (New York: American Federation for the Arts, 1969), curated by Charmion von Wiegand

Continue on p. 113

101

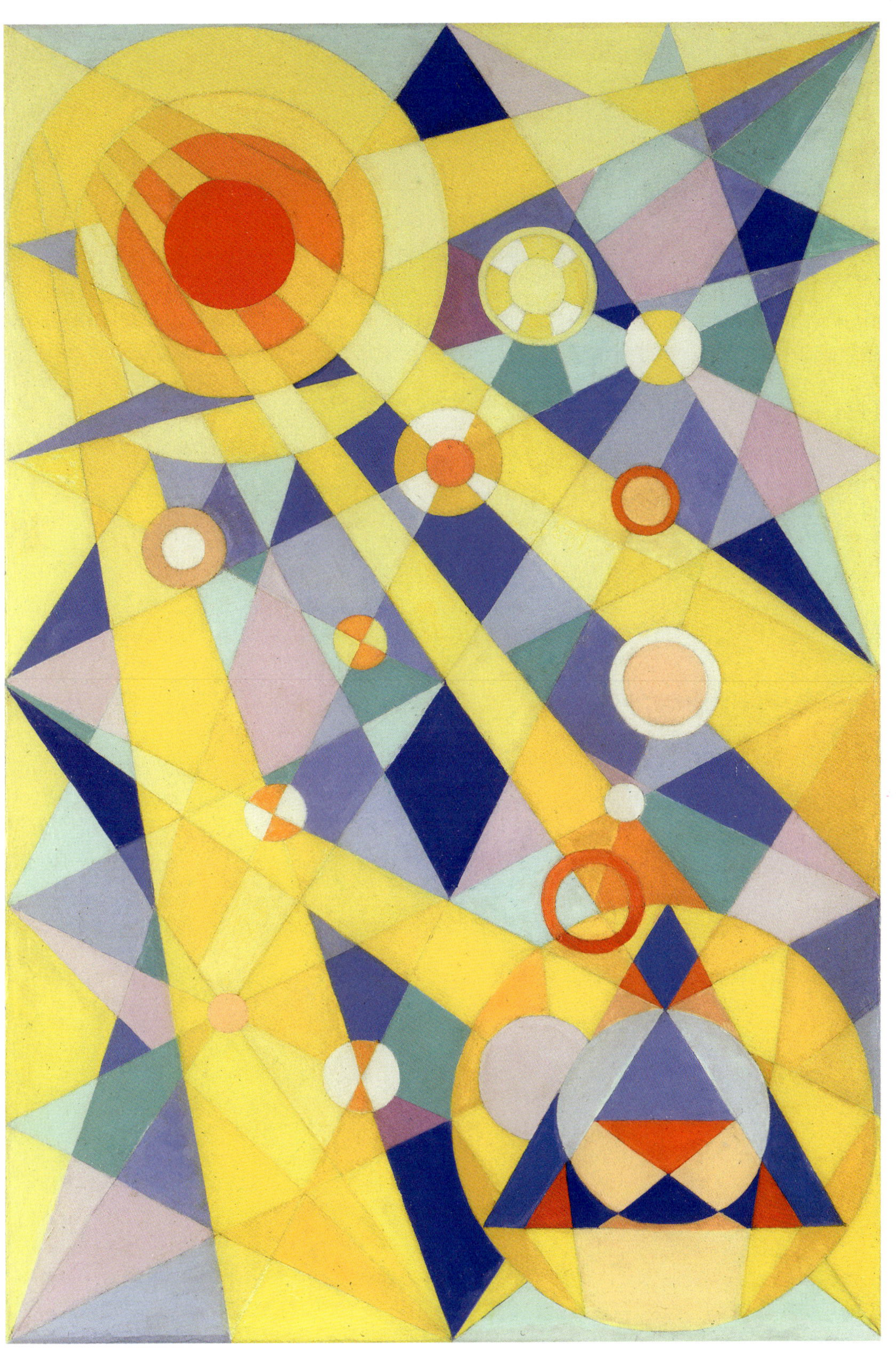

Now the First Day, 1950
oil on canvas, 76.2 × 50.8 cm
Private Collection, New York

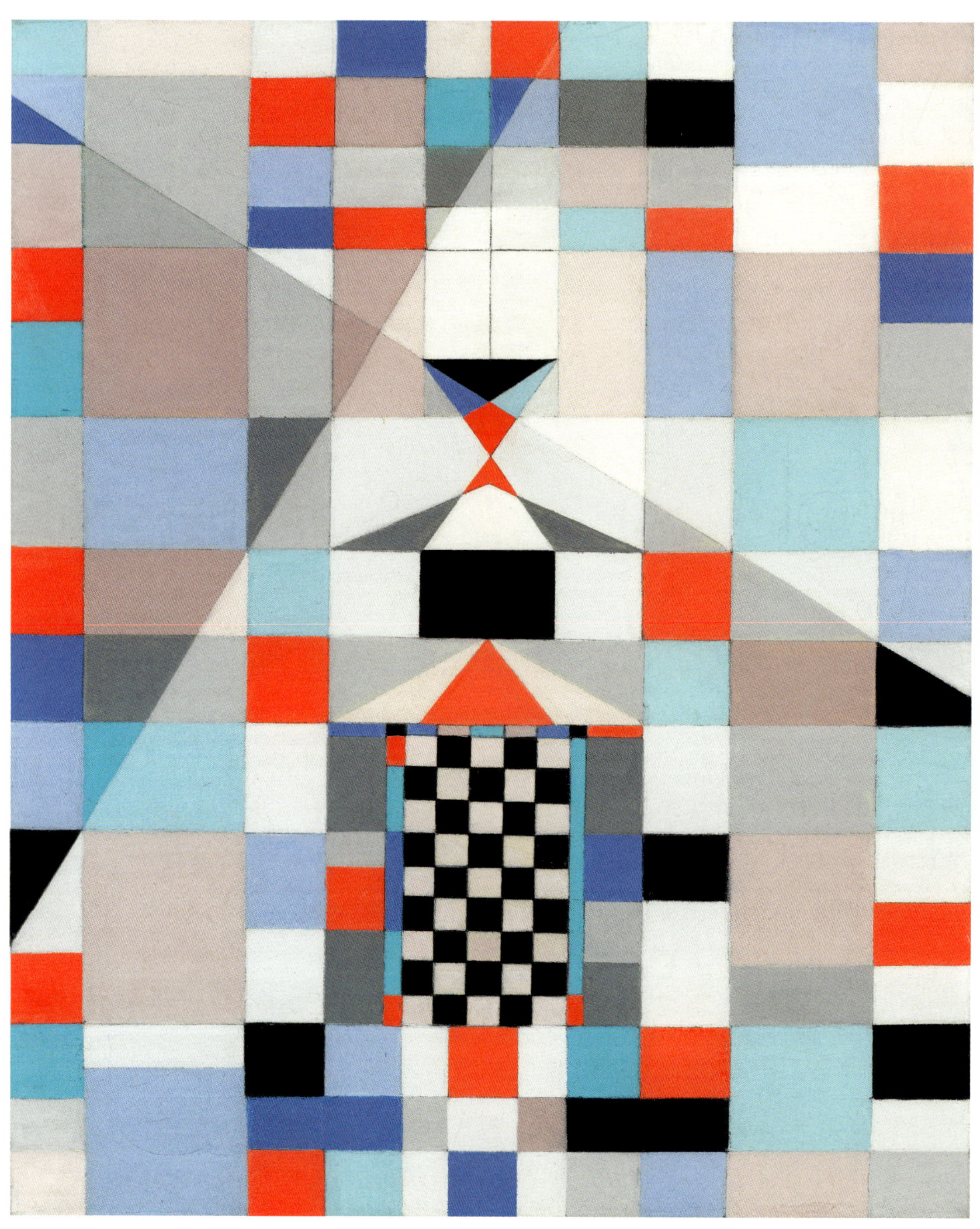

Tabernacle, 1950–1952
oil on canvas, 71.1 × 56.2 cm
Cincinnati Art Museum, Bequest of Mary E. Johnston

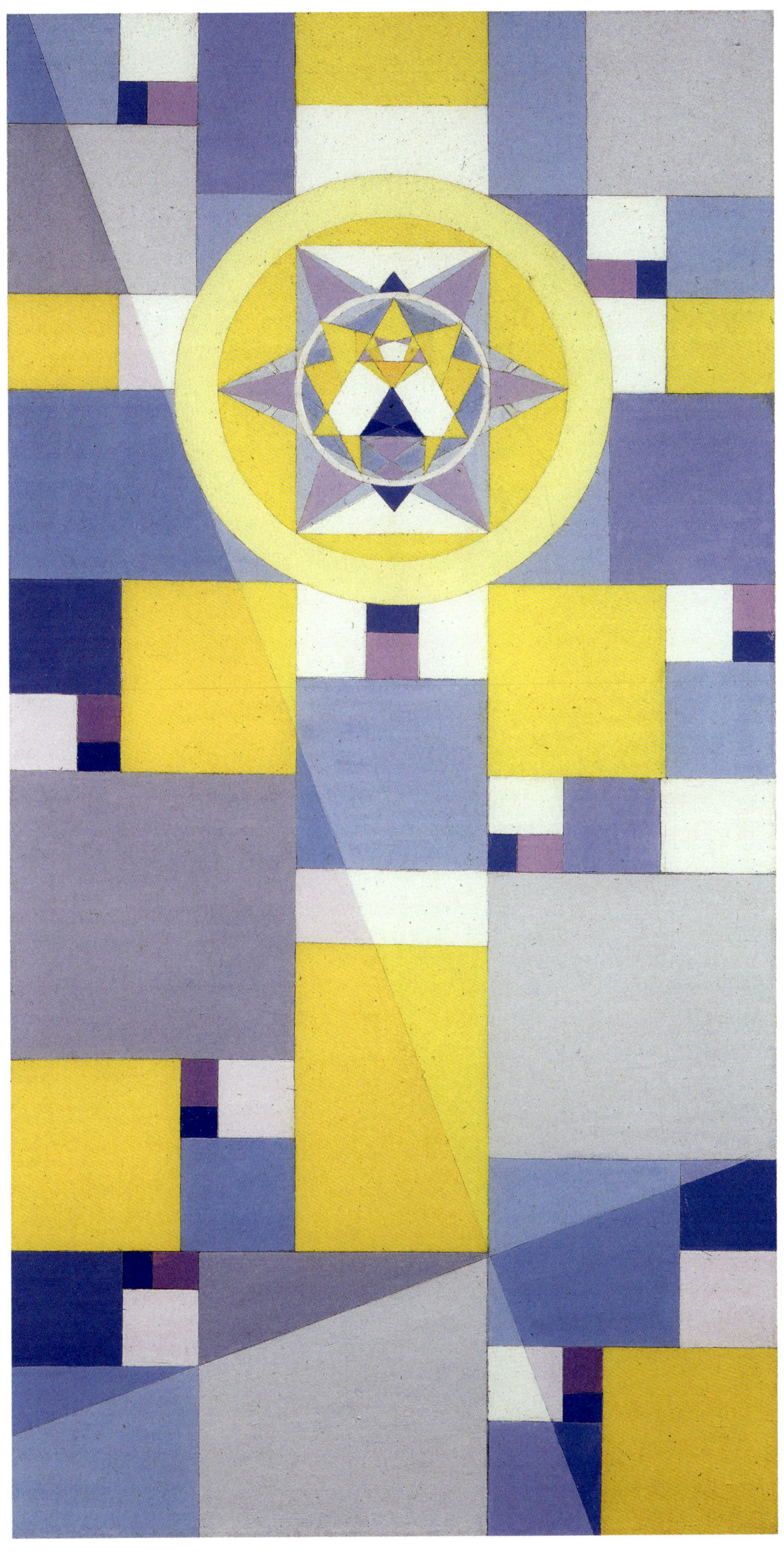

The Golden Flower, 1951–1952
oil on canvas, 101.6 × 50.8 cm
Private Collection, New York

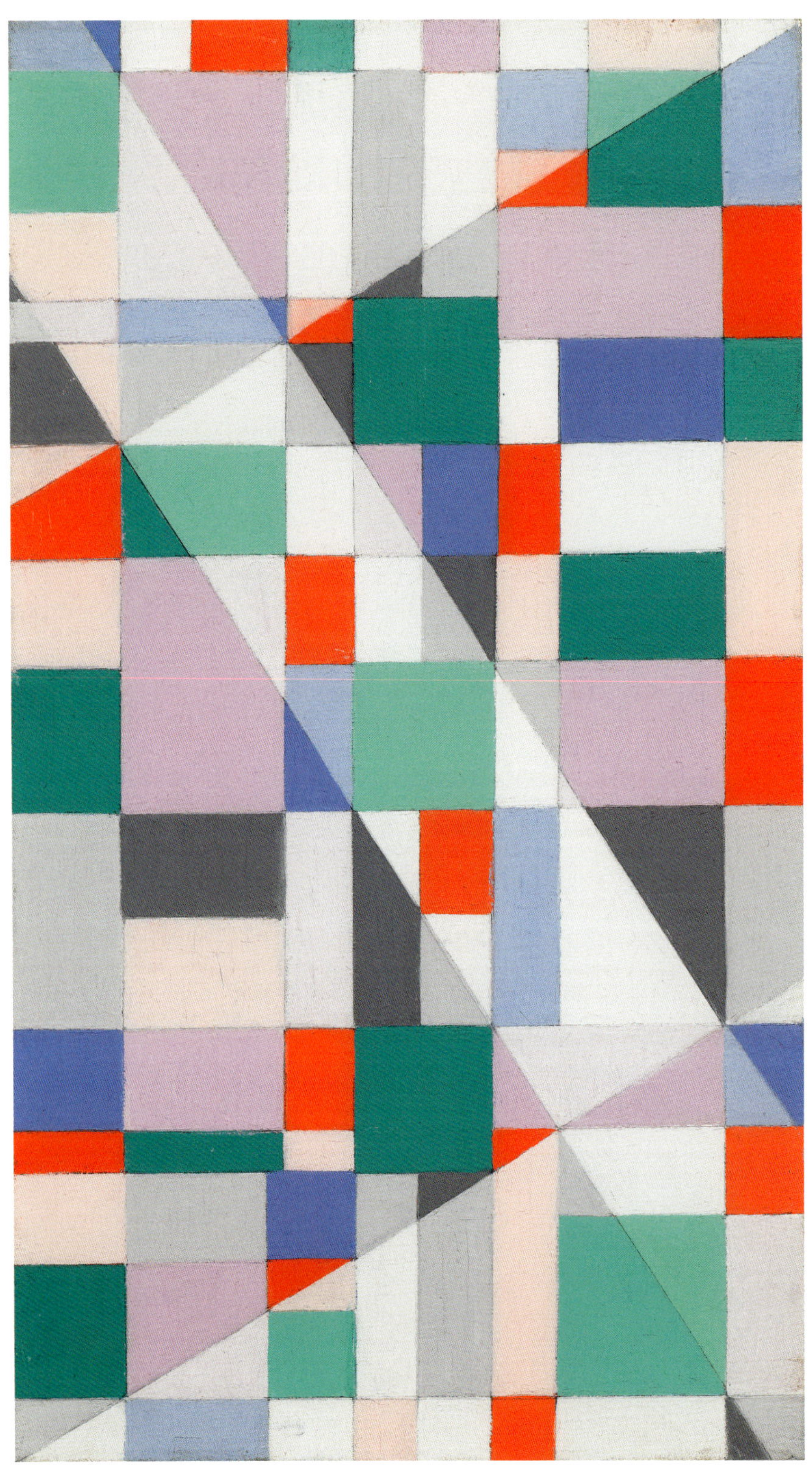

The Terrace of Jade, 1952
oil on canvas, 55.9 × 30.5 cm
Seattle Art Museum, Gift of Zoe Dusanne

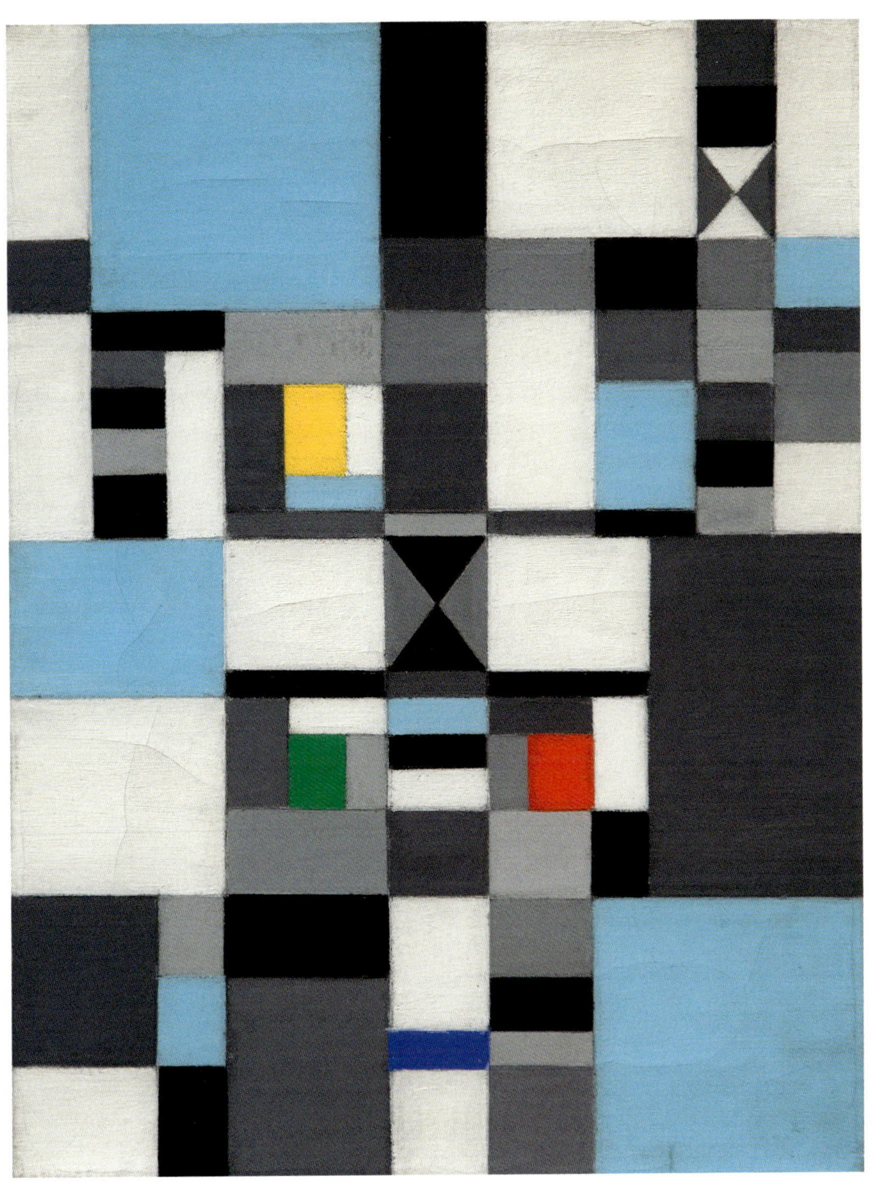

Composition, 1953–1954
oil on canvas, 41 × 30 cm
Collection of the Arithmeum/Forschungsinstitut für Diskrete
Mathematik, Rheinische Friedrich-Wilhelms-Universität Bonn

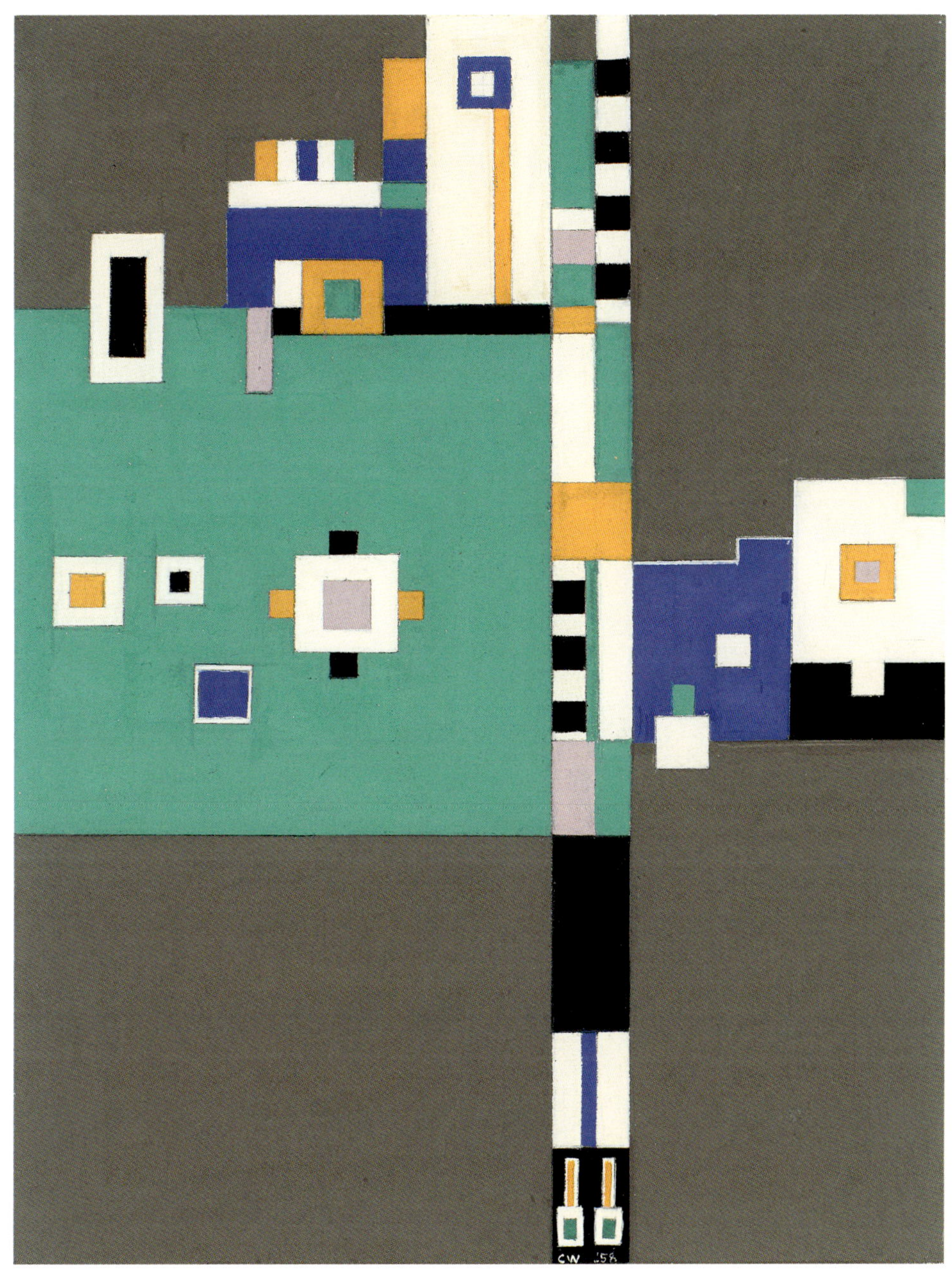

Gouache #88: Southern Sanctuary, 1958
gouache and graphite on paper
mounted on illustration board, 47.6 × 34.9 cm
Estate of Charmion von Wiegand, Courtesy of
Michael Rosenfeld Gallery LLC, New York

Cat. 30

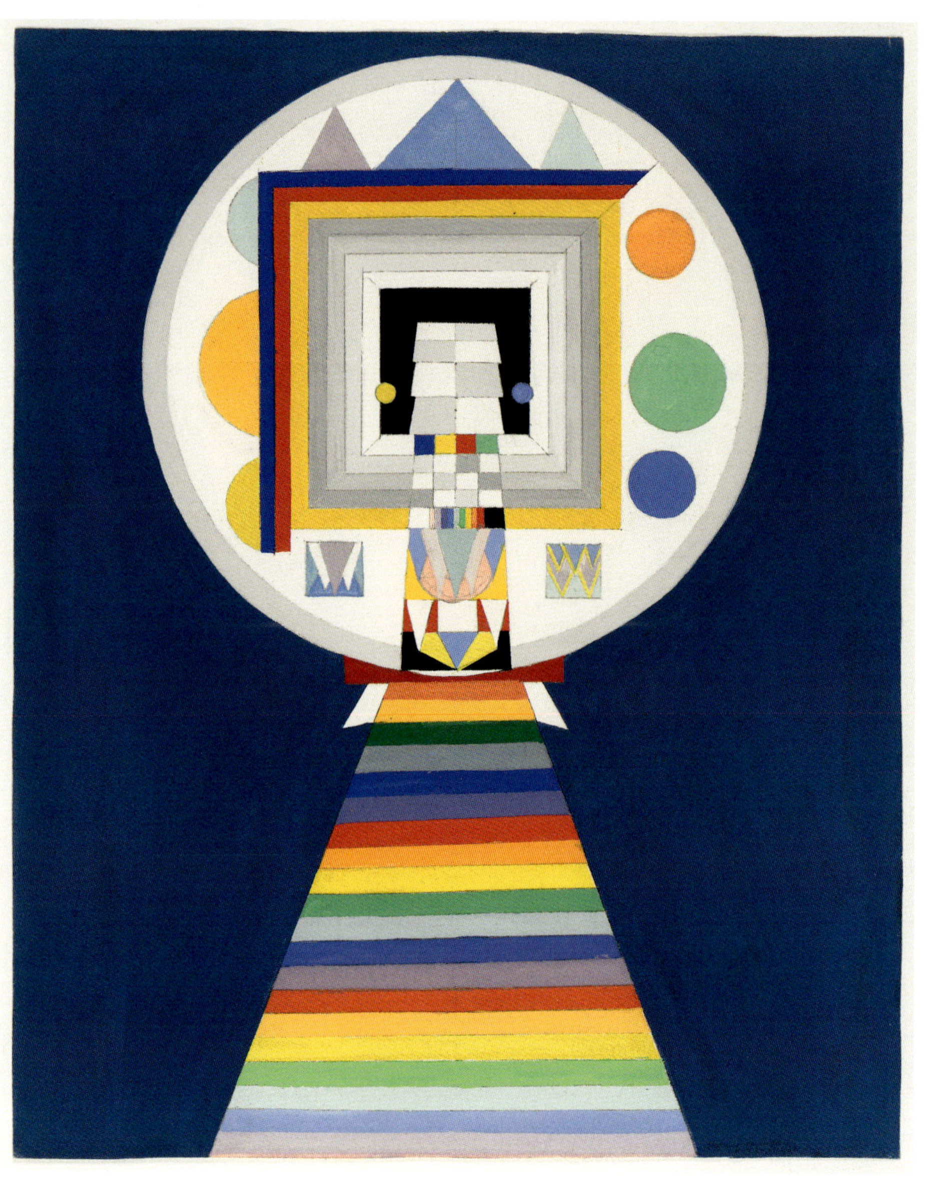

The Ascent to Mt. Meru, 1962
gouache on paper, 59.4 × 46.7 cm
Solomon R. Guggenheim Museum, New York,
Gift of Ruth Abrams in memory of Gerald Scoefield, 1982

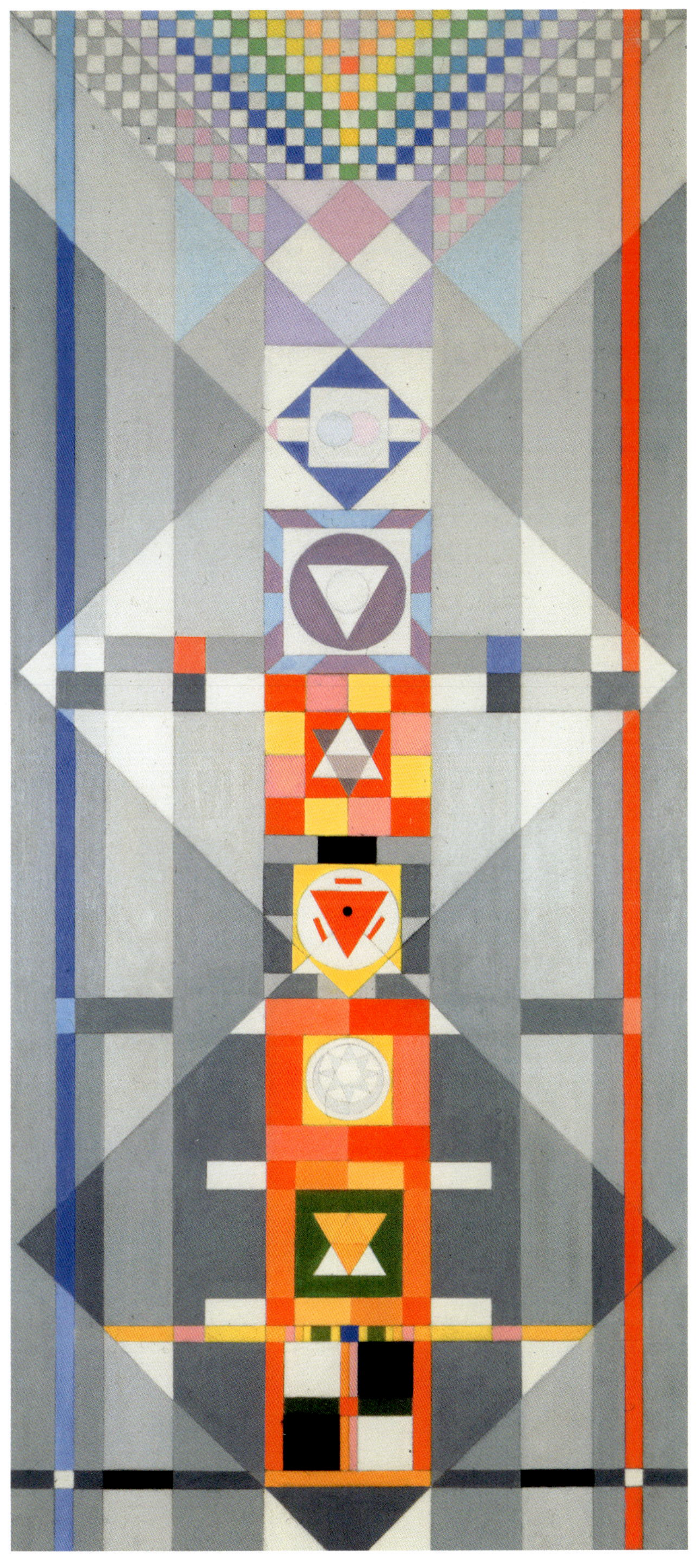

The Chakras, 1958–1968
oil on canvas, 162.6 × 71.1 cm
Carol Brown Goldberg and Henry H. Goldberg

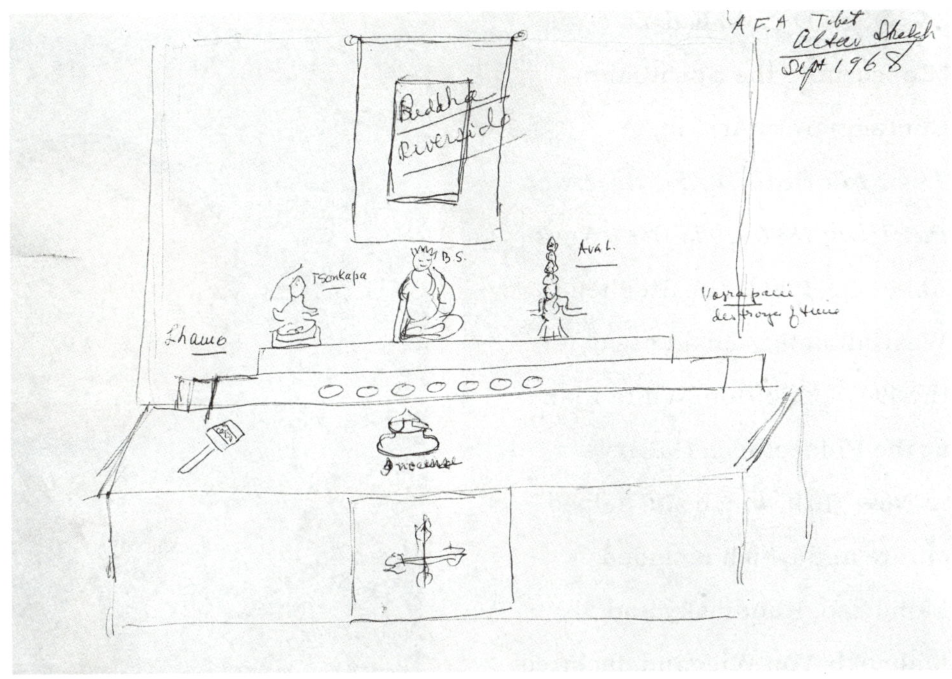

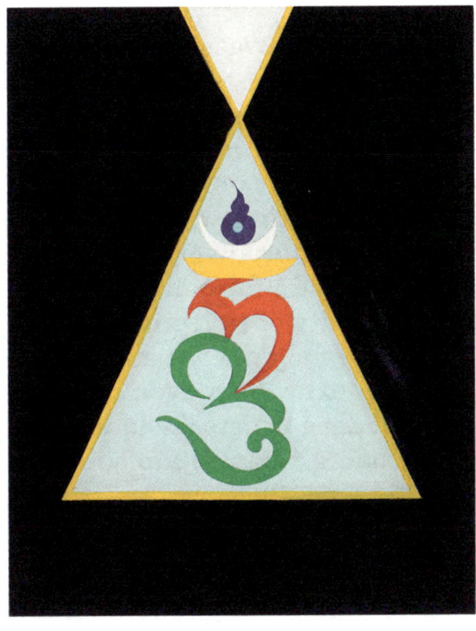

Charmion von Wiegand, *Gouache #163: The Letter Hum*, 1962, gouache on paper, 41.9 × 31.8 cm, Estate of Charmion von Wiegand, Courtesy of Michael Rosenfeld Gallery LLC, New York

Sketch for the installation of an altar in the 1969 New York exhibition *The Art of Tibet*, New York, curated by Charmion von Wiegand, Collection of Khyongla Rato

Von Wiegand's *To the Adi Buddha* invokes the primordial Buddha, considered as the undifferentiated condition of the mind, which is the goal of Buddhist ritual and meditation. The predominance of chromatic yellow and white suggests the luminous and uplifting quality of Buddhist practice, distilling the experience of Buddhism to an aspirational vision or visualization. The Sanskrit letter or seed *(bija)* mantra HUM, inscribed at the bottom of the picture, is the mantra of Enlightenment *(bodhi)*.

Invocation to the Adi Buddha suggests the culmination and ultimate purpose of the Tibetan altar, being the representation and co-ordinated evocation of body, speech, and mind. Inscribed at the bottom of this picture is the seed mantra OM. The colors of the picture evoke the expanded mantra OM (white) AH (red) HUM (blue), being the mantra of purification which, when used in meditation, refines mind, body, and speech, to promote an intensive awareness—the experience of Wisdom *(prajna)*.[31] These paintings visualize the *experience* of Buddhist meditation as sound, form, and color, developing ideas first explored in the earlier painting *Region of the Unstructured Sound*.

In these late paintings, Von Wiegand synthesized her study of Tantric geometries, Tibetan Buddhist color symbolisms, and Blavatsky's esoteric visual theories, drawing on personal and seemingly eclectic strategies developed over a long period of study and spiritual inquiry. She transforms the representation of the Tibetan altar into a visual expression of its experiential effects, as though a "visionary painting." In her essay "The Adamantine Way" (1969), written during the same period in which these paintings were made, Von Wiegand wrote, "The highest category [of Tibetan art] is the visionary paintings, which were made either by the person who had a vision while in a trance, or a monk or saint who dictated a vision he experienced to the artist."[32] It is as though this goal of visionary painting was something that Von Wiegand was seeking in her own work, describing her search for a higher purpose in art. Accordingly, it is in these paintings, suggesting luminosity, clarity, and transcendence, that Von Wiegand's art finds its aesthetic resolution and ultimate purpose. Her careful research, critical writing, curatorial work, and Buddhist practice all combined to inform an approach to painting that was at once formally elegant, in keeping with the values and ideals of her mentors, yet also a resonant expression of a profound and fulfilling inner, spiritual life.

33   See Donald Kuspit, "Concerning the Spiritual in Contemporary Art," in *The Spiritual in Art: Abstract Painting 1890–1985* (New York: Abbeville, 1986), 313. Stephen Westfall notes, "In an essay for the 1947 exhibition 'White Plane' at the Pinacotheca Gallery in New York, which she helped curate and which included Mondrian, Kandinsky and Malevich, Von Wiegand declared Kandinsky to be the most significant artist of the twentieth century. She had been reading the 1946 edition of *The Spiritual in Art*." Westfall, "Abstraction and Invisible Realms," 14.

34   Von Wiegand, "The Oriental Tradition in Abstract Art," in *The World of Abstract Art*, ed. American Abstract Artists (New York: George Wittenborn, 1957), 60–62.

35   Donald Kuspit, "Ceramics et al.: Critical Consciousness of the Arts," artnet, 2010, accessed December 18, 2019, http://www.artnet.com/magazineus/features/kuspit/critical-consciousness-of-the-arts-3-29-11.asp.

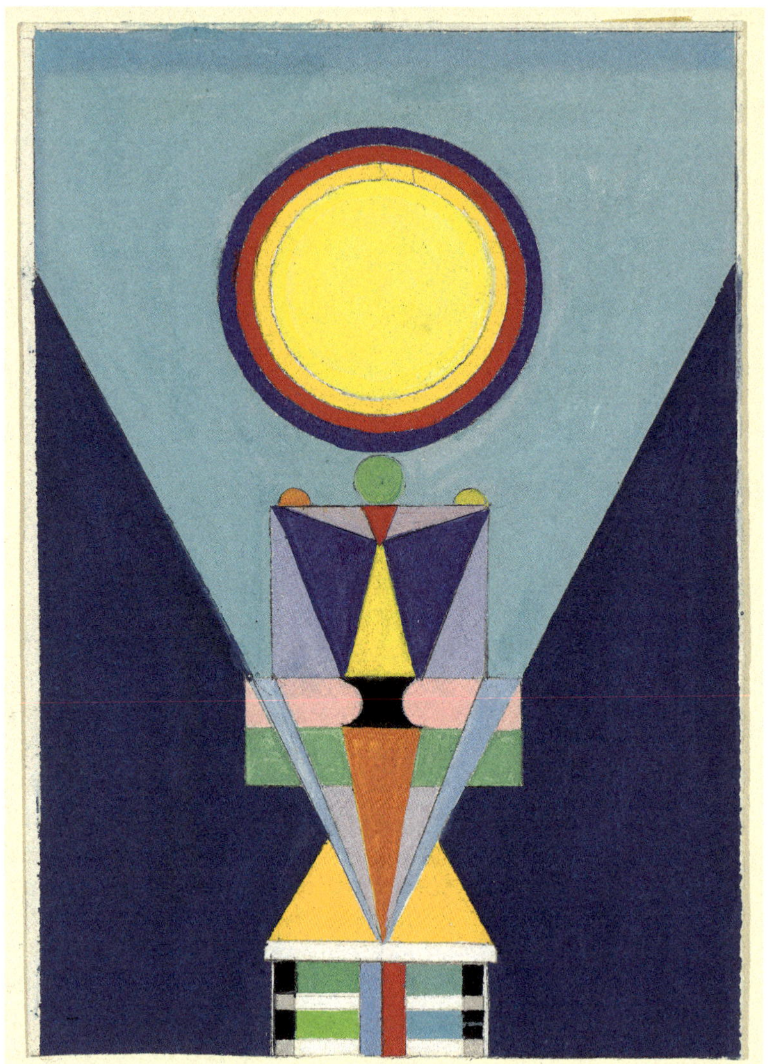

Charmion von Wiegand, *Untitled*, 1967, gouache on paper mounted on cardboard, 19.6 × 15.6 cm, Solomon R. Guggenheim Museum, New York, Gift of Mrs. Kay Hillman, 1979

Von Wiegand belonged to a school of thought, from Wassily Kandinsky onwards, that defined the "spiritual" as "the search for the abstract in art."[33] In this regard, she considered her work a critique of "the new abstraction" as it was appearing in New York in the form of Abstract Expressionism, which she described as a "novel means of expression to the exclusion of meaning."[34] She was painting at a time when abstraction itself had become concerned with gesture, materialism, risk-taking, and individuality, where painting was being read in formalist terms, rather than "experienced" as a "dialectical activity of reflective consciousness."[35] She was also painting at a time of significant anti-Asian sentiment, in the post-War and Cold War context, where even the United States Congress were denouncing modern artists, including those influenced by Buddhism and Asia, as being "shackled to communism."[36] Von Wiegand wrote in a letter to Tobey in 1968: It is the metaphysical content [...] which their materialistic view, they fear and detest because it shows up their ignorance of other dimensions of the mind. [...] But the metaphysical view is really very American--a strong strain from the indigenous Indian to the Transcendentalists and on. Mechanization has smothered it for the time being, but the best segments of the hippy movement are bringing it back in a funny way. It's not new at all: these mantras, mandalas and meditations, for Vivekananda came in the beginning of the century and Blavatsky founded the Theosophical Society in a boarding house in the west thirties. And what of Bahai? The foundation is laid for revival.[37]

36   See speech of Hon. George A. Dondero, "Modern Art Shackled to Communism," in *Congressional Record. Proceedings and Debates of the 81st Congress, First Session*, Tuesday, August 16, 1949, Papers found in Charmion von Wiegand Personal Papers, Marilyn Pearl Gallery Records, Folder 4.15, Archives of American Art, Smithsonian Institution.

37   Von Wiegand, letter to Mark Tobey, December 18, 1968, Mark Tobey Papers, Archives of American Art, Smithsonian Institution, reel 3200.

38   Edelman, "Departing the Plane," 201.

Detail of the exhibition invitation to a group show with Clarence Carter, Ray Johnson, Rita Simon, and Charmion von Wiegand at the Sid Deutsch Gallery, New York, 1977

Even though Von Wiegand was regularly exhibiting in New York, from the mid-1940s until her death, her artistic interests and concerns could be thought of as anachronistic with the kind of work that was being promoted by the critics of her day. Nevertheless, she was singular in her pursuit of an art that was genuine to her, working against the grain of dominant art world values. In Buddhism, Von Wiegand found a unique source of inspiration for abstraction; her work reveals the impact and potential of Buddhism as it coincided with the Western imagination. In this regard, she was not unlike numerous New York artists who may be considered her peers, for example, John Cage, Philip Guston, Franz Kline, Agnes Martin, Ad Reinhardt, Sari Dienes, even Ray Johnson. But where these artists drew on Buddhism (and Zen specifically) to re-imagine and redefine art as a conceptual and experimental category, Von Wiegand's commitment was to the exploration of the metaphysical potential of painting, investigating an interdependent relationship between the artist and the cosmos.[38]

Given the significant inspiration that Von Wiegand found in Tantric and Buddhist symbolisms and esoteric iconographies, she was perhaps one of the first American artists to produce an image of "modern Buddhism"—that is, an image of Buddhism as a transcultural phenomena constituted through the encounter between East and West.

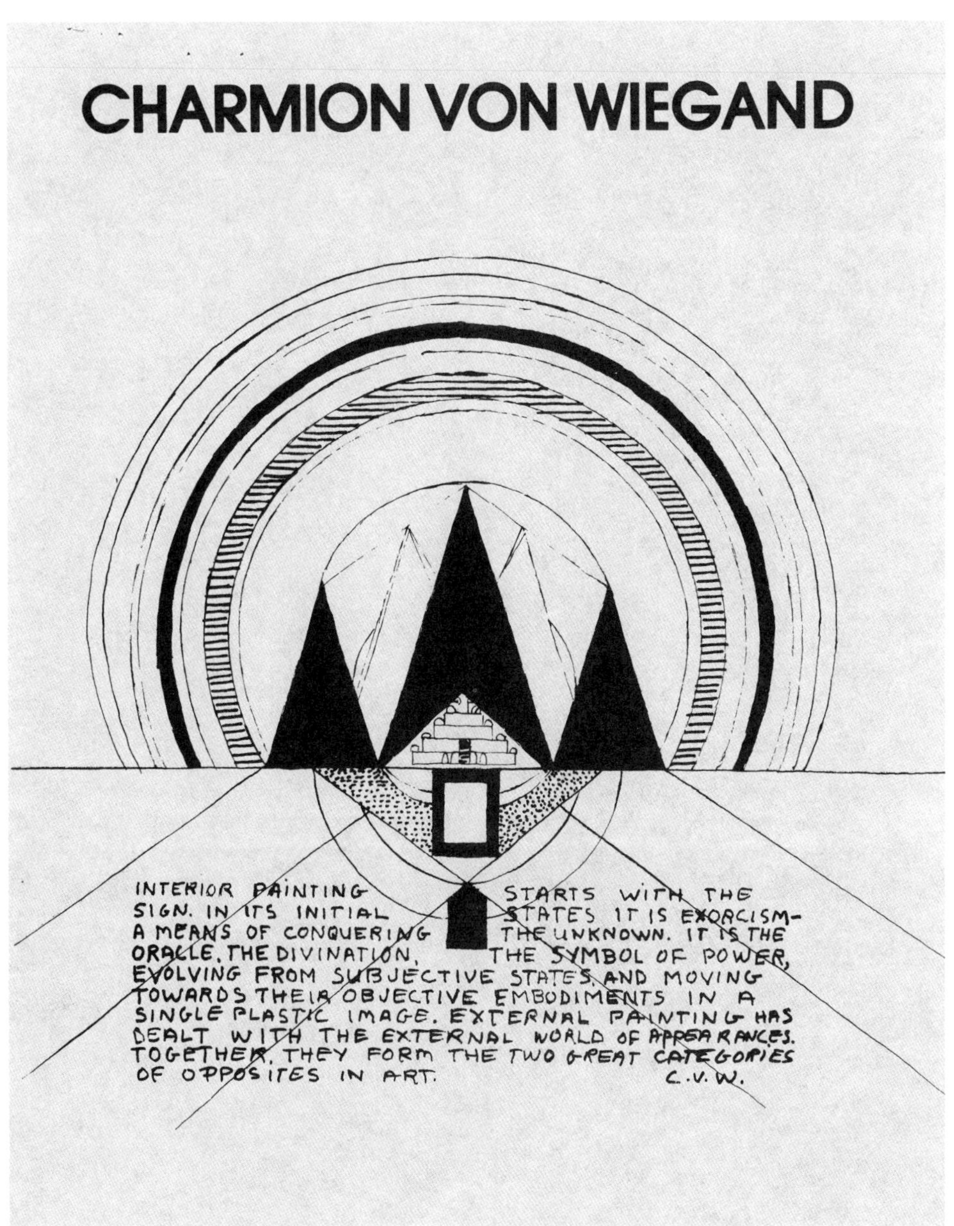

If it is possible now, in the twenty-first century, to properly examine
the rapprochement between East and West in the development of
artistic modernities and histories of abstraction, then Von Wiegand
will be assigned a meaningful place within that history. Von Wiegand's
late works (ca. 1950–1970) encompass and narrate the appearance of
Buddhism in the West—from its introduction into progressive artistic
and intellectual circles via Orientalist and Theosophical texts and
interpretations, to its arrival in the United States as a form of practice brought by refugee immigrants. These paintings demonstrate
Von Wiegand's sincere dedication to Tibetan Buddhism, which included deep study, commitment to a teacher, participation in a religious community, meditation, and practices of merit-making and
charity. At the end of her life, Von Wiegand's estate was donated to
the Tibet Center, New York, as a notable gesture of commitment
to Buddhism and its proponents.

FELIX VOGEL

AUTONOMY—SPIRITUALITY—UNIVERSALISM

THE MEANING OF ABSTRACTION

1   Max Weber, "Science as a Vocation," 1919, in Max Weber, *The Vocation Lectures*, ed. David Owen and Tracy B. Strong, trans. Rodney Livingstone (Indianapolis: Hackett, 2004), 1–31, here 13.

2   For a paradigmatic example of this, see T. J. Clark, *Farewell to an Idea: Episodes from a History of Modernism* (New Haven, CT: Yale University Press, 1999), 7.

3   Of essential importance was the exhibition *The Spiritual in Art: Abstract Painting, 1890–1985*, Los Angeles County Museum of Art, 1986. Among the more recent shows on the subject were *Enchanted Modernities: Mysticism, Landscape and the American West*, Nora Eccles Harrison Museum of Art, Logan, UT, 2014 and *World Receivers. Georgiana Houghton—Hilma Af Klint—Emma Kunz*, Lenbachhaus, Munich, 2018–2019.

History (or Histories) of Abstraction

According to one widespread assumption in art history, Modernism was a reaction to the "disenchantment of the world"[1] brought about by modernity.[2] This assertion makes a good starting point from which to explain various Modernist phenomena, from art's striving for autonomy and the emergence of avant-gardes, to the development of abstraction. What makes this one-size-fits-all explanation problematic, however, is its focus on developments in the West and its exclusion of numerous tendencies that are ostensibly irreconcilable with Modernism's progressive narrative. Among these tendencies is abstract painting's spiritual dimension. Despite numerous attempts,[3] this still ranks among the most woefully neglected fields of art history, although it would enable us to form a more complex picture of Modernism. After all, spirituality should not be understood as a relapse into a premodern—pre-secular—understanding of art, but rather as a reaction to crisis-fraught modernity itself.

One prominent example of the way spirituality has been airbrushed out of abstract painting is the 2012 show *Inventing Abstraction* at the Museum of Modern Art in New York, whose curator, Leah Dickerman, claimed, Theosophical and cosmogonic images "may resemble abstract art. But these are not art at all, for despite any formal similarity they were intended to produce meaning in other discursive frameworks."[4] It is a categorical statement that remains problematic, even if we set aside the question of what Dickerman means by "other discursive frameworks" and ignore the fact that numerous pioneers of abstraction, among them Wassily Kandinsky, Hilma af Klint, and František Kupka, all felt drawn to Theosophy, to a greater or lesser extent. To justify the putative autonomy of (abstract) art, Dickerman tries to exclude all things extraneous to art itself—in fact, anything and everything pertaining to the development of a work and its intended purpose.

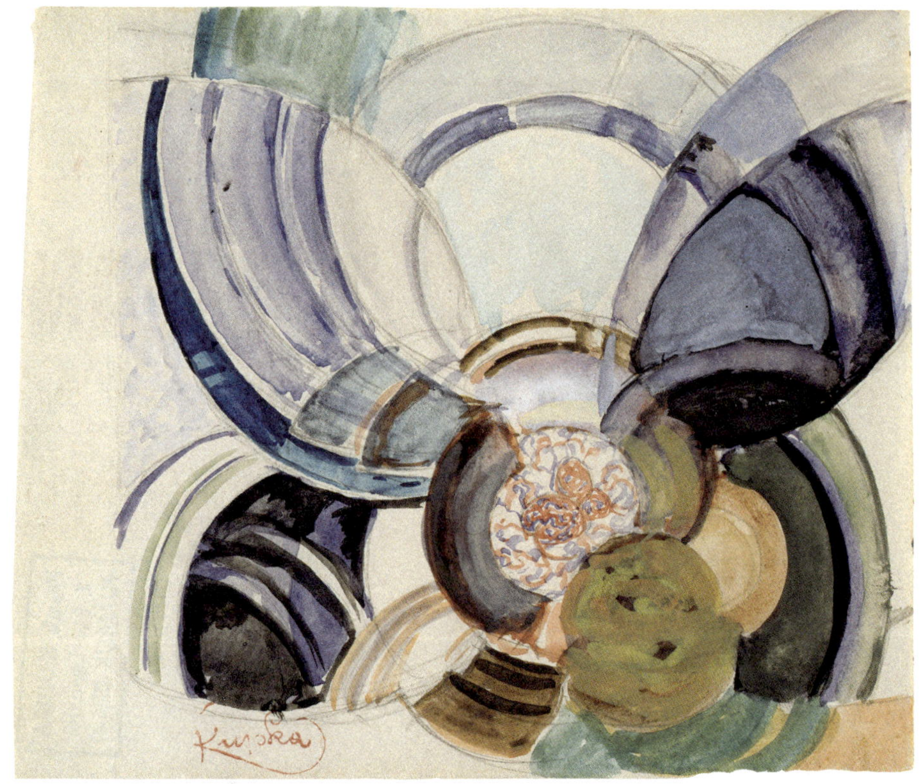

František Kupka, *Autour d'un point (Around a Point)*, ca. 1920–1925, watercolor, gouache, and graphite on paper, 20.1 × 23.8 cm, Peggy Guggenheim Collection, Venice (Solomon R. Guggenheim Foundation, New York)

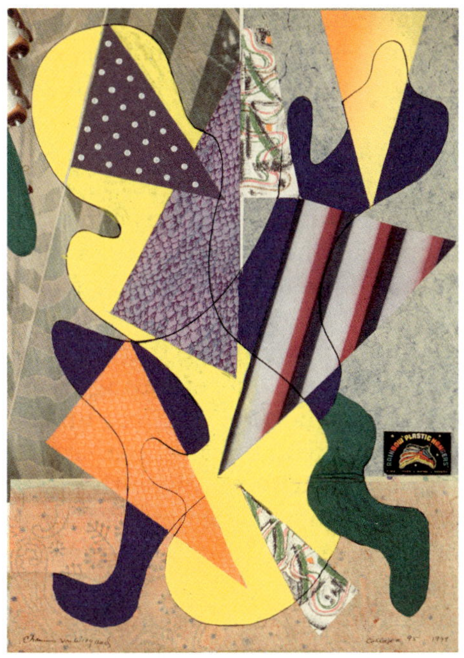

4   Leah Dickerman,

Inventing Abstraction,

1910–1925: How a Radical Idea

Changed Modern Art

(London: Thames & Hudson,

2012), 12–37, here 13–14.

5   Many thanks to Martin

Brauen for pointing this out to me.

6   Charmion von Wiegand,

"Expressionism and Social

Change," *Art Front* (November

1936): 10–12, here 10.

Charmion von Wiegand, *Collage #95*,
1949, tempera, ink, and collage
on paper, 49.8 × 34.9 cm, Estate of
Charmion von Wiegand, Courtesy
of Michael Rosenfeld Gallery LLC,
New York

From today's perspective, Charmion von Wiegand occupies an interesting position in the history of Modernism and hence of abstract art, and not just as a painter, but also as an art critic and curator. Her oeuvre exemplifies the contradictory history of Modernism. In what follows, the concepts of autonomy, spirituality, and universalism will be used to show that abstract art has never been a single, monolithic entity and that the processes by which Modernism came about were themselves fraught with conflict.

Even just the question of what abstraction actually means in the oeuvre of Charmion von Wiegand is complicated, inasmuch as her visual logic, aesthetic methods, and aims vary from work to work, and while they all warrant the epithet "abstract," they are not in essence congruent. They include automatic drawings and their translation into collages as well as the oil paintings, which—following the Surrealists—can be interpreted as an attempt to generate non-representational images from the unconscious. While paintings such as *City Lights* (1947; cat. 10) can certainly be viewed as imitations of Piet Mondrian, they can also be understood, as with other works belonging to this phase, as a literal *refiguration* of Mondrian's Neo-Plasticism. After all, we read them not as geometric forms without external referents, but rather as the abstraction of an urban environment.

Created just two years later, the work *Radiating Plane* (1949; cat. 13) must be regarded as part of a phase characterized by Von Wiegand's adoption of a non-representational idiom that managed entirely without any external points of reference at all. Other paintings, especially those belonging to her late phase, further complicate the relationship between the abstract and the non-representational, as well as that between means and ends. One good example of this is *The Ascent to Mt. Meru* (1962; cat. 31). A Western reading of this painting would interpret it as the geometric abstraction of a mountain depicted from different angles simultaneously—assuming there were any (external) points of reference at all. At the same time, the painting is bound by a traditional Tibetan style of representation in which showing an object at once from above and from the side is entirely normal.[5] In this sense, *The Ascent to Mt. Meru* is a mandala, which inevitably raises the question of whether it perhaps functions more as an invitation to meditation, the abstraction being a deliberate means to an end.

Whether as a painter, an art critic, or a curator—or, indeed, as president of the American Abstract Artists (AAA)—Von Wiegand repeatedly concerned herself with the development, the meaning, and the process of abstraction. Even if it stands to reason that her texts should not necessarily be read as an explanation of her own artistic practice, it is still worth taking a closer look at her concept of abstraction.

In her early work of criticism, "Expressionism and Social Change" (1936), Von Wiegand does not yet take a clear stance on non-representational art (that of Kandinsky, for example). She describes it rather as "subjective painting"[6] and regards its forms, detached from all worldly points of reference, as a problem, as is evident in her review of the pamphlet *Five on Revolutionary Art* (1935):

> As regards abstract art, it is obvious that forms cannot be set aside like empty jars in a cold storage plant to be filled later with a new content. Splitting the two is idealism. If the forms of abstract art are to have relevancy for the future society, they must inevitably undergo profound changes during a period of social revolution.[7]

7   Charmion von Wiegand, review of *Five on Revolutionary Art, Art Front* (September–October 1936): 10–11, here 10. Lori Cole discusses this episode in greater depth in her essay "Charmion von Wiegand and the Creative Work of Criticism," in the present publication, pp. 31–40.

8   Charmion von Wiegand, "The Oriental Tradition and Abstract Art," in *The World of Abstract Art*, ed. American Abstract Artists (New York: George Wittenborn, 1957), 55–67, here 55.

9   Ibid., 58.

10   Hilla Rebay, "Value of Non-Objectivity," in *Third Enlarged Catalogue of the Solomon R. Guggenheim Collection of Non-Objective Paintings* (New York: Solomon R. Guggenheim Foundation, 1938), 4–14, p. 6.

At the same time, she welcomed the engagement with art history of the Far East taking place in the abstract art of the West (by which she meant non-representational art, without differentiating) as a positive development.

Von Wiegand's essay "The Oriental Tradition and Abstract Art" (1957), which the AAA published as part of an anthology of essays, rests on the hypothesis that non-Western cultures of image-making have always been more open to abstract tendencies than have those in the West, where not until the twentieth century did such an assimilation take place:

> Today we seem to be approaching a period when the transformation of artistic values, begun in this century, is accelerating its pace. From Giotto to cubism, western art has had a strong unity and relatively little outside cultural influence. But in the fifty years of its existence, modern art has broken sharply with the past. The seemingly contradictory insurgent movements of the twentieth century have all pressed toward the same goal: the destruction of the natural image.[8]

She explains the fundamental shift (and putative global alignment) brought about by "the birth of abstract art" in greater detail somewhat later on:

> The birth of abstract art represented a basic shift from a sensorial culture toward a new ideational one. Once the image of individual man dominating nature—the central theme of the Renaissance—was done away with, the boundaries of art were extended to include the whole universe and man's mind. Man now took his place in the cosmos along with all other living organisms. This "death of humanism" was actually the extension of its ethos on a higher level. Thus Western art was brought close to the metaphysical speculations of Oriental thought: Vedantism, Buddhism, Taoism, and Confucianism.[9]

What Von Wiegand identifies here is not just a clean break with Western tradition and the primacy it accords to mimesis. Of far greater weight, in her view, is the fact that abstraction opens up completely new scopes for the visualization of inner states.

Abstract and Non-Objective Painting

Although she did not explicitly label it as such, Von Wiegand's essay "The Oriental Tradition and Abstract Art" was her contribution to a debate that, by the 1950s, had been raging for a good two decades and can be traced back to the early days of the twentieth century. At its core was the question of the origins, goal, and relevance of abstract, that is to say, non-representational art, in other words, nothing less than the meaning of abstract art.

The exhibition of Solomon R. Guggenheim's collection titled the *Museum of Non-Objective Painting*, which toured between 1936 and 1938 before being shown in its own showroom in New York beginning in 1939, sparked a dispute over abstract art's relevance that was not confined to the art world alone. The opinions were essentially divided into three camps, each of which accorded non-representational art a different meaning.

The artist and curator Hilla von Rebay, who had been entrusted with the conception of the exhibition, took an important stance in the ensuing debate on abstraction and non-representationalism, in part because her choice of title—specifically the term "non-objective art"—marked a departure from the more usual term "abstract art," and in part because she championed the "spiritual dimension" of art, albeit a

11   Ibid.

12   Hilla von Rebay defined non-objective art in relation to the art that preceded it, positing a teleological progression from mimesis to abstraction, the *telos* being the non-objective painting. Yet decades earlier, Wilhelm Worringer had argued the exact opposite, namely that art originated in abstraction (by which he meant, in principle, non-representationalism or non-objectivity), while the imitation of nature—by means of "empathy"—had been a much later development in art. Cf. Wilhelm Worringer, *Abstraction and Empathy: A Contribution to the Psychology of Style*, trans. Michael Bullock (1907; Chicago: Ivan R. Dee, 1997).

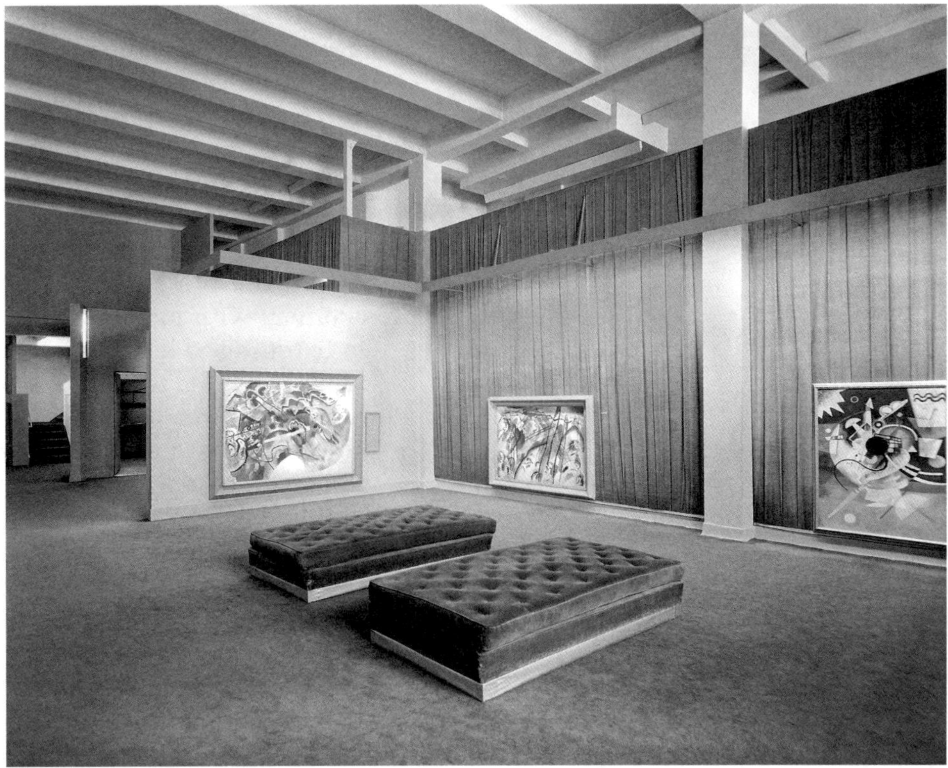

Exhibition view *Kandinsky Memorial Exhibition*, Museum of Non-Objective Painting, 1945
© Solomon R. Guggenheim Foundation Archives, New York

term hardly any more precisely defined. Rebay drew the dividing line between abstract and non-objective paintings along their specific referentiality: "The abstract picture abstracts the object to its last constructive part but discards perspective, while light and darkness are used as tonal qualities only."[10] While the abstract picture retains some residual relation to reality, in her view, this quality is missing entirely from the non-objective picture:

> [The] Non-objective picture stands by itself as an entirely free creation, conceived out of the intuitive enjoyment of space. It is the visual essence of rhythmic balance in form, design, and color. Secondary to the creation of theme, forms, and motifs are the combinations and shades of color and tone-values in Non-objective painting. The Non-objective picture is far superior to all others in its influential potentiality, educational power, and spiritual value to humanity.[11]

Non-objective art, it follows, is self-referential and autonomous. It is an art that no longer represents external referents, and it elevates visual expression above all else. For Rebay, non-objective painting differs from "representational" works in terms of both its production aesthetic and, owing to its greater spiritual impact, its reception aesthetic.[12]

This view was rejected by Edward Alden Jewell, art critic for the *New York Times*, who in the summer and autumn of 1939, after the opening of the Museum of Non-Objective Painting, published several articles on the problem posed by non-representational art and in doing so provoked numerous letters to the editor, including from Hilla von Rebay herself. Jewell kicked off the debate with his piece "The Guggenheim Non-Objective Art," in which he did not come out against the artists exhibited, but rather against the understanding of non-objective art espoused by Rebay:

> Very nice decoration indeed may be thus produced; decoration, too, that frequently recommends itself to architectural use. That the non-objectives get, as a rule, beyond that, I cannot concede. And too often their confections appear chiefly characterized by aspects of the geometrician's logic or the oculist's chart.

13   Edward Alden Jewell, "The Guggenheim Non-Objective Art," *New York Times* (June 4, 1939): 157.

14   Edward Alden Jewell, "Abstraction and Music: Newly Installed WPA Murals at Station WNYC Raise Anew Some Old Questions," *New York Times* (August 6, 1939): 137.

15   Stuart Davis, "Abstraction is Realism," *New York Times* (October 8, 1939): 144.

16   Hananiah Harari et al., letter to the editor, *Art Front* (October 1937): 20–21, here 20.

> Non-objective art may be ingenious, may be highly imaginative, may be beautiful. What I am not for a moment prepared to concede is that it mirrors in paint the vague cosmic platitudinizing offered in print (and frequently in very odd English) by way of official explanation.[13]

Jewell thus takes a stand against any kind of spiritual meaning, which for him smacks of the formation of a cult. He continued this line of argument in still more articles, including one piece in which he used the murals at the WNYC broadcasting company to compare Abstract Expressionism with music.

> On listening to a symphony one does not ask what it means. One just listens to it and is moved by it according to the mood of its composition. On looking at a painting, if it is a story-telling picture, there is no need to ask what it means, since it tells you itself. And in looking at a symphonic painting there is also no need to ask what it means, since its meaning lies in the harmonious variety of its color, size and direction of intervals. Therefore the one thing to do when before a painting of this type is just to look at it and enjoy it.[14]

A "story-telling picture" is Jewell's term for representational art, whereas he refers to non-representational art as "symphonic painting." As crude as we might find his underlying assumption that music is "meaningless," it does lend expression to the idea that non-representational art has no meaning beyond itself.

The third camp in the discussion espoused a political understanding of non-representational art. The American painter, Stuart Davis, for example, contributed several pieces to the *New York Times*, including one titled "Abstraction is Realism" in which he argued the following:

> But the outstanding error is the assertion that abstract art is "relative" and that "non-objective" art is "absolute." [. . .] Why is abstract art realistic, and what does it mean? What is meaning? Meaning is objective process, a real happening, which is proved by its social communicability. Meaning is a quality found only in association with experience common to many people. For an event to have meaning for us, we must have had experience with the objective elements that compose it. Abstract art is realistic and has meaning because it expresses common experience.[15]

For Davis, abstract art is the outcome of an engagement with our experience of the material world, which to his mind automatically makes it political. A letter from artists who, like Davis, allied themselves with the left-wing popular front pointed in much the same direction. The signatories, Hananiah Harari, Jan Matulka, Herzl Emanuel, Byron Browne, Leo Lances, Rosalind Bengelsdorf, and George McNeil had their letter published in *Art Front*, the magazine of the New York Artists' Union. In it, they explicitly took a stand against Hilla von Rebay:

> We wish it understood that with the works of art themselves and with the artist who created the works in Mr. Guggenheim's collection, we will not disagree. But we cannot accept with approbation the opinions which Baroness Rebay seems to have that abstract art has "no meaning" and represents nothing, that it is the "prophet of a spiritual life."[16]

Instead, the artists took the alternative view that abstract art does indeed relate to the "great realities" of life:

> It is our very definite belief that abstract art forms are not separated from life, but on the contrary are great realities, manifestations of a search into the world about one's self, having basis in living actuality, made by artists who walk the earth, who see colors

17   Ibid., p. 21.

18   Von Wiegand, "The Oriental Tradition and Abstract Art," 62.

19   Ibid., p. 60.

20   Cf. Clement Greenberg, "Avant-Garde and Kitsch," *Partisan Review* 6, no. 5 (Fall 1939): 34–49; Clement Greenberg, "Towards a Newer Laocoon," *Partisan Review* 7, no. 4 (July–August 1940): 296–310; Clement Greenberg, *Modernist Painting: The Voice of America Forum Lectures* (Washington, D.C.: U.S. Information Agency, 1960).

21   See Piet Mondrian, *The New Plastic in Painting*, 1917, in Piet Mondrian, *The New Art—The New Life: The Collected Writings of Piet Mondrian*, ed. Harry Holtzman and Martin S. James (Boston: G.K. Hall, 1986), 27–74, here 42; Piet Mondrian, *Le Néo-plasticisme* (Paris: Éditions de l'Effort Modern, 1920).

22   Quoted in Mark A. Cheetham, *Rhetoric of Purity: Essentialist Theory and the Advent of Abstract Painting* (Cambridge: Cambridge University Press, 2009), 106.

(which are realities), squares (which are realities, not some spiritual mystery), tactile surfaces, resistant materials, movement.[17] Even though Charmion von Wiegand was not among the letter's authors, her own texts in *Art Front* indicate that by the end of the 1930s she, too, was of the same opinion. At the same time, the debate shows that the idea that abstract art has a spiritual dimension had existed right from the start, and not just by individuals, but also by institutions. Even before the establishment of Abstract Expressionism, there could be no talk of just *one* abstract art, and even less so of just *one* way of interpreting it.

Autonomy and Spirituality

The idea of a non-representational or non-objective art—what Von Wiegand called the "destruction of the natural image"—was the starting point for the demand for more autonomy in art and thus became central to Modernism's perception of itself. Even Von Wiegand's argument that Abstract Expressionism marked the achievement of a "novel means of expression to the exclusion of meaning"[18] must be viewed as part of abstract art's striving for absolute autonomy. She understood this new tendency as an engagement with the medium of painting itself, which no longer referenced anything extraneous to itself:

> "For certain painters nothing exists but the canvas, the artist and the operation of painting—the establishment of direct, immediate, bodily, or psychic sensation with the minimum of conscious determination."[19]

The medium-specific, self-referentiality of Modernist painting is closely associated with the ideas of the art critic Clement Greenberg. His theory of art rested on the two central concepts of "purity" and "flatness,"[20] and according to his doctrine, the arts throughout history have increasingly concentrated on the limitations of their own specific medium, hence the reduction of painting to the two-dimensional surface of the canvas. The "purest" art of all for Greenberg is the one that comes closest to this ideal and that no longer contains any illusionist or narrative elements. As examples of this, he names the works of Morris Louis, Kenneth Noland, and Jackson Pollock.

The idea of a formalism of purity is also of the utmost relevance to the theoretical and painterly work of Piet Mondrian: i.e., an artist to whom Charmion von Wiegand explicitly declared herself indebted. In several different texts Mondrian wrote about the purity of Neo-Plastic painting, which he attributed to the purity of the painting medium.[21] Purity, for him, was a paring down to certain primary geometric shapes and colors, which he described in rather less technical terms than Greenberg. For him, moreover, colors and shapes were part of a larger metaphysical context.

Another argument frequently adduced in the discussion of art's autonomy is its freedom from purpose: Art, it is argued, should be sufficient unto itself, not a means to an end, but an end in itself. The De Stijl architect J.J.P. Oud, to single out an example close to Mondrian and hence to Von Wiegand, likewise saw "purity" as the highest quality of art. For him, however, purity was not tied to any formal properties or to the medium, but rather to the relationship between means and ends: "Impurity in art [...] arises as soon as means are considered aims."[22] Thus Oud allied himself to a tradition that had originated in the German idealism of the eighteenth century and writers like Karl Philipp Moritz, Immanuel Kant, and Friedrich Schiller, who espoused

23   Mondrian, *The New Plastic in Painting*, 42.

24   Cheetham, *Rhetoric of Purity*, 40.

25   Ibid., 117.

26   Cf. Carel Blotkamp, *Mondrian: The Art of Destruction* (London: Reaktion, 1994), 111.

27   Piet Mondrian, *Natural Reality and Abstract Reality: A Trialogue (While Strolling from the Country to the City)*, 1919–1920, in Piet Mondrian, *The New Art—The New Life: The Collected Writings of Piet Mondrian*, ed. Harry Holtzman and Martin S. James (Boston: G. K. Hall, 1986), 82–123, here 89–90.

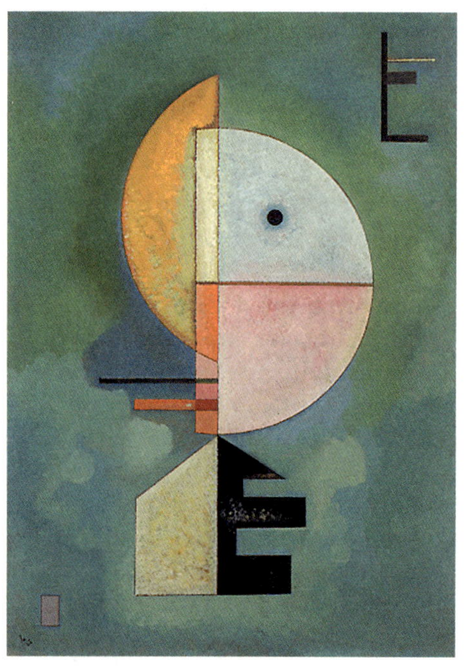

Wassily Kandinsky, *Empor (Upward)*, 1929, oil on cardboard, 70 × 49 cm, Peggy Guggenheim Collection, Venice (Solomon R. Guggenheim Foundation, New York)

Morris Louis, *Delta Khi*, 1960, acrylic resin on canvas, 264.2 × 322.6 cm, Kunstmuseum Basel, Gift of the Marcella Brenner Revocable Trust

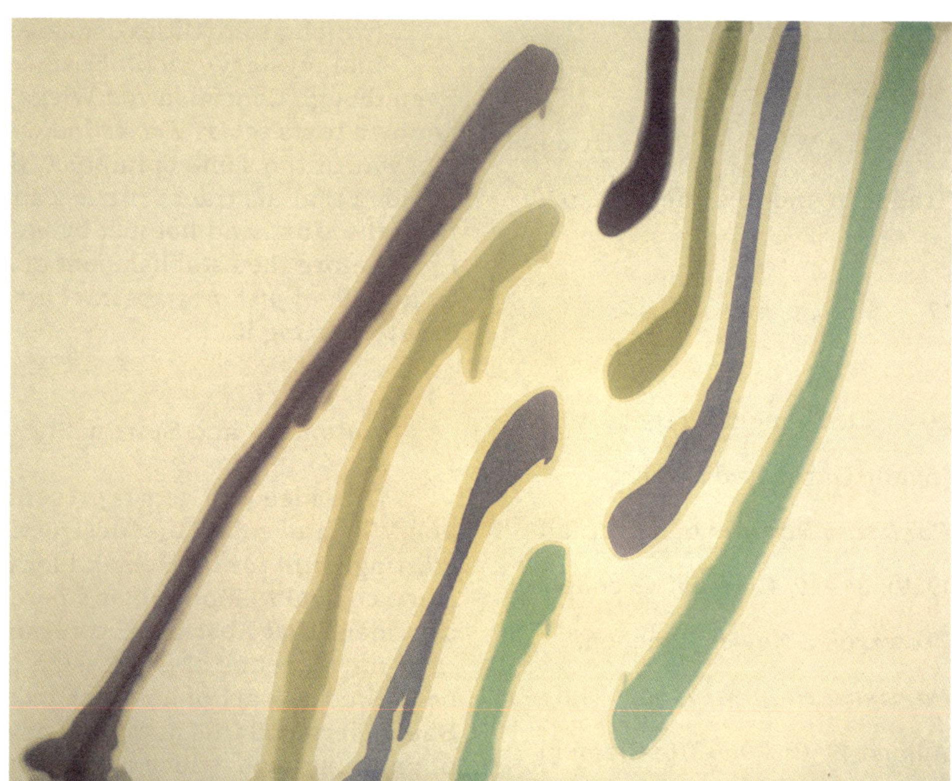

the notion of art as being without any purpose or objective. Mondrian's own writings show him taking a rather surprising stand in this respect. In *The New Plastic in Painting* (1917), for example, he writes, "Art—although an end in itself, like religion—is the means through which we can know the universal and contemplate it in plastic form."[23] But how can something (art) be purposeless and, at the same time, serve a purpose? According to Mark Cheetham, this definition of art is paradoxical only at first glance: "Art as an end in itself, as an autonomous [...] system, is abrogated in Mondrian's thinking [...] in deference to a greater good."[24] This paradox is part of the larger autonomy-heteronomy debate: Art's "autonomous" status is the precondition for the possibility of achieving an effect outside art. Kandinsky, too, whose writings, like those of Mondrian, had a huge influence on Von Wiegand, makes a similar claim for art in his book *Concerning the Spiritual in Art* (1912), in which he sees art's autonomy fulfilled exclusively in relation to a "transcendental absolute."[25]

How important Mondrian's interest in Theosophy was to his art and what we should make of his statement that his entire output was influenced by Helena Blavatsky's treatise, *The Secret Doctrine* (1888), is immaterial at this juncture.[26] Of central importance to Mondrian's Neo-Plasticism was the quest for transcendence (or the "absolute"). Another example of this is a passage from his essay composed as a trialogue, *Natural Reality and Abstract Reality* (1919–1920), in the third scene of which his protagonist "Z" say the following:

> This contemplation, this plastic vision, is most important. The more consciously we are able to see the immutable, the universal, the more we see the insignificance of the mutable, the individual, the petty human in us and around us. The aesthetic vision, man possesses the means to unite himself with the universal abstractly, that is, consciously. Through all vision as disinterested contemplation [...] man transcends his naturalness. [...] But in the moment of aesthetic contemplation the individual as individual falls away. The universal is born.[27]

28   Charmion von Wiegand,

"The Adamantine Way,"

Art News 68 (April 1969):

38–41, here 39.

29   Charmion von Wiegand,

"The Meaning of Mondrian,"

Journal of Aesthetics and Art

Criticism 2, no. 8 (Autumn 1943):

62–70, here 68–69.

30   Oral history interview with

Charmion von Wiegand by

Paul Cummings, October 9 and

November 3, 1968. Archives

of American Art, Smithsonian

Institution, 22.

Whether this idea of the quest for "the immutable" or "the universal" originated in Theosophy is a secondary matter. The two aspects worth noting are, first, the understanding of "disinterested contemplation" as the means by which the transcendent experience of art's paradoxical autonomy as discussed earlier is brought about; and, second, Mondrian provides us with instructions regarding how (his) art is to be received and how it fulfills a specific purpose—in other words, how the contemplation of art becomes a means of self-transformation.

Viewed against this backdrop, Von Wiegand's work after 1950 raises the question of whether the belief in abstract painting's transcendental meaning was also pivotal to her early work, specifically her engagement with Mondrian. In her discussion of the exhibition *Adamantine Way* (1969), she wrote about Tibetan art in a way that is powerfully redolent of the theses that Mondrian laid out in *Natural Reality and Abstract Reality*:

> There are two ways to an understanding of this art: the long study of a complex pantheon of deities, their symbolic forms and their religious meaning, or the direct path of immediate experience through seeing, feeling and participation. Tibetan art operates so directly on the viewer that all he needs to appreciate it is an open mind and a seeing eye. It is a magic instrument deliberately designed to destroy ignorance and transform the consciousness, to bring one face to face with the reality underlying the world of appearances.[28]

It is particularly noteworthy that in her essay "The Meaning of Mondrian" (1943), Von Wiegand makes no mention at all of the Theosophical elements in Mondrian's painting. On the contrary, that text is entirely compatible with a formalistic history of abstraction with a slant distinctly reminiscent of Greenberg, as is borne out by her assertion that Mondrian "stripped the canvas of its illusionistic veil of pigment, revealing it in the stark nakedness of white."[29] In an interview from 1968, moreover, Von Wiegand went on record as saying that when she first began studying Buddhist art, she saw an "aesthetic conflict"[30] with the ideals of Neo-Plasticism, but that this problem soon lost all relevance for her.

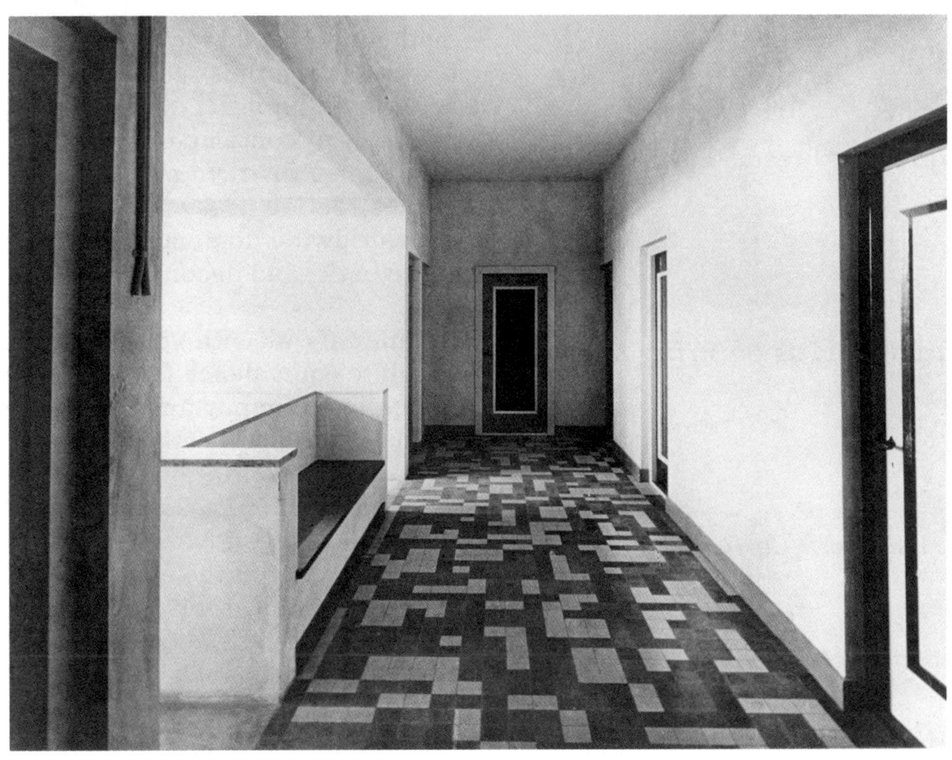

View of the tiled floor designed by Theo van Doesburg for the *De Vonk* holiday home in Noordwijkerhout, Netherlands

Universalism

Having seen how Charmion von Wiegand grappled with the abstract and the non-representational in her own artistic output, it comes as no surprise to discover that by the 1950s and 1960s, the fusion of different traditions of abstraction was informing not just her painting, but also her writing. Even the aforementioned essay, "The Oriental Tradition and Abstract Art," was premised on the assumption that the establishment of abstract art in the West would bring it closer to the image-making traditions of the Far East. The consequences of this would be far-reaching:

> During and after the first world war, the pioneers of abstract art formulated a new plastic language in which local, particular and national differences were gradually absorbed into a universal expression [...] But today everything vitally creative in art takes place, for the most part, in the abstract domain; all the esthetic arguments are conducted on this level.[31]

Tradition and Abstract Art," 56.

32   Ibid., 62.

Ultimately, Von Wiegand was also concerned with the equivalence—even the equation—of completely different pictorial traditions: here the autonomy of modern art in Europe and North America, there the religious-spiritual art of Asia. By implication, spirituality is thus upheld as a legitimate criterion for abstract art in the first place. Von Wiegand even saw the triumph of Abstract Expressionism as but further progress toward the putative leveling of local cultural traditions and peculiarities:

> Whatever beautiful works of art the abstract expressionists are creating, the movement as a whole has been one further step in the disintegration of the Western tradition. In this crisis Western art can either move backward into its own past, turn in on itself and [...] mechanically repeat its formulas; or it can move forward and seek a new level on the basis of a world concept of art.[32]

33   Werner Haftmann, *Die*

Her idea of a "world concept of art" was, in short, an attempt to describe nothing less than the consolidation of abstract art, which is historically and temporally broadened in order to lend it legitimacy—on the grounds that it has always existed all over the globe. Such a notion rests on an understanding of art as autonomous and of its forms as detached from their local and historical context. Aesthetic methods, spiritual and religious ends, political demands, and local traditions are thus reduced to a single common denominator defined solely by a superficial similarity. This places Von Wiegand in the company of contemporary authors like Werner Haftmann, who in his 1954 book, *Painting in the Twentieth Century*, developed the idea of "abstraction as a world language," with which he sought to explain the worldwide dominance of abstract art after 1945 in an ahistorical, formalistic, and decontextualized fashion.[33]

Malerei im 20. Jahrhunderts

(Munich: Prestel, 1954),

translated as *Painting in the*

Behind this, as with Von Wiegand, lay the endeavor to establish an absolute equivalence for which cultural and historical differences were of negligible importance. Such a view is not unproblematic, since from today's perspective, certain tendencies would be understood as "cultural appropriation." The argument becomes more understandable, though not necessarily less in need of further explanation, when the historical context is thrown into the equation and the specific understanding of the meaning of abstraction is interpreted historically. Writing in the early 1950s, Haftmann's primary concern was the rehabilitation of so-called "degenerate art" and the aspiration that West Germany, firmly anchored within the bounds of Western liberalism, could reconnect with the international art scene. Von Wiegand's art criticism and paintings from the 1950s onward, by contrast, must be

Twentieth Century

(New York: Praeger, 1960).

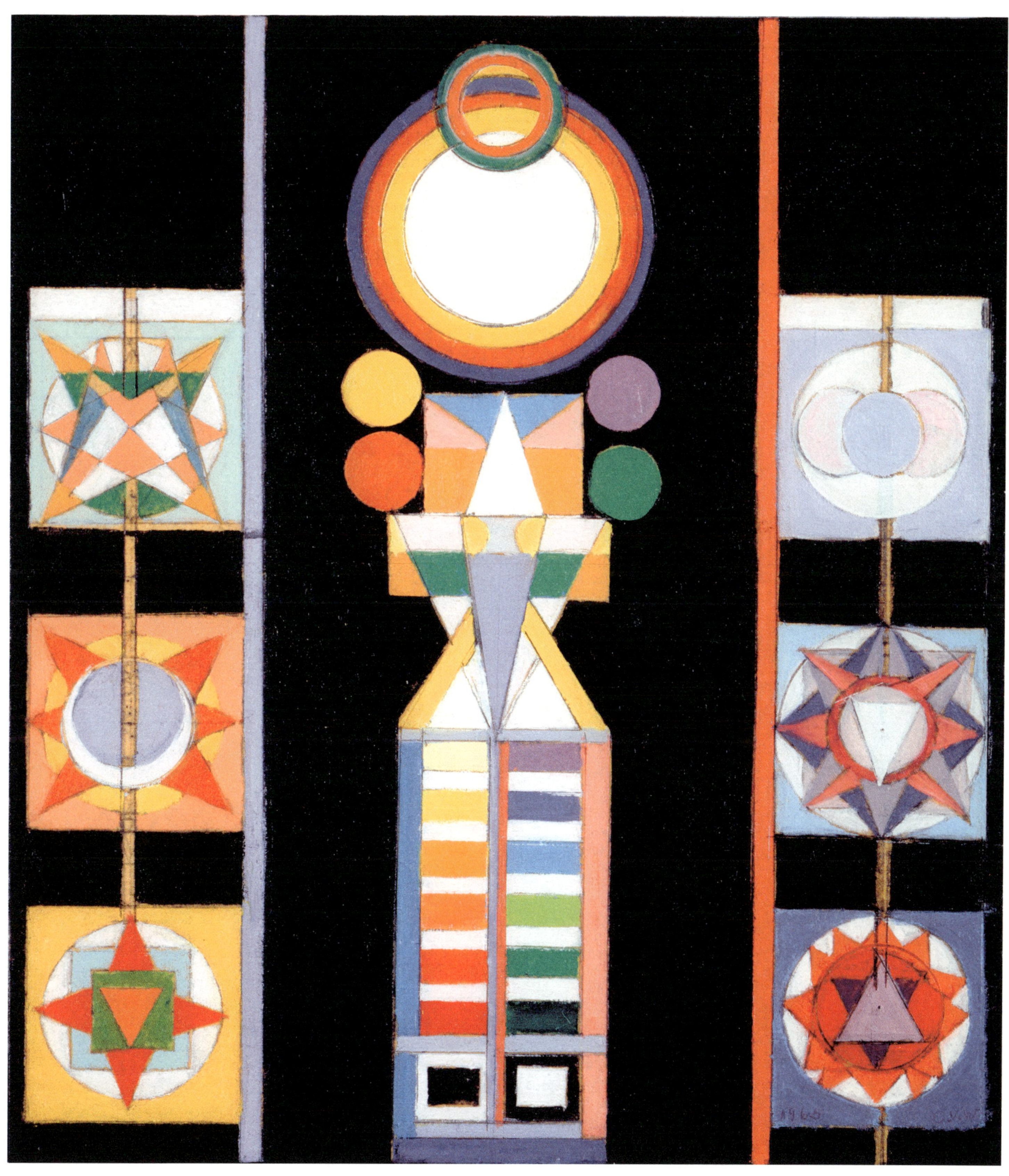

Charmion von Wiegand, *The Adamantine Way*, 1964–1965,
oil on silk on wood, 27.9 × 24.1 cm, Estate of Charmion von Wiegand,
Courtesy of Michael Rosenfeld Gallery LLC, New York

understood within the (cultural-)political context of McCarthyism, that is to say, the persecution of those on the left, which certainly included the artist herself, who wrote articles for various left-wing publications, and others in her circle.

Against this backdrop, a (self-)perception of abstract art that is not only apolitical, but also inclusive of spiritual and even religious tendencies, without substantially changing the art itself is likely to become the consensus definition. As an artist who in her own works found many different answers to the question of what abstract painting actually means, Charmion von Wiegand occupies an important position in the process by which Modernism was negotiated.

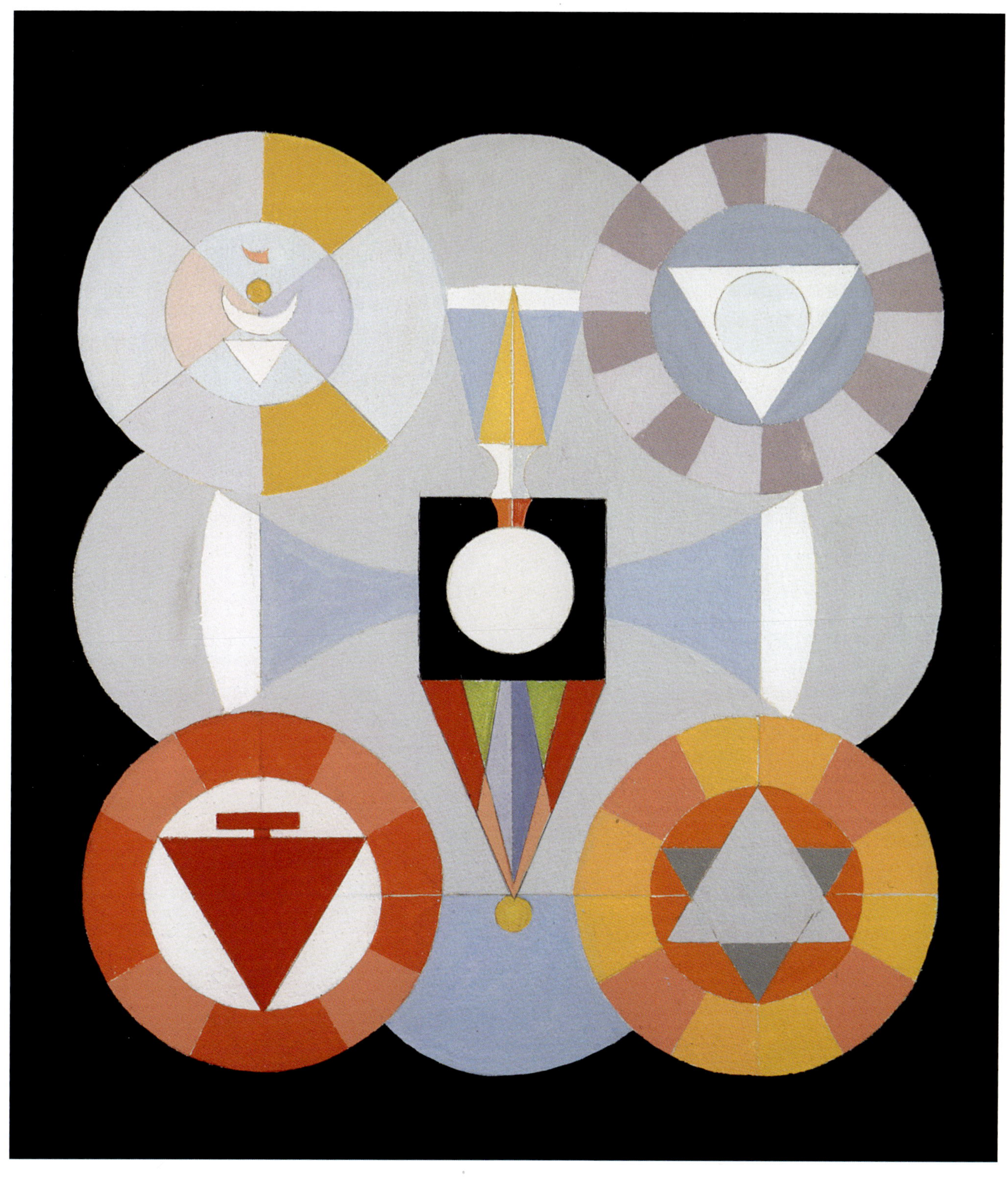

Gouache #180: The Chariot, 1962
gouache and graphite on paper, 49.6 × 42.2 cm
Estate of Charmion von Wiegand, Courtesy of
Michael Rosenfeld Gallery LLC, New York

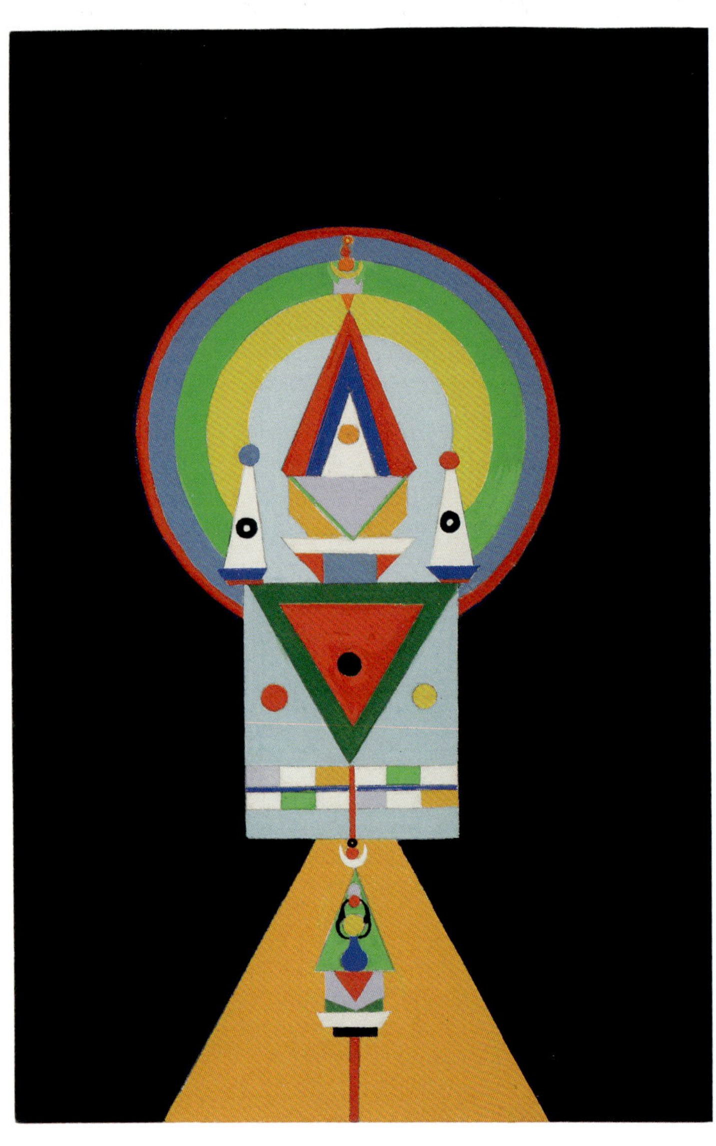

To the Winter Goddess, 1963
gouache on paper, 49.2 × 30.5 cm
Collection of the Herbert F. Johnson Museum of Art, Cornell University,
Gift of Miss May E. Walter

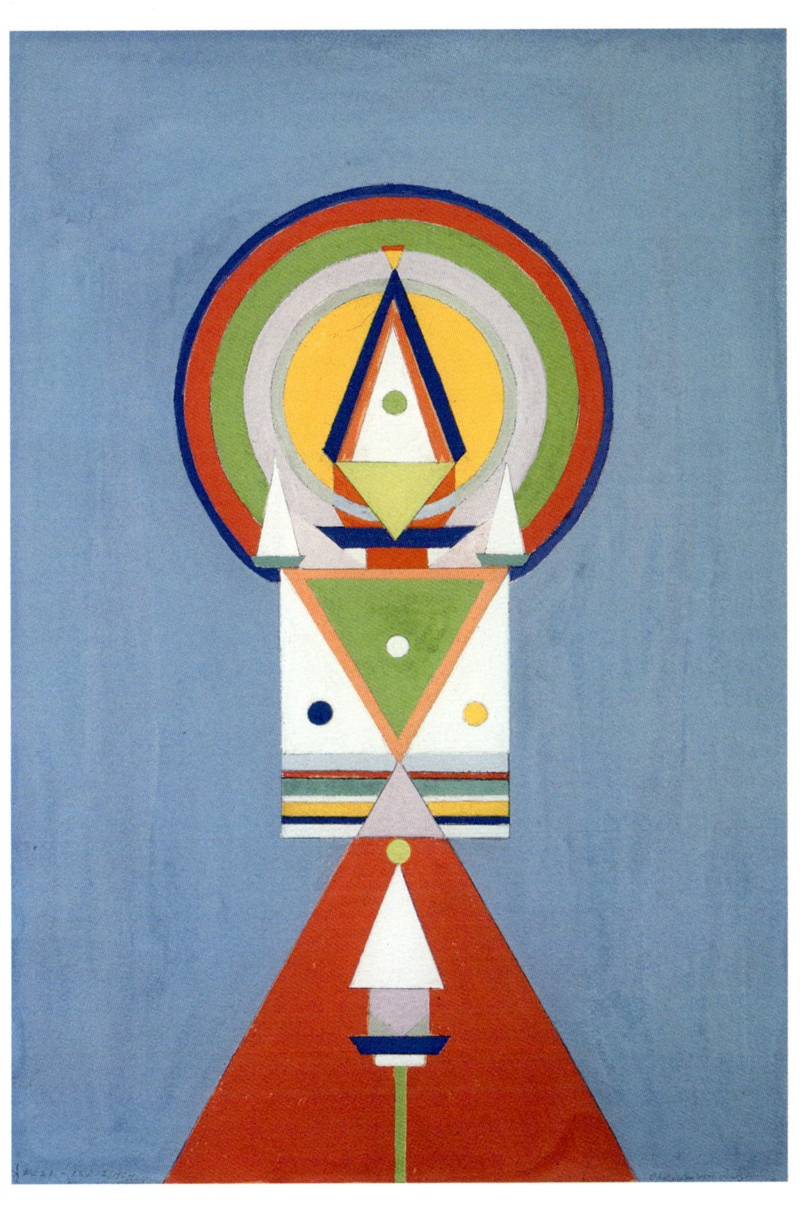

Gouache #233: To the Goddess of Spring, Vasantadevi, 1964
gouache on paper, 54 × 35.6 cm
Estate of Charmion von Wiegand, Courtesy of
Michael Rosenfeld Gallery LLC, New York

Cat. 35   133

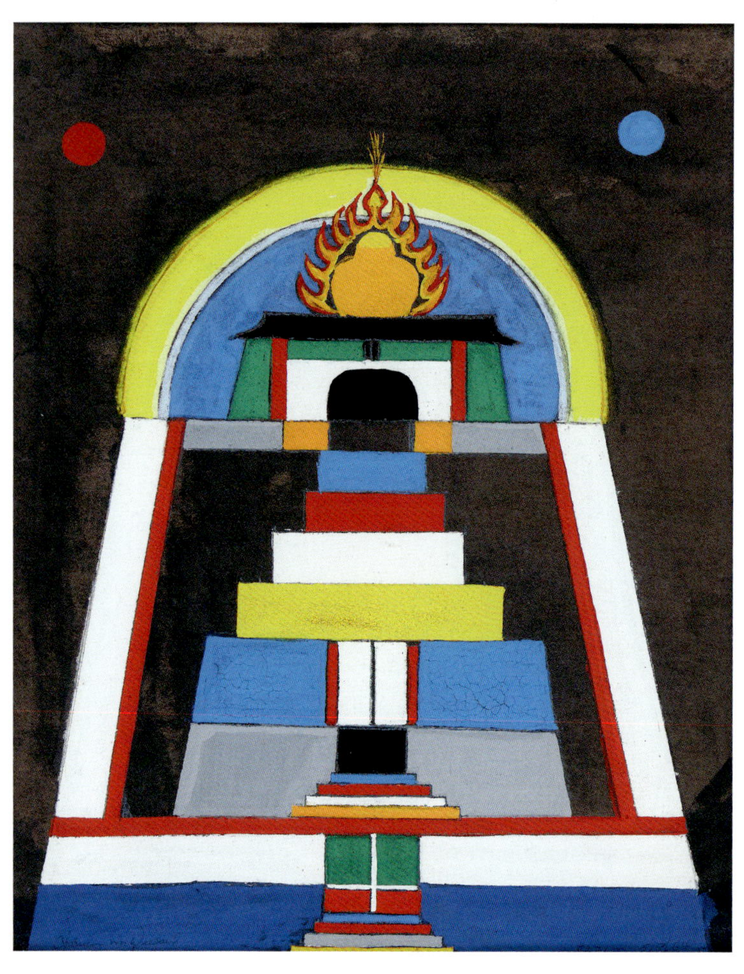

Untitled, 1964
gouache on paper, 31.5 × 24.1 cm
Sonam Dolma and Martin Brauen, Bern

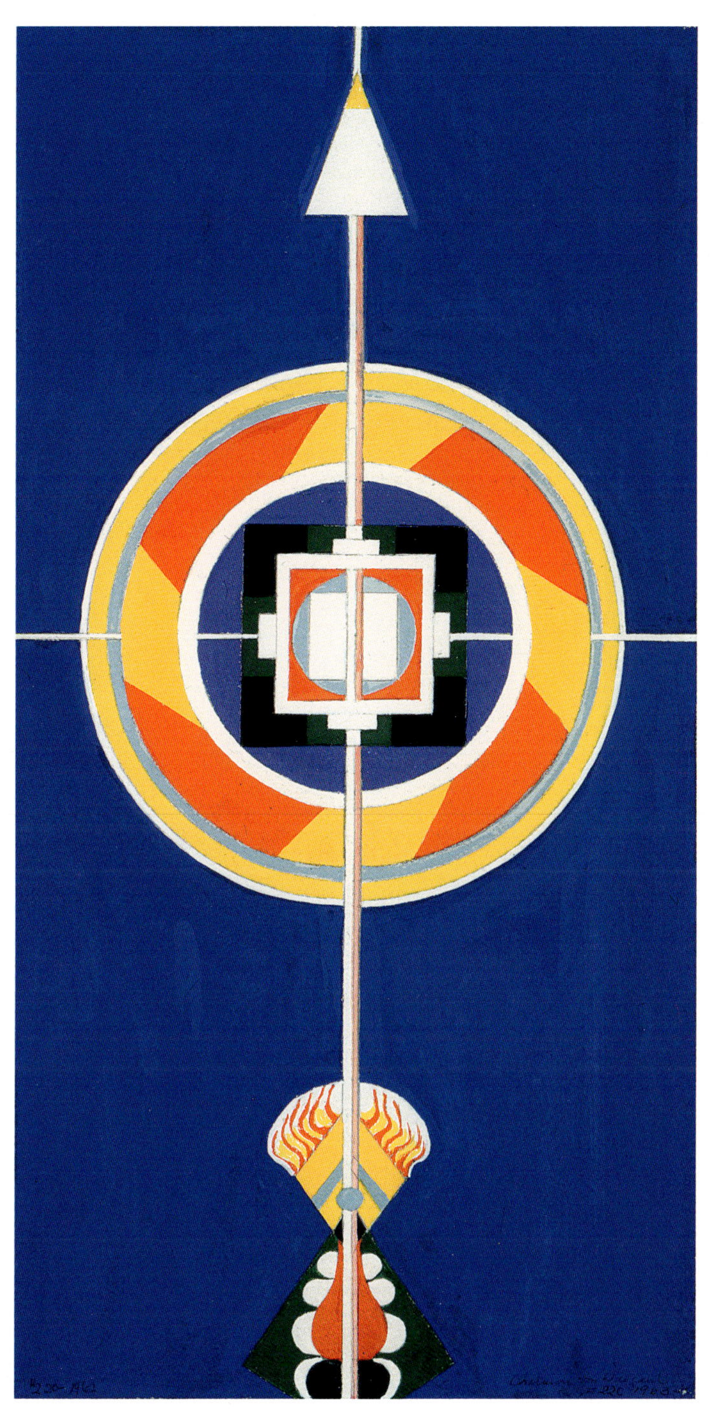

Mandala of the White Arrow, 1963–1964
gouache on paper, 55.9 × 27.9 cm
Private Collection, New York

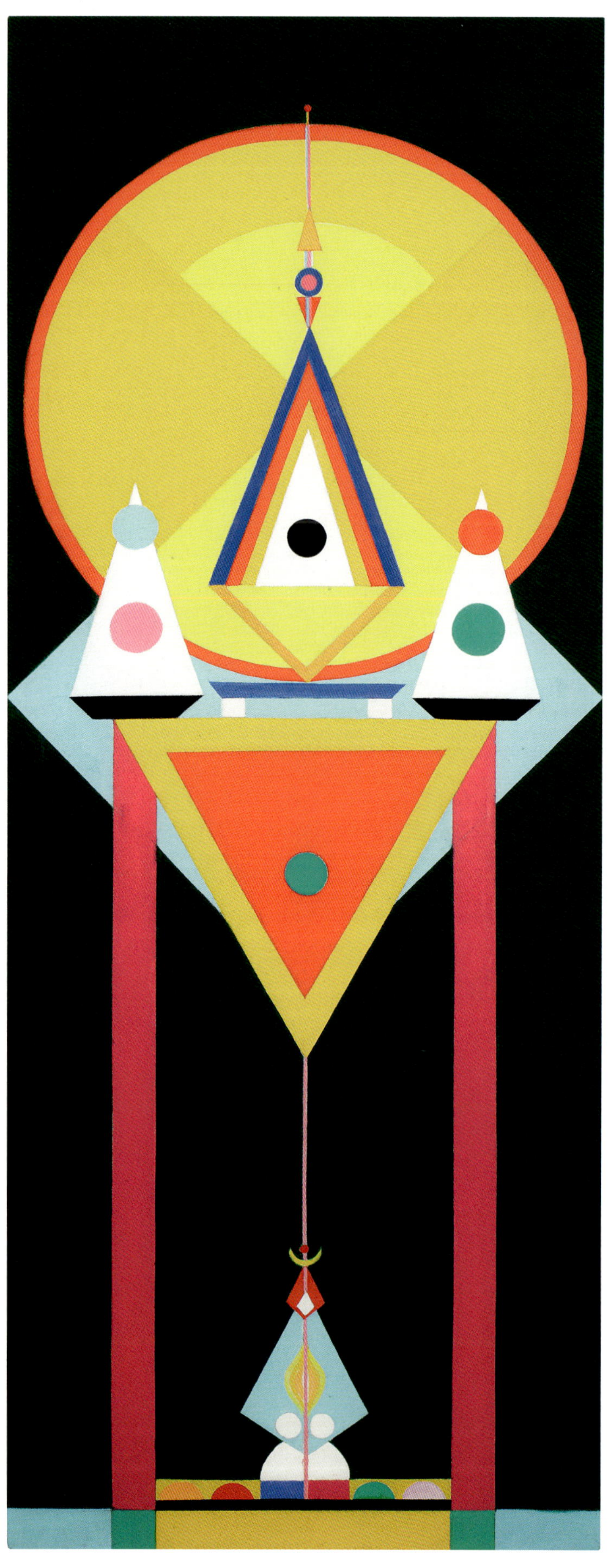

Offering of the Universe, 1964
oil on canvas, 183 × 71 cm
Estate of Charmion von Wiegand, Courtesy of
Michael Rosenfeld Gallery LLC, New York

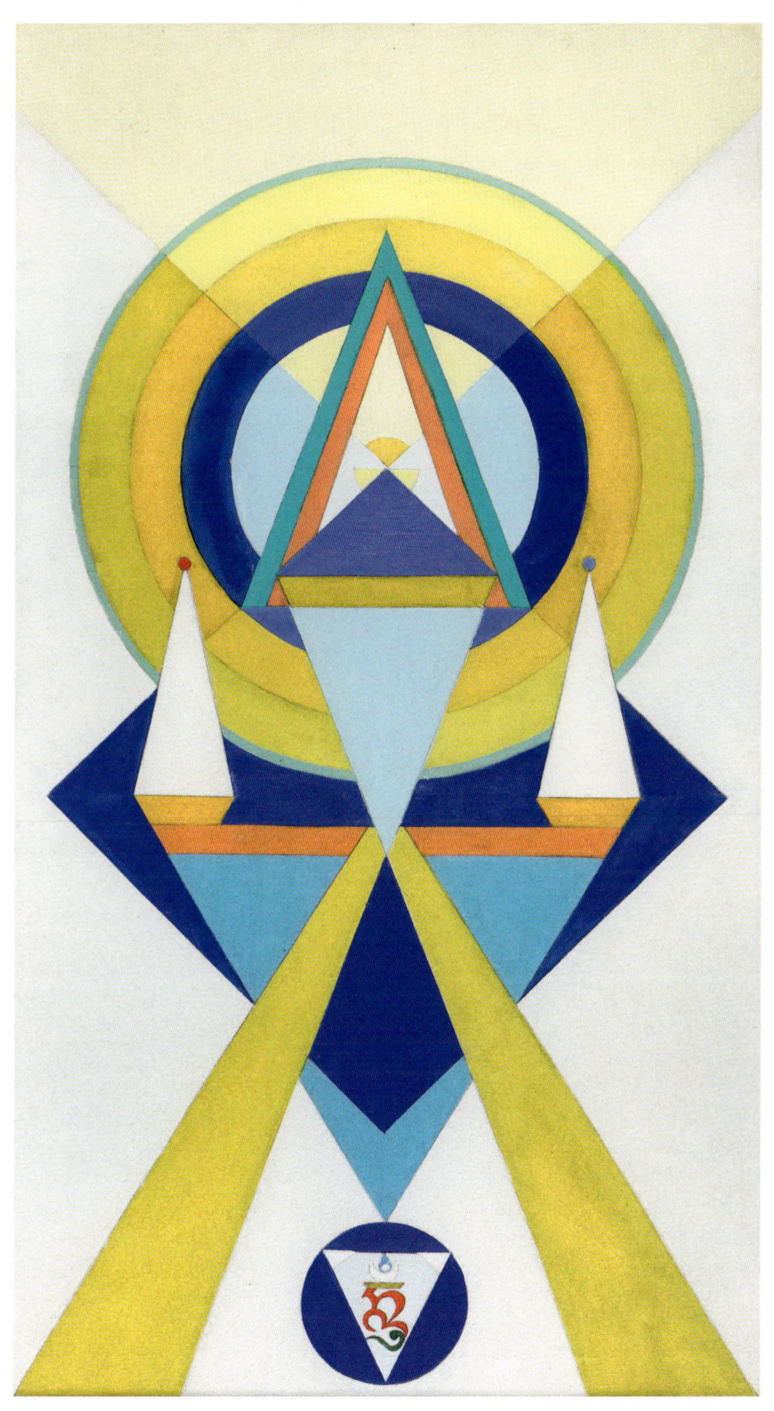

To the Adi Buddha, ca. 1968–1970
oil on canvas, 127 × 68.6 cm
Estate of Charmion von Wiegand, Courtesy of
Michael Rosenfeld Gallery LLC, New York

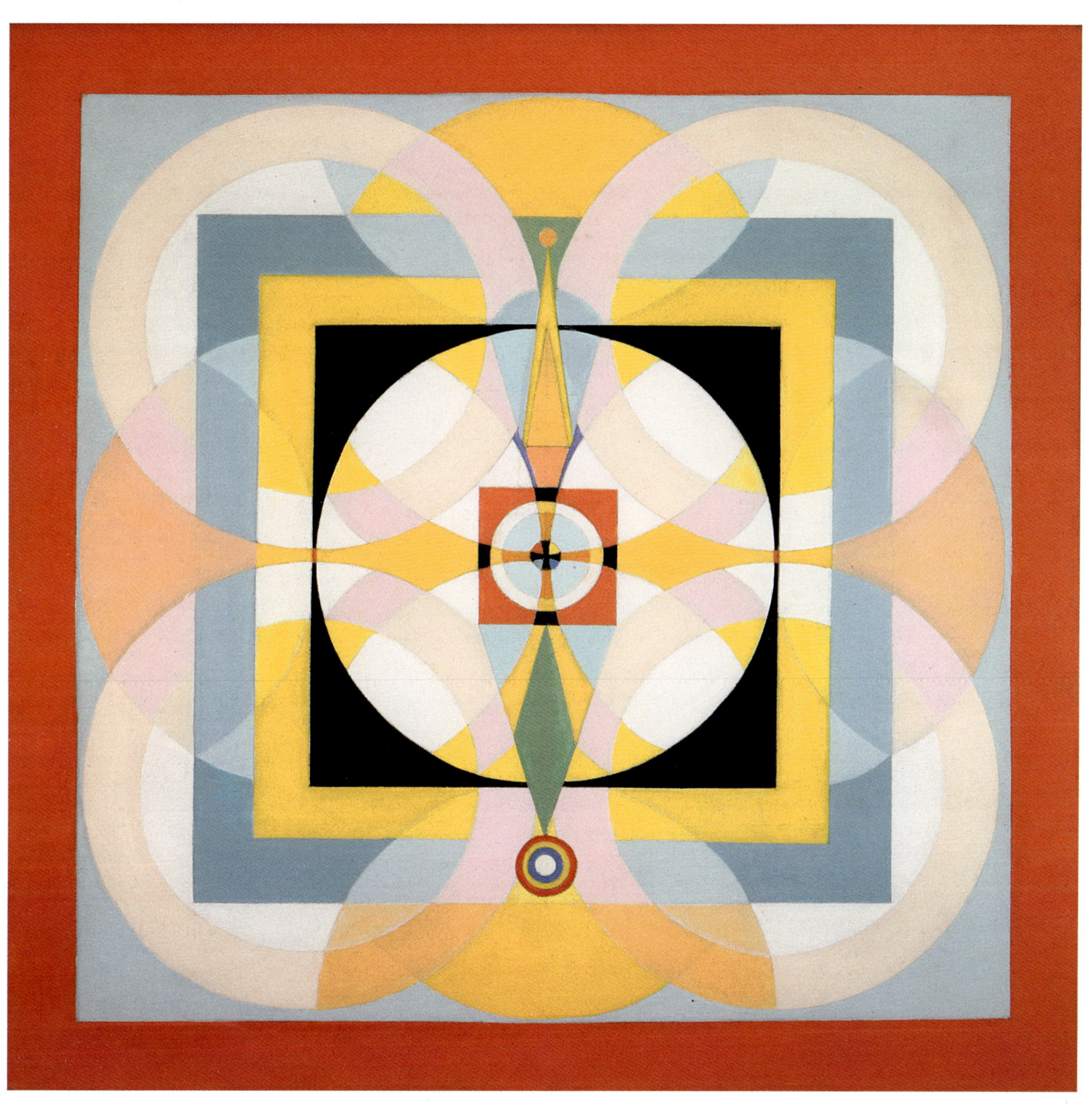

The Kundalini Lotus, 1968–1969
oil on canvas, 88.9 × 88.9 cm
Private Collection, New York

Cat. 40   139

RAMONA WARSZAWSKI

NORA WEBER

MAJA WISMER

BIOGRAPHY

AND

CHRONOLOGY

1896

1896 born in Chicago, childhood in Arizona and San Francisco. 1911–1915 formative years in Berlin, where her father, the journalist Karl von Wiegand, is on assignment.

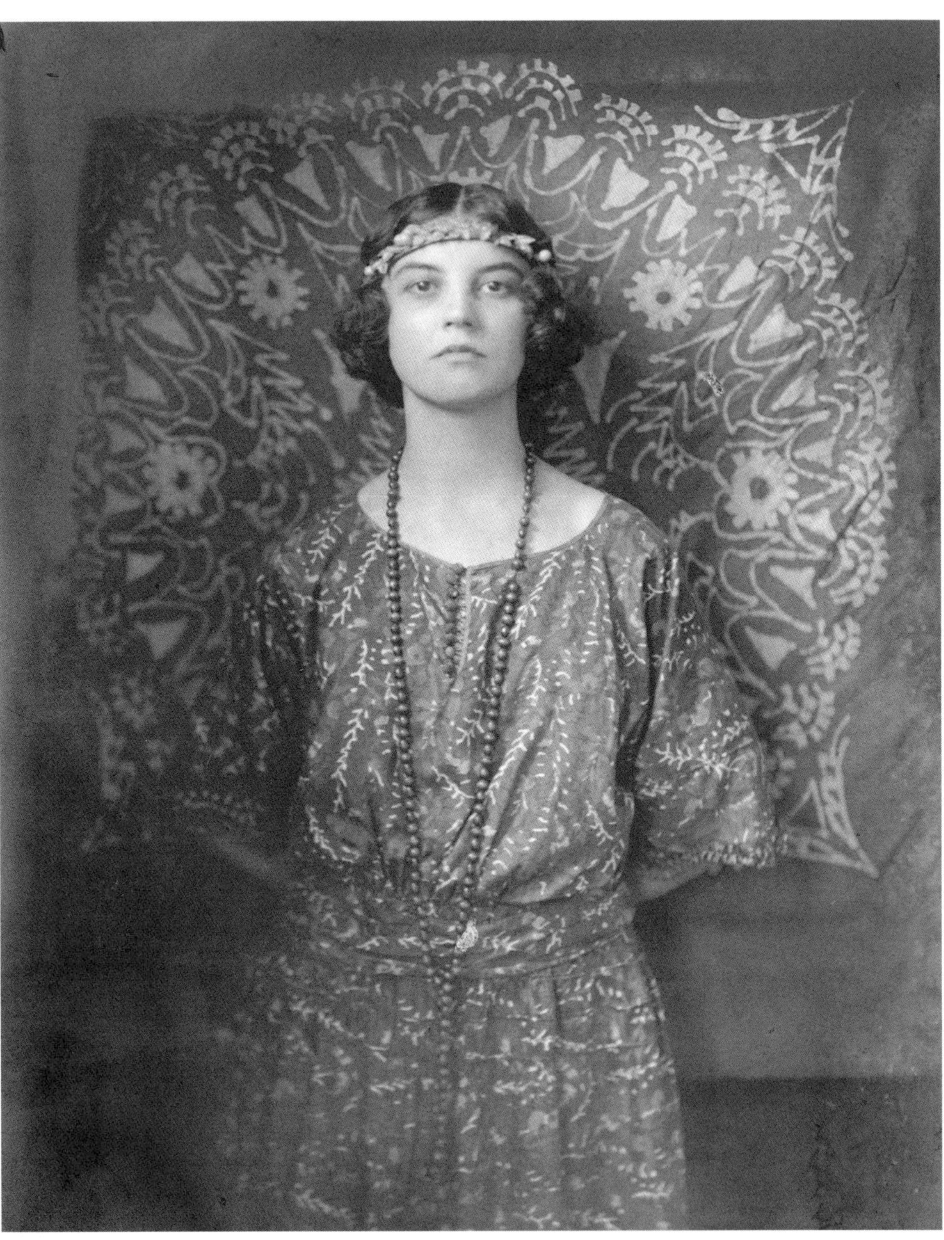

Charmion von Wiegand, date and photographer unknown, Collection of Khyongla Rato

1915

1915 returns to the United States, where she enrolls at Barnard College in New York City before transferring to Columbia University to study art history and journalism. As a student, Von Wiegand begins drawing and taking an interest in Chinese, Persian, and Indian art.

1919

1919 marries the business executive Hermann Habicht and moves to live with him in Darien, Connecticut. That same year she meets the poet Hart Crane, who encourages her to publish her

1922

1924
1926

1928

1929

1932

poetry in literary journals like *The Double Dealer*. Crane introduces her to theories of modern art and shares with her an interest in esoteric subjects. 1922 begins writing works for the stage, inspired in part by the philosopher and choreographer George Ivanovich Gurdjieff, whom she meets in person at a 1924 performance in Greenwich Village and who will be her role model for a time.

1926 begins psychoanalysis with Dr. L. Pierce Clark, a former president of the American Psychopathological Association. Through writers like Hart Crane she meets one of her most admired artists, Joseph Stella, who introduces her to Italian Futurism. 1928 first exhibition of her paintings in *The Independent Show*.

Von Wiegand and Habicht divorce, allowing her to pursue her interest in the life and politics of the Soviet Union. 1929 travels to Moscow. The city and its industrial architecture inspire numerous sketches and paintings.

At this time, she becomes an avaricious reader of Marx, Engels, Lenin, and Trotsky. Her dispatches from Moscow are informed by her socialist views. Hence her argument that art should no longer be something elitist and exclusive, but revolutionary. Hired by the Hearst Corporation in New York, she is the only female correspondent on assignment there. 1932 the political situation escalates under Stalin and Von Wiegand returns to the United States together with the journalist Joseph Freeman, co-founder and editor of the Marxist magazine the *New Masses* and later the *Partisan Review*.

Back in New York, Freeman and Von Wiegand marry. At this time, she is active mainly as a journalist and, being passionate about art, writes with ever greater self-assurance for several art magazines (*Art Front*, *Art News*, *The Journal of Aesthetics and Art Criticism*, and *New*

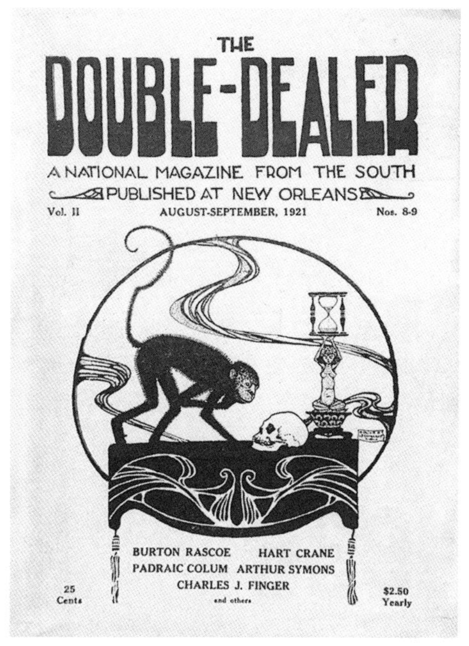

Cover of the American literary journal *The Double Dealer* (vol. 2, nos. 8–9), August–September 1921

1936

Theatre). Her texts show her grappling with the social and political role of art.

1930s the United States is riven by social disparities. President Franklin D. Roosevelt's New Deal and the Federal Art Project (FAP) of the Works Progress Administration (WPA) are among the policies adopted to counter the Great Depression. Several independent artists' groups come into being, among them the American Artists' Congress (AAC), whose founding in 1936 Von Wiegand discusses in her first article for *Art Front*: "This is the first time in American history that artists have organized on so wide a scale for the purpose of protecting their crafts, and culture in general, in a social situation fraught with danger."

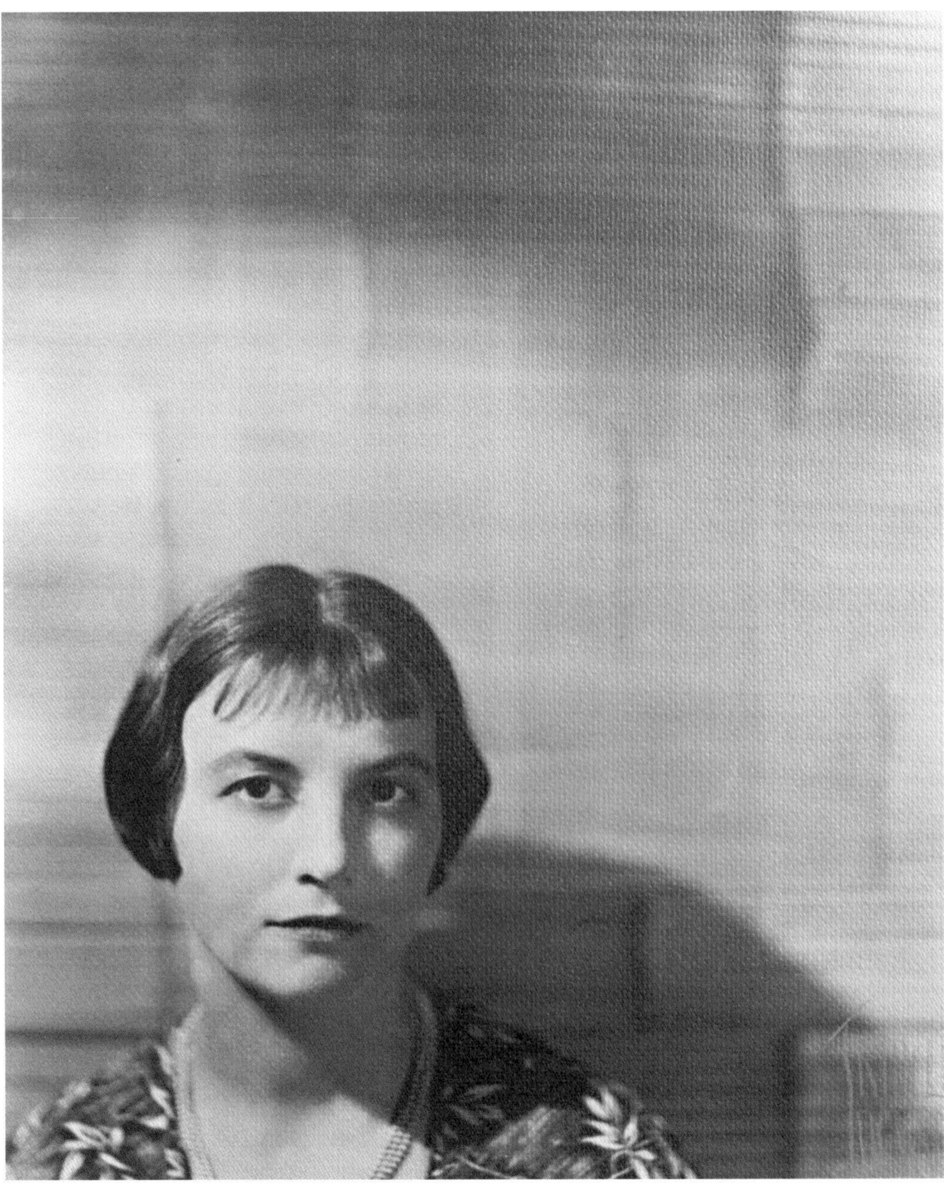

Charmion von Wiegand, date unknown, photograph by Ray Lee Jackson, NBC Studios, Collection of Khyongla Rato

1936–37

1939

1940–41

1942

She also reviews the exhibition *Fantastic Art, Dada, Surrealism* on show at the Museum of Modern Art from December 1936–January 1937. The artist and filmmaker Hans Richter and the scenographer Frederick Kiesler become friends and discussion partners with Von Wiegand. 1939 publication of Clement Greenberg's article "Avant-Garde and Kitsch" in the *Partisan Review*. This influential article will form the theoretical basis for Abstract Expressionism, which will come to dominate the trans-atlantic art world. Most importantly, it breaks with the political demands of American art criticism of the 1930s.

1940–1941 works together with the artist Carl Holty on the manuscript of a *History of Abstract Art*, which will never be completed. After reviewing the pamphlet *Five on Revolutionary Art* in which Herbert Read hails Piet Mondrian as a "true revolutionary artist," she longs to meet Mondrian in person. Holty organizes a meeting with the artist, who has just moved to New York from London. Von Wiegand and Mondrian will remain in close contact right up to his death in 1944. She witnesses the creation of Mondrian's late New York works, such as *Broadway Boogie Woogie* (1942–1943) and *Victory Boogie Woogie* (1942–1944), which signal a veering away from his iconic, Neo-Plasticist works of the 1920s and 1930s.

1942 opening of Peggy Guggenheim's Art of This Century gallery. Frederick Kiesler, who designed much of the interior, introduces Von Wiegand to Guggenheim. In the same year, Von Wiegand and Stephan C. Lions curate *Masters of Abstract Art*, a benefit show for the Red Cross held at Helena Rubinstein's New Art Center in New York. Von Wiegand also helps Mondrian with the English version of his article "Toward a True Vision of Reality," which is published to coincide with his

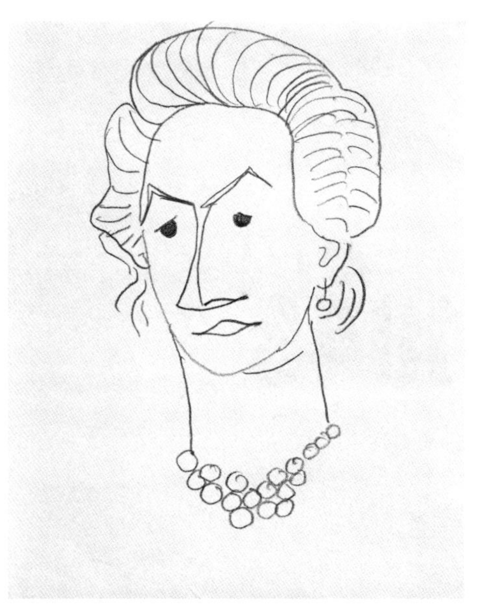

Portrait of Charmion von Wiegand, most probably by Frederick Kiesler, pencil on paper, Collection of Khyongla Rato

show at the Valentine Dudensing Gallery in New York, his first solo exhibition in the United States. She will henceforth edit and translate many of Mondrian's writings and becomes an associate member of the American Abstract Artists (AAA).

1943 writes "The Meaning of Mondrian," the first comprehensive article on the Dutch artist to be written from an American perspective, published in the *Journal of Aesthetics and Art Criticism*. In it she writes, "While it is doubtful if all the European art expressions recently transplanted to our shores can survive when confronted by the robust virility of America, the art of Mondrian offers a new beginning. Between his work and the

First page of Charmion von Wiegand's corrected typescript "Statement of Piet Mondrian" from July 24, 1941, Collection of Khyongla Rato

July 24, 1941

From Handwritten manuscript of P.M. with my English corrections.

Statement of Piet Mondrian.

An example of the cultural significance of Mondrian's Art can be seen in the following:

He said that his art is sensual . I retorted that I saw it as sensuous. * He replied that when sensuous means a deeper grade of sensual, then the definition sensuous will just be what I mean to say. But will it be directly understood that in this case, sensuouness remains unified with sensuality?

The word "sensuality" embraces the whole of human sensex faculty and Art is produced by this whole. Every art must be the expression of our whole being and can be approached [approved] only with our whole being. But the kind of expression depends on the grade of profoundity that its sensuality has (contains) .

This fact explains the culture of Art moving toward pure abstraction. For true abstraction is not rejecting or eliminating parts of the whole of reality, but in intensifying it. The culture of Art is an continuous attempt to move toward ~~profoundxxx~~ more profoundness.

Based not on philosophical but on pure plastic and technical ~~experience~~ [experience], Mondrian says that it cannot be enough emphasized that abstraction is not rejection but intensification. Thus ~~it~~ an abstract work is not the creation of another reality but of another vision of the one and always the same reality.

This fact makes a work living and concrete.

Mondrian's vision of art is an example of cultural interest. He sees , the most abstract (work) as a "substitute" for what he calls "true life". True life , he defines as human life freed from external (objective) and internal (subjective) oppression.

He sees human life as slowly marching toward true life and men fighting for that state of life.

* ("I could not find this word in the dictionary.") P/M/

environment of our great cities there exists an unconscious but spontaneous affinity."

Writing in the catalog to the *American Modern Artists* exhibition at the Riverside Museum in New York around the same time, Barnett Newman notes, "We have come together as American modern artists because we feel the need to present to the public a body of art that will adequately reflect the new America that is taking place today and the kind of America that will, it is hoped, become the cultural center of the world."

1944 death of Piet Mondrian in March. Robert Motherwell publishes two articles that will define how contemporary American art is understood and lay the foundations for the American avantgarde. In "Painter's Objects," published in *Partisan Review*, Motherwell takes Mondrian, especially his New York paintings, as an example to explain what he means: "For the first time a subject is present, not by virtue of its absence, but actually present, though its appearance is torn away, and only the structure bared. The Modern City! Precise, rectangular, squared, whether seen from above, below, or on the side; bright lights and sterilized life; Broadway, whites and blacks: and boogie-woogie, the underground music of the at once resigned and rebellious, the betrayed . . . Mondrian has left his white paradise, and entered the world."

Several American artists explicitly acknowledge their indebtedness to Mondrian, among them, along with Robert Motherwell, are Alexander Calder and Lee Krasner. Von Wiegand's most important influences during this period are Wassily Kandinsky, Hans Arp, and Hans Richter, who through his experiments in automatic drawing hopes to liberate drawing from any particular artistic concept and make it entirely intuitive. She produces drawings, paintings, and collages

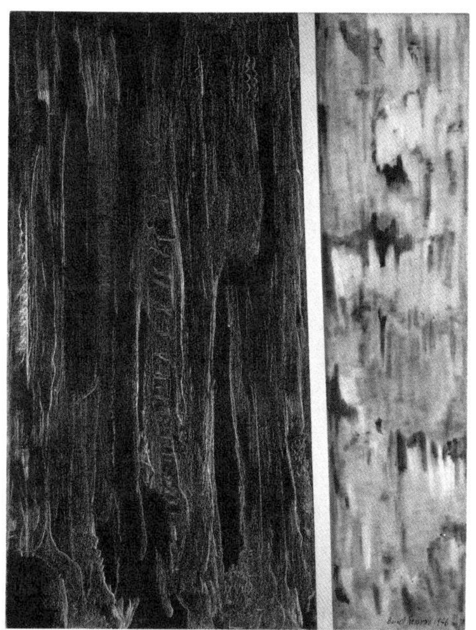

Barnett Newman, *The Command*, 1946, oil on canvas, 122 × 90.5 cm, Kunstmuseum Basel, Gift of Mrs. Annalee Newman in honor of Arnold Rüdlinger and Dr. Franz Meyer

Lee Krasner, *White Squares*, ca. 1948,
enamel and oil on canvas, 61.1 × 76.5 cm,
Whitney Museum of American Art,
Gift of Mr. and Mrs. B. H. Friedman

1945

1947

1948

full of organic forms, followed soon after by compositions inspired by Mondrian's "grids."

1945 Von Wiegand and several other women artists, including Louise Bourgeois, Hedda Sterne, and Alice Trumbull Mason, take part in *The Women*, a group exhibition at Peggy Guggenheim's Art of This Century gallery that one critic describes as "refreshingly unladylike."

1947 Von Wiegand becomes a full member of the AAA, the organization of whose international touring shows she will be actively involved in for the rest of her life. She also curates several exhibitions for Rose Fried's Pinacotheca Gallery in New York, among them *The White Plane*, for which she assembles works by Mondrian, Kandinsky, and Burgoyne Diller. Inspired by Kandinsky, Hans Arp, Joan Miró, and Kurt Schwitters, her main interest alongside painting during this period is collage.

Also in 1947, the Seattle-based gallerist Zoë Dusanne introduces Von Wiegand to the painter Mark Tobey, with whom she will correspond regularly on spiritual subjects and their shared interest in East Asian cultures and religions.

1948 Von Wiegand, Katherine S. Dreier, and Naum Gabo together

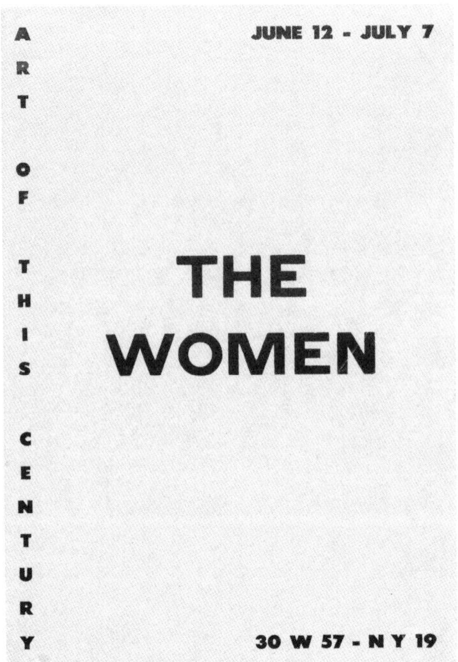

Announcement for the group exhibition
The Women, 1945, Art of This Century,
New York

1949

write the text for Schwitters's first solo show in the United States, which also takes place at Rose Fried's Pinacotheca Gallery. Von Wiegand likens the impact of Schwitter's collages to that of Taoist painting. 1949 Congress of Religions in New York where Von Wiegand and Freeman meet Louis James, President of the New York Theosophical Society. Its library containing publications by the founder of the Theosophical movement, Helena Petrovna Blavatsky, and her successors, Annie Besant and Charles Webster Leadbeater, will prove a valuable resource for Von Wiegand.

She intensifies her own spiritual practice throughout the 1950s, becoming increasingly immersed in Zen Buddhism. Crucial to its spread in the West is Japanese author Daisetsu Teitaro Suzuki, who through the Eastern Buddhist Society founded in 1921 brings both Zen Buddhism and Mahayana Buddhism to Europe and the United States. Von Wiegand attends a lecture by Suzuki at the Church Peace Union in New York in 1951 and is a regular auditor of his lectures at Columbia University from 1952 onward.

1951
1952

1952 solo exhibition at the Saidenberg Gallery in New York is Von Wiegand's first show to include works with explicitly Far Eastern references. One of these is eventually selected for the exhibition of *American Watercolors, Drawings and Prints* at the Metropolitan Museum. 1953 the staunchly left-wing Freeman has to answer for himself before the House Un-American Activities Committee. Although he is acquitted, he will henceforth publish only as a ghost writer. That same year he gives his wife a copy of the *I Ching Book of Changes*. Von Wiegand makes productive use of its Taoist principle of sixty-four hexagrams and their interpretation by means of

1953

chance in a series of paintings. Zen Buddhism is a major source of inspiration for numerous New York-based artists during this period, among them John Cage, Agnes Martin, and Ad Reinhardt. 1952–1954 president of the AAA. 1954 first exhibition at the gallery Cittadella d'Arte Internazionale e d'Avanguardia in Ascona, Swtizerland. Many more will follow. 1955 writes to her father, we live in a jungle and can trust no one [...] so while I have come to detest politics of all kinds, it is not necessary to become cynical but rather more compassionate towards human beings.

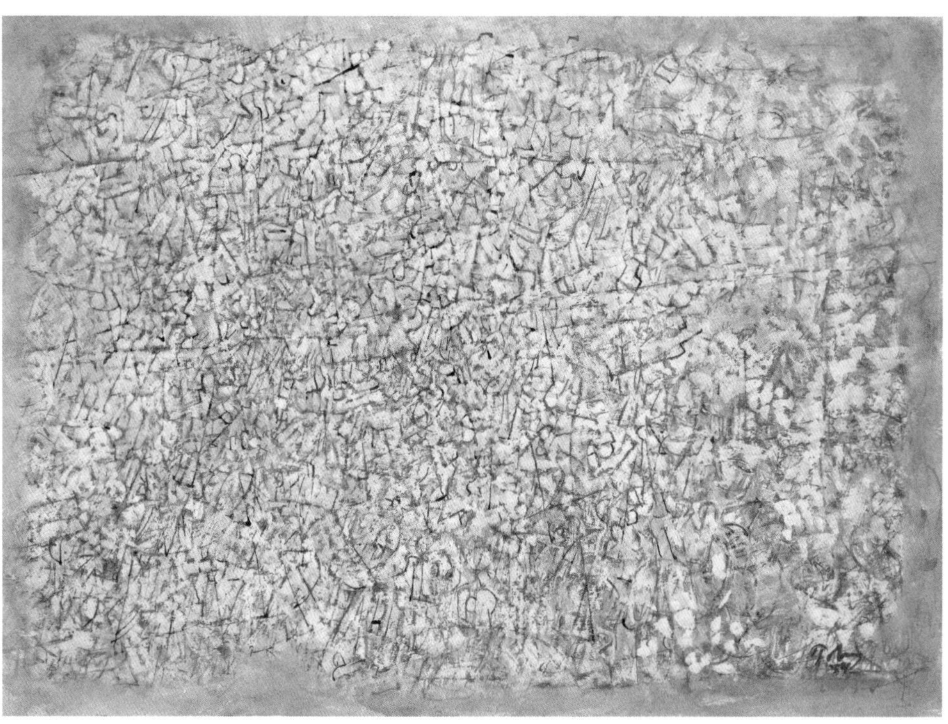

1957 takes up yoga with Yogi Vithaldas, one of the first yogis active in the United States. This enhances Von Wiegand's interest in Tantra, after which chakras will figure in many of her works. Her article "The Oriental Tradition and Abstract Art" is published in the AAA's book *The World of Abstract Art* that same year. 1959 her "The Vision of Mark Tobey" is published in *Arts Magazine*. In it she asserts, "like every creative artist of our time, Tobey has felt the impact of Cubist space, and, most

Mark Tobey, *The Wall*, 1954, tempera on paper, 23.7 × 31.8 cm, Kunstmuseum Basel, Kupferstichkabinett, Gift of Marguerite Arp-Hagenbach

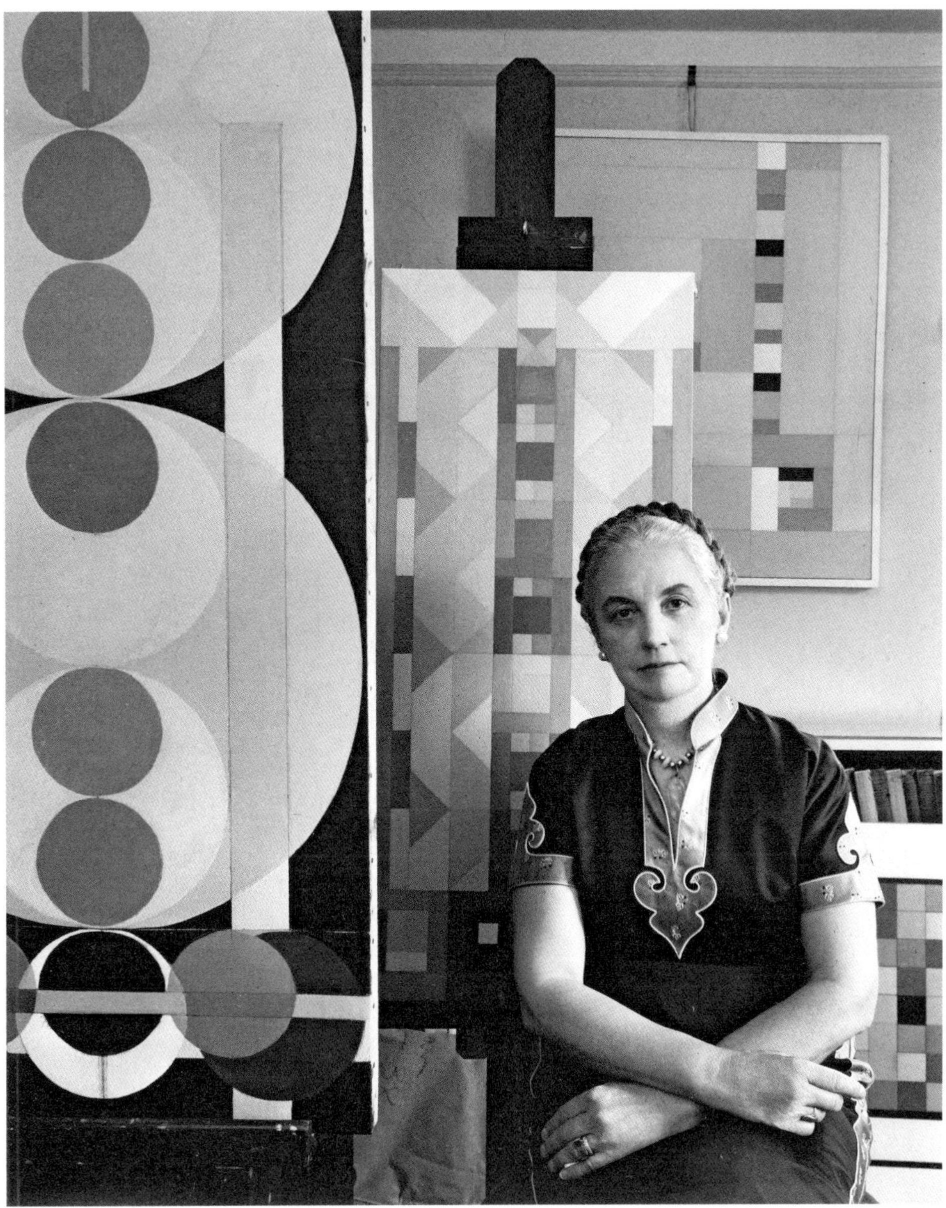

overwhelmingly, the space of Far Eastern art. It is a space of fusion, for it seeks to build a bridge between East and West in this time of world expansion."

1960 *Konkrete Kunst— 50 Jahre Entwicklung* (*Concrete Art—50 Years of Development*), a group exhibition at the Helmhaus Zurich curated by Swiss Concretist Max Bill, in which Von Wiegand also takes part. "1941 meets mondrian in new york and embraces neoplasticism," notes the catalog, adding, "through her organization of exhibitions and journalist activities does much to promote the new art in america." Tobey moves to Basel where Von Wiegand will visit him several times on her regular trips to

1960

Arnold Newman, Portrait of Charmion von Wiegand, 1961

151

1961

1962

Europe. 1961 publishes the essay "Mondrian: A Memoir of His New York Period" for the *Arts Yearbook* and has her first solo show at the Howard Wise Gallery in New York. A small-format work by her is included in the survey *The Art of Assemblage* at the Museum of Modern Art. 1962 inclusion of her monumental painting *Triptych, Number 700* (1961; fig. pp. 6/7) in the *Geometric Abstraction in America* exhibition at the Whitney Museum of American Art.

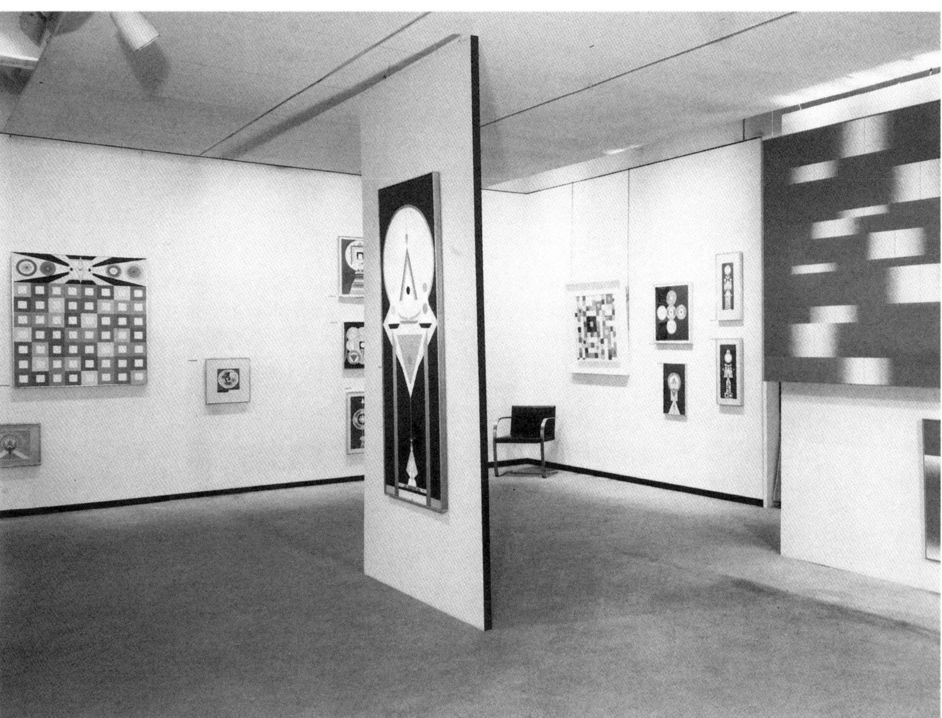

1965

1967

1968
1969

1965 attends the Oriental Congress in New York where her encounters with Tibetan refugees and the texts and images they have brought with them inspire her to organize an exhibition of Tibetan art for the American Federation of Arts (AFA). Death of Joseph Freeman.

1967 meets her future Buddhist teacher Khyongla Rato Rinpoche through the Theosophical Society. Von Wiegand will help him write up his autobiography.

1968 Paul Cummings interviews Von Wiegand for the Archives of American Art. 1969 the Cranbrook Academy of Art awards her first prize for her 1963 work, *To the Winter Goddess* (cat. 34). She organizes and

Exhibition view with works by Charmion von Wiegand and Herbert Bayer in the show *Three One-Man Shows: Herbert Bayer, Charles Howard, Charmion von Wiegand*, Howard Wise Gallery, New York (April 27–May 15, 1965), photograph by Geoffrey Clements, New York, Collection of Khyongla Rato

1970

1971

1973
1974
1975

1976

1977

curates the exhibition *The Art of Tibet* for the American Federation of Arts.

1970 first trip to India where she visits the exiled Dalai Lama before traveling on to Tibet. The following years will see an ever-greater preoccupation with Tibetan art and religion.

1971 is interviewed as both an expert and an eyewitness for the exhibition catalog *Piet Mondrian 1872–1944: Centennial Exhibition* at the Guggenheim Museum in New York.

Takes part in various shows in Europe and the United States, including two retrospectives at Fiamma Vigo's galleries in Rome and Venice in 1973 and, in 1974, at the gallery Annely Juda Fine Art in London. 1975 *The Paradox of Transformation*, a wide-ranging exhibition dedicated to Von Wiegand at the Andre Zarre Gallery in New York. Her long-time friend and fellow artist, Sonia Delaunay, writes about her in the catalog: "Von Wiegand is one of the very few artists who understands color theories and utilize them to perfection. Her accomplishment in this area is enormous and should not be overlooked." Khyongla Rato Rinpoche founds the first Tibet Center in New York and asks Von Wiegand to sit on its Board of Advisors.

1976 International Women's Arts Festival in New York at which Von Wiegand and other women artists, such as Sari Dienes, Alice Neel, Louise Nevelson, and Georgia O'Keeffe, are honored for their "outstanding cultural contributions."

1977 Von Wiegand is one of five American women artists to take part in the inaugural show of Paris's Centre Georges Pompidou, *Paris–New York*. Mail Art artist Ray Johnson invites her to take part in a small group show at the Sid Deutsch Gallery in New York. The exhibition brochure quotes her as follows: "Interior painting starts with the sign. In its initial states it is exorcism—a means

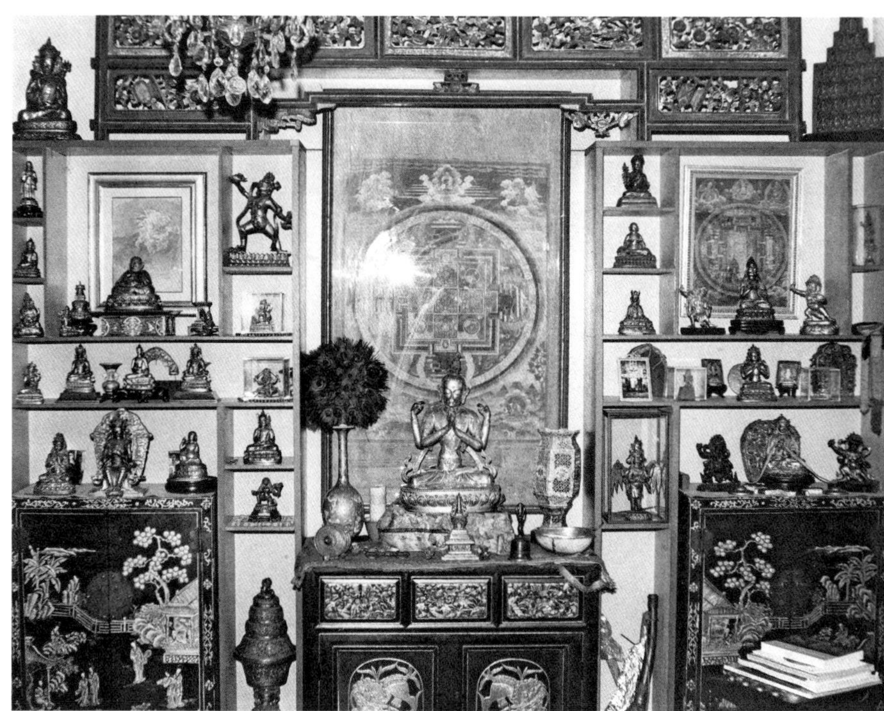

1978

1980

1982

1983

of conquering the unknown.
It is the oracle, the divination,
the symbol of power, evolving
from subjetive states and
moving towards their objective
embodiments in a single plastic
image." 1978 America's Public
Broadcasting Service (PBS)
commissions and broadcasts
the documentary *The Circle of
Charmion von Wiegand*,
produced by the artist Ce Roser.

1980 becomes a member of
the American Academy of Arts
and Letters. Von Wiegand is
one of the twenty women artists
featured on the title page of
Art News under the headline,
"Where Are the Great Women
Artists?" The whole issue
is devoted to the art world's
gender gap.

1982 first museum retro-
spective at the Bass Museum of
Art in Miami Beach, Florida,
accompanied by a small catalog.
Von Wiegand is awarded the
Women's Caucus for Art Lifetime
Achievement Award and takes
part in the Honor Award Exhi-
bition of the National Women's
Caucus for Art Conference in
New York.

1983 dies in New York, aged
eighty-seven. She leaves her
estate to the Tibet Center of
New York.

Charmion von Wiegand's own private
altar, date and photographer unknown,
Collection of Khyongla Rato

CONTRIBUTORS

MARTIN BRAUEN studied Buddhism at the University of Delhi and Cultural and Social Anthropology at the University of Zurich. His field research has taken him to Ladakh, Nepal, Bhutan, Tibet, and Japan. After serving as Head of the Department of Tibet, the Himalayas, and the Far East at the Ethnographic Museum at the University of Zurich, he became Chief Curator of the Rubin Museum of Art in New York. He is now an independent curator and freelance writer.

LORI COLE is Clinical Associate Professor and Associate Director of the interdisciplinary master's program XE: Experimental Humanities & Social Engagement at New York University. She has previously held fellowships at Brandeis University and the Whitney Museum of American Art, and has lectured at the Museum of Modern Art. Her writing has been published in *Artforum*, *Cabinet*, *Journal of Surrealism and the Americas*, and *The Oxford Critical and Cultural History of Modernist Magazines*. She is the author of *Surveying the Avant-Garde: Questions on Modernism, Art, and the Americas in Transatlantic Magazines* (2018).

JOSEF HELFENSTEIN was Director of the Kunstmuseum Bern's Collection of Graphic Art and the Paul Klee Foundation from 1988 to 2000. From 2000 to 2004, he directed the Krannert Art Museum at the University of Illinois at Urbana-Champaign and concurrently held a professorship in the university's art history department. Before taking the helm as the Kunstmuseum Basel's director in 2016, he was Director of the Menil Collection, Houston, Texas, from 2004 until 2015.

HAEMA SIVANESAN is Chief Curator of the Glenbow Museum in Calgary. Until April 2021, she was curator at the Art Gallery of Greater Victoria in British Columbia with a Bachelor of Architecture from the University of New South Wales, Sydney. She is a past curatorial fellow of The Andy Warhol Foundation, New York (2018–2019) and recipient of a multi-year research and exhibition development grant from the Robert H. N. Ho Family Foundation, Hong Kong (2016). Her current research is focused on the influence of Buddhism on contemporary art in North America.

NANCY J. TROY is Victoria and Roger Sant Professor in Art at Stanford University, California. In addition to *The De Stijl Environment* (1983), she is the author of *Modernism and the Decorative Arts in France: Art Nouveau to Le Corbusier* (1991), *Couture Culture: A Study in Modern Art and Fashion* (2003), and *The Afterlife of Piet Mondrian* (2013), in which she examines the artist's work and legacy as it circulated after his death in both elite and popular culture. Currently, Troy is preparing a book on the intersecting trajectories of Mondrian, Yves Saint Laurent, and Pop Art in America during the 1960s.

FELIX VOGEL is professor of Art and Knowledge at the University of Kassel. Prior to this he taught art history at the University of Basel. He received his doctorate in art history from the University of Fribourg, Switzerland, in 2017. His dissertation, "Empfindsamkeitsarchitektur. Der Hameau de la Reine in Versailles" will be published by *Passages* at the Centre allemand d'histoire de l'art (Paris) in 2021. His current research project is titled "Art & Language: Theory—Practice—Display." Besides the eighteenth century and Conceptual Art, Felix Vogel is interested in the history of exhibitions, transcultural art history, and the theory and history of abstraction.

RAMONA WARSZAWSKI received her Bachelor of Arts in Art History and Philosophy from the University of Basel.

NORA WEBER is a master's student in Art History and Religious Studies at the University of Basel.

MAJA WISMER is Head of Art after 1960 and Contemporary Art at the Kunstmuseum Basel. She previously worked on exhibition and publication projects in the fields of modern and contemporary art in Berlin, Glarus, Munich, Riga, and elsewhere. From 2012 until 2014, she was Renke B. and Pamela M. Thye Curatorial Fellow at the Busch-Reisinger Museum, Harvard Art Museums, Cambridge, Massachusetts.

PHOTO CREDITS

Albright-Knox Art Gallery, Buffalo, NY: p. 81

Archives of American Art, Smithsonian Institution, Washington, D.C., Ben Shahn papers, 1990, bulk 1933–1970: pp. 32, 37

Archives of American Art, Smithsonian Institution, Washington, D.C.: p. 115

Arithmeum/Forschungsinstitut für Diskrete Mathematik, Rheinische Friedrich-Wilhelms-Universität Bonn, Bonn: p. 107

Jonathan Boos, New York, Gavin Ashworth, New York, NY: p. 83

bpk-Bildagentur/The Metropolitan Museum of Art, New York, NY: p. 53

Bridgeman Images: p. 47

Brooklyn Museum, Brooklyn, NY: p. 79

Cincinnati Art Museum, Cincinnati, OH: p. 104

The Cleveland Museum of Art, Cleveland, OH: p. 89 below

Matt Flynn, New York, Cooper Hewitt, Smithsonian Design Museum © 2021 Cooper Hewitt, Smithsonian Design Museum, New York, NY/Art Resource, New York/Scala, Florence: p. 39

Fondazione Marguerite Arp, Locarno, Roberto Pellegrini: pp. 49, 55

The Getty Research Institute, Los Angeles, CA, David Alfaro Siqueiros papers: p. 34

Grey Art Gallery, New York University Art Collection, New York, NY: p. 51

The Historic New Orleans Collection, New Orleans, LA: p. 143

Herbert F. Johnson Museum of Art, Cornell University, Ithaca, NY: p. 132

Collection of Khyongla Rato, Robert Stout: pp. 33 above, 44, 57, 58, 61, 62, 64, 65, 68, 69, 70, 71 left above, 86, 92 right above and below, 93, 96, 98, 100, 113 right, 144, 145, 152, 154

Kunstmuseum Basel, Basel, Jonas Hänggi: pp. 94, 95 left; Martin P. Bühler: pp. 124 above, 147, 150

Kunstmuseum Den Haag, The Hague: p. 87 below

The Museum of Modern Art, New York, NY © 2021 Digital image, The Museum of Modern Art, New York/Scala, Florence: pp. 71 right, 87 above, 97

The Museum of Modern Art Archives, New York, NY. Photo: Soichi Sunami © 2021 Digital image, The Museum of Modern Art, New York/Scala, Florence: pp. 36, 71 left below

The Museum of Modern Art Library, New York, NY: p. 72

The Newark Museum, Newark, NJ: pp. 75, 82

Arnold Newman Properties/ Getty Images: p. 151

Het Nieuwe Instituut, Rotterdam, OUDJ, ph96: p. 125

RKD – Netherlands Institute for Art History, The Hague: p. 85

Michael Rosenfeld Gallery LLC, New York, NY: pp. 19, 21, 24, 25, 27, 33 below, 52, 74, 78, 88, 89 above, 92 left, 95 right, 103, 105, 109, 111, 113 left, 119, 127, 131, 133, 135, 136, 137, 139, 142, 144, 145, 146

Seattle Art Museum, Seattle, WA: cover, pp. 20, 23, 106

Smithsonian American Art Museum, Washington, D.C.: p. 50

Solomon R. Guggenheim Foundation, New York, NY, David Heald: pp. 110, 114, 118, 124 below

Solomon R. Guggenheim Museum Archives, New York, NY: pp. 121, 148 below

Walker Art Center, Minneapolis, MN: p. 77

Love Weber, Bern: p. 134

Whitney Museum of American Art, New York, NY © 2021 Digital image, Whitney Museum of American Art/Licensed by Scala, Florence: pp. 6/7, 18, 35, 48, 148 above

IMPRINT

This catalog is published on the occasion of the exhibition

Charmion von Wiegand. Expanding Modernism

originally planned for September 12, 2020–January 10, 2021 at the Kunstmuseum Basel; the exhibition is scheduled to take place in 2023.

Transparent Front Cover:
Charmion von Wiegand, *The Terrace of Jade*, 1952, oil on canvas, 55.9 × 30.5 cm, Seattle Art Museum, Gift of Zoe Dusanne

Transparent Back Cover:
Charmion von Wiegand, sketch for "The Relationship Machine," August 3, 1941 (detail), Collection of Khyongla Rato

In respect to links in the book, the Publisher expressly notes that no illegal content was discernible on the linked sites at the time the links were created. The Publisher has no influence at all over the current and future design, content, or authorship of the linked sites. For this reason, the Publisher expressly disassociates itself from all content on linked sites that has been altered since the link was created and assumes no liability for such content.

A CIP catalog record for this book is available from the British Library.

Library of Congress Control Number: 2021935292

PUBLICATION

Editors
Kunstmuseum Basel and
Maja Wismer

Texts
Martin Brauen, Lori Cole, Josef
Helfenstein, Haema Sivanesan,
Nancy J. Troy, Felix Vogel,
Ramona Warszawski, Nora Weber,
and Maja Wismer

Text and Picture Editing
Maja Wismer

Translation
German–English
Bronwen Saunders, Basel
(Contributions by Martin Brauen,
Josef Helfenstein, Felix Vogel,
Ramona Warszawski, Nora
Weber, and Maja Wismer)

Editorial Direction Prestel
Andrea Bartelt-Gering

Copyediting
José Enrique Macián,
Valencia and Brighton

Design and Layout
Julia Born, Zurich

Typesetting
Dorothee Dähler, Zurich

Production
Corinna Pickart

Separations
Reproline Mediateam,
Unterföhring

Printing and Binding
Eberl & Koesel,
Altusried-Krugzell

Typefaces
Catalogue LL, Lineto
Forum, Source Type
Studio 42, Luca Pellegrini

Paper
Munken Polar, Enviro Ahead,
Pergamenata

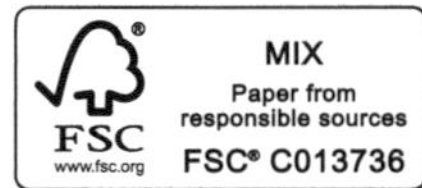

Penguin Random House
Verlagsgruppe FSC® N001967

Printed in Germany

ISBN 978-3-7913-5975-5
(English trade edition)
ISBN 978-3-7913-9017-8
(English museum edition)
also available
ISBN 978-3-7913-5974-8
(German trade edition)
ISBN 978-3-7913-9016-1
(German museum edition)

www.prestel.com

EXHIBITION

Curators
Maja Wismer with Martin Brauen

Coordination
Charlotte Gutzwiller,
Monika Mascus

KUNSTMUSEUM BASEL

Director
Josef Helfenstein

Head of Art and Research,
Deputy Director
Anita Haldemann

Head of Art Care
Werner Müller

Head of Finance
and Operations
Matthias Schwarz

Head of Marketing
and Development
Mirjam Baitsch

Head of Exhibitions
and Collections
Charlotte Gutzwiller

Exhibition Manager
Matthias Fellmann

Curator of Programs
Daniel Kurjaković

Art Education
and Outreach
Hannah Horst and
Christine Müller Stalder

Communication
and Social Media
Karen N. Gerig and
Dominik Asche

Marketing
Christian Selz and
Vera Reinhard